THE EXPLODING GALAXY:

PERFORMANCE ART, LSD AND BENT COPPERS IN THE SIXTIES COUNTERCULTURE

WRITTEN BY JILL DROWER

FOREWORD BY
JOHN OLIPHANT
&
HUGO WILLIAMS

SCRUDGE BOOKS
LONDON

SCRUDGE BOOKS LIMITED
Kirk Rice, 13 Princeton Court
53-55 Felsham Road, Putney
London, SW15 1AZ

ISBN number: 978-0-9927775-2-4

Published by Scrudge Books Limited

British Library Cataloguing in Publishing Data

A catalogue record for this book is available from the British Library

Designed by Jill Drower

Design Consultant: Roger Pons-Bolton

Cover Design: Roger Pons-Bolton

In heaven where time is measured in epochs of trillions of years, *lexakinesis* takes a prominent role – most noticeably in the library. Here the books, stacked for league upon league upon vast bookcases, suffer a form of degredation whereby the letters on the page of one book begin to slide down the manuscript and fall onto or sometimes into the book below. This is called *lexakinesis*.

'Encyclopaedia of Unusual Processes'
From *Bramblespit and other Poems and Stories* by Roly Drower

This book is dedicated the memory of my brother

Roly Drower

1953 – 2008

About This Book

This memoir was originally published in 2014, under the name *99 Balls Pond Road: The Story of The Exploding Galaxy*. It is one of very few accounts by women 'who were actually there' during London's sixties counterculture. On the whole, apart from accounts from the few, among them, Sheila Rowbotham, Jenny Diski, Karen Moller and Sara Maitland or musicians such as Marianne Faithful or Carol Grimes, the English hippie movement has been largely seen through the prism of male ambitions and male memories. In this book Drower evokes the spirit of the time, with all its innocence, its hopes for the world, its contradictions and its glaring hypocrisies.

This smaller-format, text-only version of the book is produced largely for the academic market with the budgets of students in mind. It is relevant to those studying art history, the sixties counterculture, the emergence of feminism, cultural studies or anthropology. The larger format, fully illustrated version is still available.

Acknowledgements

There are a number of people I would like to thank for their support during the research and production of this book.

Firstly there are the witnesses - those people who were either members of the Exploding Galaxy or were close to the group who have kindly shared their memories of the time. They are: Annabel Bradshaw (previously, Annabel Rutter), Guy Brett, Pete Brown, Nick Butt, Michael Chapman, Chris Clarke, Caroline Coon, David Curtis, Hermine Demoriane, Patrick Deval, Jeff Dexter, Drumbeat, John Dugger, John Dunbar, Gerald Fitzgerald (also known as Mr Agoshaman Ceribel), Andrew Forrest, Lesley Forrest, Carol Grimes, Sue Hall, Jim Haynes, Hertzmark, Mitja Hinderks, Jane Hope (Ellis), John (Hoppy)Hopkins, Michael Horovitz, Jenny House, Josephine Johnson, Annabel Keeler (previously Annabel Drower), Christian Ledoux, Malcolm Le Maistre, Umiak Mahoupe (previously, Julia Price), Josephine Marston, John Oliphant (also known as Rakis), Clay Perry, Maggie Perry, Judith Pertz, Edward Pope, Rag Doll (also known as Steve Thornton), Eve Ridoux, Vidya Anand Sagar, Nick Sawyer, Maya Sendall, Stanley Siegel, Lizzie, Simon Shirley, John Schofield, Jenny Spires, Ray Stephenson, David Thorp, Monica Threlfall, Audrey Vipond, Hugo Williams and Tony Whooley.

I would also like to thank all those who supported the practical side of the production of this book. In particular, I would like to thank: Rasheed Araeen, Roger Bolton, Gill Dow, Roger Ede and Adrian Whitaker. Thanks also go to David Medalla, for giving me the best part of my education and to Sylvina Boissonas, for her courage in making those funding decisions that defied all convention. Finally, I would like to thank my husband, Constantine Benckendorff, for his patience in accepting the ever-shifting deadline, John (Hoppy) Hopkins for his wisdom and good suggestions and John Oliphant for his unstinting encouragement via email from afar.

Chapters

Foreword

EVEN IN OUR world of instant imagery and information, it seems we must wait patiently before a period of time is deemed worthy of 'serious' examination. The first issue of *The Sixties*, an academic journal dedicated to the time in which this work is set, appeared only in 2008. The curious had to depend on accounts offered from the periphery by the Mr Joneses, written in the comfort of their campus offices but back then nowhere to be seen. Other accounts, including those by Joe Boyd and Barry Miles, who were both emphatically 'there', have added greater authenticity, although their books, *White Bicycles* and *London Calling*, are written from a male perspective, and tend to focus on the authors' own roles as bringers and messengers of change.

If the past is a foreign country, Jill Drower's work is a guide, written with great accuracy, elegance and humility, to remote and previously unexplored valleys of London's alternative culture in those years. Her story begins in the art world, with the opening of a gallery forgotten by all but the cognoscenti. There is considerable interest at present in the work of once obscure groups active in the 1960s in carrying art into new territories, as, in New York, the MoMA's show on Japan's Hi Red Center group recently demonstrated. But Drower here draws attention to, and documents meticulously, the work of the Exploding Galaxy, a group that worked on our doorstep but has, with the exception of David Medalla, been almost completely neglected. She traces the group's contribution to the seminal events marking the emergence of the London Underground, from the 14-Hour Technicolor Dream to the Legalise Pot Rally, that are given the attention and space they deserve by someone who was present and deeply involved.

Her narrative extends beyond the world of London's galleries, clubs, performance spaces and exploration sites in those years. Even to those who shared that experience, especially us males, the descriptions of these legendary moments through the eyes of a 15-year-old girl and the observations of the women interviewed, on stage but ornamental and largely silenced, introduce a fresh perspective on the 'sexual revolution' as it played out in group and personal relationships. Indeed, we are prompted to ask whether there was much of a revolution at all. Social-class differences that persisted in the 'summer of love', a theme glossed over in idealised versions of the changes, also come under the microscope.

The work incorporates oral history, recording the linguistic peculiarities that developed so rapidly among those involved. Historians of fashion will find the nuanced descriptions and the visual evidence of what was worn of great interest. Meanwhile, Londoners' complex and rapidly shifting notions of class and status were reflected in their geographical reference points. The Islington of widespread light industry and brick-throwing fascists may seem fanciful to today's reader.

This account may well not please all those Exploders mentioned within. Reading through, I found it a hall of mirrors where our vanity, moral superiority, spiritual materialism, utter sense of entitlement and ultimate corruptibility made me shudder at times. But it is a story that fills important gaps in our own histories, marking what was certainly a turning point for each one of us, and enhancing our insights into who we were, or thought we were.

John Oliphant, Tokyo, 1 January, 2014

AN ANNEXE OF THE GALAXY

The Exploding Galaxy flashed brightly in the black and white world that was just coming to an end as I was growing up. When I first met them, my opinion of art was fixed firmly against what I thought of as amateur. I came from a theatrical family, dedicated to extreme professionalism and mockery of anything less. Whether it was holiday pantomimes, school plays, or cabaret flamenco

– anything short of Yehudi Menuhin or John Gielgud – we would be told how ludicrous they were, how comically inept. It seemed to be the only thing my parents agreed about and so we went along with it. How we laughed! They would wrap themselves in contempt for less immaculate performers as a form of protection from the rawness of appearing in public.

Professionalism is a counterfeit art. It gets swept away from time to time. Brando did it in the fifties, Gerald du Maurier in the twenties, playing one scene with his hands in his pockets. My own allegiance to the dégagé light comedy and perfect timing way of life (which was supposed to be so difficult) was exactly the sort of thing the sixties in general and the Exploding Galaxy in particular were trying to explode, 'but just too late for me'. I came to know them by a series of seemingly random chances. I'd known Guy Brett at school and when I came to London in 1964 I rented a room in his house off the Edgware Road. His brother was at the Architectural Association and one day we all went to a ball there. I had a double ticket, but couldn't find anyone to go with. I asked Hermine to dance and two days later she moved into my room. Guy was the Art Critic of *The Times* by now, influenced by David Medalla.

It was the time of Kinetic Art and David was curator of Signals Gallery in Wigmore Street. Art was moving away from my protected world, but Hermine kept after it. Soon after we got married and moved into a house in Islington, Medalla instigated The Exploding Galaxy Dance Drama, a commune in nearby Balls Pond Road. They would come round here for communal hot baths and snacks, there being no services at No. 99. Hermine would go jumble saling with them, or scrudging (looking for things in the street). It was now that our marriage took a crash course in hippie. Dance dramas were performed at the Roundhouse and Parliament Hill, where we later had annual birthday parties for our daughter like a kind of ghost tribute to the Galaxy. In those days I was about halfway between the thinking of the Galaxy and that of the other inhabitants of Balls Pond Road. Today I feel more sympathetic to what they were trying to do, which was personified for me by the form of Jill Drower, flitting magically through psychedelic happenings like a dryad of the night.

Every so often a particular kind of professionalism wears itself out and then a cult of inspired amateurishness rises up for a moment and creates innovation through chaos. As Jean Cocteau said, all art is amateur. The Galaxy finally exploded when a Paris heiress started dispensing large amounts of francs for them all to go to India. 'Free money for artistic projects. Please come to 31 Rue de l'Echaudé. Telephone...' ran the ad in the *Herald Tribune* in 1968. Hermine was included in the gold rush. In order to be different, she took our three-year-old daughter all over South America. But that's another story.

Hugo Williams, London, 27 October 2013

A Walk in Dalston

WE MET IN the early summer of 2013, Edward and I. I had invited him on a hunt – not a scrudgehunt as in the sixties, but the search for a particular building, where, in 1968, Exploding Galaxy members had produced our greatest unscheduled art event.

We travelled up remnants of the North London line, alighting at Canonbury Station. It was here, on the bridge between platforms, that a group of us had all those years ago created the refrain, 'No two elephants are the same', a cheerful transformation of an enamel sign we had seen. This had become a Galaxy catch phrase.

Our journey down Balls Pond Road and to the streets beyond was as much a journey back through time as through space. Nothing brought this home to me more than the sounds, or rather the absence of sounds, on that walk in June 2013. As we left the the train, there was just the mild hum, woosh and click of the automatic doors. In the 1960s, overground travel was always accompanied by banging as you left the train – the shutting of the doors on the old slam-shut carriages.

The soundscape that morning was poignant. No sounds of industry. In 1967 a walk through the area bounded by Kingsland Road in the East and Essex Road in the West would have been accompanied by continual whirring and grinding coming from industries of all kinds – metal workings, garages or carpentry shops. In the sixties, even the private homes in those back streets housed family industry – trinket making, garment production and the like. There was also the dressing-gown factory in Tottenham Road. We knew all this because we had harvested material offcuts from local bins to make costumes and artworks as we went about our daily wanderings.

We did not know noise pollution. We just accepted an assortment of lively sounds – the cock crowing in a local garden and the day punctuated like clockwork by the after-lunch playground din from the primary school nearby.

The visual changes were similar. The houses were the same ones, but whereas before the paint was peeled, mortar absent and the brickwork split, now all was freshly painted and carefully tended.

Only the Duke of Wellington pub appeared almost exactly the same. It has mercifully kept its 19th century identity, although the back part appears to have been extended out into where there was once a milk depot. Across the road, our old Turkish café was now a smart housing development.

Nothing could have prepared us for the biggest change, which lay waiting for us at Dalston Junction. The place was altered beyond all recognition. The old theatre, once a circus, was gone. This had during our time been the Four Aces Club where Desmond Dekker and Stevie Wonder had performed. Its exquisite interior started to decay after Hackney Council took the roof off. By flattening and rebuilding the centre of Dalston, London has gained a brand new station and large quantities of housing, little of it affordable.

It was here in the redevelopment that we found the Hackney Archive and here that Edward picked up the lead that would take us to our destination, the site of our greatest scrudge event – an abandoned manufacturer of cake-makers' supplies.

1

Signals of Wigmore Street

I dream of the day when I shall go to the centre of the earth and in the earth's core place a flower sculpture.

DAVID MEDALLA [1]

MY INTRODUCTION TO the world of kinetic art came when, at the age of 15, I accidentally broke a work by the Venezuelan artist Jésus-Rafael Soto. It was displayed on the wall in the basement of 99 Balls Pond Road, Hackney, and at the time I was doing a twirling dance with an opened Edwardian parasol, which I had recently bought at a shop called Granny Takes a Trip. The wooden tip caught on something – threads of taut nylon, a vibrating illusion – and *oops*, the half-joined strands hung limply down. I had just obliterated an artwork which would now fetch a small fortune.

I did see other works at the house that night, including the majestic columns of David Medalla's bubble machine boxes, tilting lifeless against a wall. The house was still smart, but lacked electricity, as this had been cut off. The occupants were clearly passionate about art but had fallen on hard times. What I did not know was that the building had been bought by Paul Keeler almost exactly one year before, shortly after Europe's showcase gallery, Signals, had opened its doors in central London, and that this property was all that remained of that very special gallery's spirit.

I did not know either, on that evening of the parasol and the Soto, that this building was to become my home from home as a weekend hippie for the next two years. Wednesday 5 April 1967 marked my symbolic enrolment into a singular kind of finishing school that later came to be known as the Exploding Galaxy, a school through which I was to embark on a radical re-education and a journey that was both psychedelic and aesthetic.

In the months following my first visit to 99 Balls Pond Road, I became familiar with the works of the kinetic artists who had been shown at Signals. In my own fifth-form manner, I gradually got to know the term *kinetic* and began to realise how broad it was. Kinetic artworks incorporated the idea of motion, and this could be engendered by means of a motor, as in David Medalla's mud machine, or by powerful electro-magnets as in the dancing tension of the *Homage to Nijinsky* by Takis, or by interaction with the audience/participant as with any number of works by Lygia Clark. There were people who liked to argue about labels, and I remember a debate about whether or not the virtual movement created by op art techniques should also be counted as 'kinetic'. Certainly, Soto's works, with his use of suspended Perspex and the dizzying moiré technique, would have to be included.

No one in London's art world in the mid-sixties could have failed to notice David Medalla. He had a freshness that was beguiling. This was swinging London, and there were some very exciting young artists at work who had been experimenting since the fifties and did not fit into the old-school mould. Medalla blended in with the new mood, with ideas simply tumbling out of him in every conversation. A young Filipino who had been living and working in Manila, he had until recently been extremely conventional in his approach to painting, doing landscapes, portraits and still lifes. He described himself before he turned to kinetic sculpture as 'having been living in a different time – almost a hundred years behind my other fellow artists'.

It was around this time that David Medalla and Paul Keeler had plans to start an art gallery. David had an extraordinary eye and was the driving force. Paul describes him as the one with ideas and the flair, and himself as the entrepreneur, the one who made it all happen. Both shared an interest in painters such as Charles Lutyens and Rudi Behrens, and this led to the first 'trial run' exhibition in the vast wood-panelled entrance hall of Paul's parents' home in Windsor. This was followed by an exhibition of David's paintings and drawings at the Mayflower Barn in Jordans, a village near Chalfont St Giles. The interest generated by these exhibitions led to the registering of 'Paul Keeler Fine Arts Limited' at Companies House in December 1963 and the opening of a permanent viewing space in Cornwall Gardens, their mansion flat near Gloucester Road in London.

Paul describes an overnight conversion – one day it was 'out with figurative paintings and the next, it was in with kinetic art'. On one of his visits to Paris, David had been enchanted by the work of Takis, Pol Bury and Soto. Both he and Paul were instantly convinced that these were the new Mondrians and Kandinskis and that there was a progression from Monet, Seurat and Cézanne through Klee and Malevich and on to the avant-garde sculptors who led directly to the work of Lygia Clark, Hélio Oiticica and others. They were 100 per cent certain that these artists would one day be internationally famous and displayed in the world's most prestigious museums. The problem was to convince the public and, in particular, that rare breed, the collectors, who at that moment were principally interested in acquiring work from pop artists.

The flat at 92 Cornwall Gardens was open for people to 'view by arrangement'. It was called the Centre for Advanced Creative Study and was dedicated to an exploration of the ways in which art related to science. This connection might seem strange, since we were now living in a world that was in the shadow of thermonuclear war and, during the recent Cuban Missile Crisis, had had to endure a mock execution, one that was oh-so-nearly not mock. But to the younger generation, there was no contradiction here. In addition to the destructive technology it engendered, the space/arms race had granted us permission to see our world with new objectivity. Labour-saving devices had given us the idea that our time was our own; through electron microscopes, we could see the biological as abstract forms; and machinery, previously always strictly at the service of function, could now be used solely for aesthetic reasons. The Centre was a place where such ideas could be generated and explored.

Perhaps the artist who most epitomised this fusion of art and science was Frank J Malina, the aeronautical engineer who designed and launched the first successful rocket in the US in 1945. He resigned from his job to devote himself to 'light and movement in painting'. The historian Frank Popper called him 'an artist–scientist of the space age', and described his work like this:

> In his art Malina has sought to find new methods and forms of expression and a new rhythm characteristic of our modern age. By choosing his themes in the world of science he has tried to focus attention on the interplay between science and art.[2]

David Medalla had started producing his own kinetic works – most famously, his Cloud Canyons, which did for foaming sculpture what Mark Boyle's lightshows did for projected colour. Watching either was a contemplation, the witnessing of a process as it slowly unfolded. Where Boyle used inks that merged and repelled in intense colour, Medalla used soap-foam that oozed down in dollops and then folded over on itself endlessly.

Maggie Perry, a friend of the two directors and frequent visitor to the Centre, describes David Medalla at this time:

> He was inspirational. He'd sit, first in Cornwall Gardens, then in Signals Gallery, and his mind was as if he was on acid, which everybody was then. Those were the days when it wasn't even illegal. But he wasn't on acid; he was on Coca-Cola. He just had this extraordinary wonderful sense of untamed imagination. There was one point where he said he was just about to make some robotic sculptures that would fly off into Cornwall Gardens and pick up rubbish, and bring it back to the house. And we would all sit there entranced by this. Quite honestly, he was in a state of extraordinary creativity and we all just got carried away. Nobody cared if he really had translated Homer when he was 12. It didn't matter; because the whole time in the sixties anything and everything was possible.

David's work soon graduated towards biokinetics. Still using a motor to initiate random movement, he produced his sand machine. Edward Pope, a member of the Exploding Galaxy, first saw David's sand machine at the Indica Gallery in 1967. Edward was on an LSD trip at the time:

> I could not see the workings. All I could see moving were the conical shapes and the sand. There was an upright, and this hid the machine itself. From the top was a string threaded through what seemed like conical shells. These trailed in such a way that the particles of sand were moving all the time and they formed little furrows. The geometric effects could not be achieved without the organic materials. Of course, you could experience this just by going down to the seashore, but in a gallery it became a metaphor. The upright with the spiral going around was like a metaphor for time and life. Once you were looking at it as a work of art, the beauty of the forms of the world we live in became apparent. We live in the city where what most people see for most of the time is square or rectangular, like squares and blocks of buildings or books and shelves in a bookshop. So the spiral motion had a much deeper rhythm.

By the summer of 1964, it had become clear that Cornwall Gardens was not fit for purpose and that this project required both more space and dedicated gallery status. The exhibition 'First Festival of Modern Art from Latin America', planned for September 1964, could only be displayed in two fortnightly shifts as there were so many contributions.

By happy coincidence, at just this moment the Keeler family business was relocating to larger and more modern premises in Marylebone Lane. The original showroom, on the corner of Wigmore and Welbeck streets, would lie vacant until its lease expired. Since the showroom was situated in W1, near London's top galleries, this seemed the obvious solution.

Charles Keeler, an inventor as well as a businessman, had expanded the family business, which made and sold spectacles, by setting up a factory for the design and manufacture of optical instruments. He introduced contact lenses to Britain, and one of his most notable achievements was to set out a new calculation which allowed opticians to measure the magnification needed to enable partially sighted people to focus clearly.

Paul approached his parents to get their support, plus the money necessary for the launch of Signals, a trail-blazing art gallery that would show and sell works by artists at the cutting edge of the cutting edge. The plan was to use the small foyer and ground and first floors for one-man shows or retrospectives. The second floor would contain a 'projects hall' for exhibitions of environmental and architectural projects. A 'Room at the Top' was later set aside for a continuing exhibition to give young and experimental artists a chance to show their work.

There were three things in particular that made Signals special. The first was its size, given its highly prized West End location. Even the state-financed Institute of Contemporary Arts, then down the road in Dover Street, had less square footage. The comfortable amount of space at Signals allowed for an experimental wall, a 'blank canvas' for an artist to try something new during an exhibition. The number of floors also meant that work by unknowns could be displayed, in keeping with the gallery's openness to new voices within art.

A second attribute, and perhaps the signature feature of the gallery, was its companion magazine, *Signals Newsbulletin*. London's arts magazines, such as *Studio International*, *The Arts Review* and *Art and Artists*, had an establishment feel, both visually and in their content. *Signals Newsbulletin* was more exciting to look at – more like the ideas wall of a top designer than a stuffy arts mag. The *Newsbulletin* contained visual references that belonged to the natural world (a flock of terns in flight or a skate's teeth magnified 15-fold), or to ancient architecture (Buddhist *stupas* or the Great Wall of China). The reader was constantly invited to make connections beyond conventional art history. This was true not just visually, but also in terms of the writing, which was much more in line with what was coming from the Beat poets. By the summer of 1965, at the time of the 'The International Poetry Incarnation' at the Albert Hall, poems featured prominently in the *Newsbulletin*. Most noticeable of all was its multilingual content, including a poem by Pablo Neruda in Spanish. This was a concerted attempt to look outwards, in defiance of what was seen as British insularity. And a regular column from BBC scientist John Newham maintained the strong connection with scientific discovery.

A third significant difference in Signals as a gallery was its open approach, unlike that of many other central London galleries, which concerned themselves exclusively with selling artworks. Nick Sawyer was a student of art and Galaxy associate during the sixties. He remembers Signals at its best. A subscriber to the *Newsbulletin*, he regularly came down to London from the Scottish borders. At most of the West End galleries, he was scowled at and frozen out pretty quickly because he looked too young and too poor to have potential as a buyer. According to Nick:

> Signals was different. If you went in there, you were welcomed, introduced to artists and invited to participate in discussions. What came across above anything else was the passion in that gallery for the works they were showing. It was welcoming and unpretentious.

When the gallery was at its height, a Signals launch was the place to be seen in London, and people would fly in just to attend. The only difficulty was the paucity of sales.

Paul Keeler was an entrepreneur. He was excited by the work and wanted to promote it, and he liked talking to the artists. Selling and dealing was of less interest to him. He only came to realise the impact of this when it was too late:

> I have never been very comfortable as salesman to the very rich. As a dealer, you got to be a part of their world. You joined as a courtier, just like their barber or their interior decorator or their couturier. These were the people who were close to the super-rich, and art dealers were a part of this entourage. I never felt comfortable in that particular tribe. I was a very good promoter of the work but was not a successful dealer.

In his early twenties, Paul had until recently been an aspiring actor. Unlike his older brother, he had not worked in the family business, and so had not been initiated into the world of selling. During the life of Signals Gallery, he can remember only a handful of private buyers, the occasional museum purchase and just one single passionate collector.

There has been much speculation about the end of Signals in the autumn of 1966. It seems that, when a single theory is propounded for a historical occurrence, where there is an absence of any other explanation, this single theory gets repeated time and again until it becomes irrefutable fact. The single theory in the case of Signals is that Charles Keeler, as principal backer of the gallery, withdrew his support in protest against Lewis Mumford's 1965 address to the American Academy of Arts and Letters, which he read in *Signals Newsbulletin*. In the piece, Mumford publicly criticised US involvement in the Vietnam War, and it was followed by the poet Robert Lowell's letter declining an invitation to the White House for the same reasons. This story fits very snugly with countercultural romanticism – the narrow world of the pro-war older generation crushing the creativity of the young.

Paul is certain that his father would not have read the Mumford article, and that if he had, this would not have been enough for him to close the gallery, since he was, above all, a practical man with good business sense. Paul says:

> There was no mystery to the end of Signals. It is quite simple. Signals closed because it was not able to carry itself through financially. It is a world you enter because you believe in it. You promote the work in the hope that there is sufficient time before the money runs out. In the case of Signals, the money ran out before the collectors began to buy. If I had held on longer and had cultivated a group of collectors, then it might have been different, but the reality was that there weren't sufficient funds to launch that kind of operation. We would put a show on and get massive press interest, but hardly a work sold. In this sense, the gallery was ahead of its time... The Mumford ending is a myth, as is any version of Greek drama with a father intent on destroying his son. It was the plain old bottom line that ended Signals.

In addition to the lack of sales, there were crippling expenses. Following Soto's success at the Venice Biennale, Paul had convinced his mother that the artist was a watertight investment, and she gave him the £10,000 necessary to buy the whole collection. There was also the rental of a studio in Flood Street for Takis and the astronomical production costs of the *Newsbulletin*. The gallery was haemorrhaging money and the receivers were called in.

The artist Graham Stevens has described Signals as 'the most avant-garde gallery in the world, with nothing that could have beaten the collections they introduced' and saw its end as a tragedy. For him, the financial problem boiled down to the differences between dealing in art and selling in the optical business, which ran on entirely different business models. With spectacles or optical instruments, you manufactured and you sold quickly. With a gallery, you bought artists when they were valued at a low price and you waited. It was only by hanging on to them that you got the profit, but this required nerve. Graham describes this difference:

> You have a gallery, and you buy the artists you think are the best, at a time when they are totally unknown. They become your artist stock and over the years they get recognised, and as their reputation increases you then sell off your stock at the best point. That is the role of the dealer – to buy artists and develop the stock.

The problem is that the kind of nerve required has to be supported by wealth of the bottomless-pit variety, which was not an accurate description of the Keeler family's financial resources.

The debt at this point was approximately £10,000 and growing. This will seem a remarkably low figure to modern ears, but it was enough to threaten to topple the mother ship – Keeler Optics. Charles Keeler was forced to sell assets to compensate.

There was also history here. As manufacturers of precision instruments, Keeler Optics had had the kind of plant and know-how that had been immediately commandeered for state use at the start of the Second World War. During the six-month 'phony war' following the official declaration, the government had instructed seconded manufacturers to 'clear the decks and await instructions', and as a result

Keeler Optics had very nearly gone under. In 1966, the clock had been ticking for far longer than six months.

Towards the end, when the writing was on the wall, the industrialist Jeremy Fry was brought in. The Fry family were no longer in the business of manufacturing chocolate, after a take-over by their rivals Cadbury. Having founded Rotork Engineering, which supplied equipment to oil and gas refineries, Jeremy Fry had gained a reputation as a rescuer of theatre and arts projects and had already produced a limited edition of Takis – randomly flashing lights on reedy tensile stalks. Paul invited him up to London in the hope that he might inject funds. Fry took one long look at the books, politely said no and left.

Eventually, long after all the emotional dust had settled, the Signals directors were vindicated. In the end, the artworks they had advocated so passionately were indeed purchased by the world's major galleries. However, since that time there has been nothing in print that has commended the Keeler family for their courage against all the odds in backing this extraordinary art gallery.

I did eventually meet Jésus-Rafael Soto. It was in Paris in 1968, when he was supporting his life as an artist by playing guitar in restaurants at night. I was present at a private recital he gave to visiting members of the Exploding Galaxy. The more I learned about this artist, the more ashamed I felt about that moment when I had sliced through his delicate optical illusion.

Unlike others from the South American avant-garde, Soto did not come from the urban middle class. He was a child of the Orinoco, brought up in poverty and in close proximity to a community of Indians, whom he held in high regard. It was their ancient knowledge of forest medicine that had kept his family safe from doctors' bills. He particularly admired the way, when fishing in their dugout canoes, the Indians would aim their arrows skywards to pierce fish in the waters below. Soto talked about the Indians and his childhood:

> They dressed their own way and spurned Western society. I have great respect for Indian civilisation, so superior to ours when one considers the selfishness, deceit and bickering that goes on everywhere here. Here it is every man for himself. The Indians did not know of prisons and death penalties. I miss their friendship... My house looked out over the riverbank. We used to bathe in the river. It was full of alligators and electric eels, the *trembladores* – one sting and you're at the bottom. Many children were eaten alive by alligators. But one can spot alligators by their smell. I can't any longer. The instinct has gone. The last time I bathed in the Orinoco was in 1962. But I had lost the ability to smell out the alligators: uprooted, I had lost contact. I often regret that.[3]

Now, looking back, I think this one artist in particular has given us a symbolic message about those times. As 'beautiful people', we often stated that we were going back to 'the garden' – to a new Eden of our own making; but our urban ways were clumsy. Our motives were honourable, but we did not know how to tread carefully and were blind to some degree to our impact on the delicately established systems we wanted to enter.

Soto was unusual because he actually came from 'the garden' and could effortlessly straddle the two worlds. We 'beautiful people' wanted his kind of innocence, but our idealism lacked the necessary awareness that would allow us to step easily between the two. We were innocent in a different kind of way. Our hearts were in the right place, but we were unable to smell out the alligators lurking close by.

NOTES

1. David Medalla, MMMMMMM... Manifesto, 1965 *Signals Newsbulletin*, vol. 1, no. 8, June–July 1965.
2. From the *Unesco Courier*, September 1963.
3. *Signals Newsbulletin*, Soto issue, vol. 1, no. 10, translated by Sebastian Brett

2

Were you in Yoko's Bottoms Film?

> *I was continuing to shrink, to become... what? The infinitesimal? What was I? Still a human being? Or was I the man of the future? If there were other bursts of radiation, other clouds drifting across the seas and continents, would other beings follow me into this vast new world? So close – the infinitesimal and the infinite*
>
> FROM THE INCREDIBLE SHRINKING MAN, 1957[1]

IT WAS IN August 1966 that I first heard the term *hippie*. I was in an all-girl folk band with my sister Annabel and her musician friend Julia, and we were gigging at the Edinburgh Festival. We hung out at the Traverse Theatre, and I got chatting to the comedy trio The Scaffold. I was impressed by Mike McGear, particularly because he was Paul McCartney's brother. He said 'hippie' a lot – 'hippie this' and 'hippie that'. This was the last I heard of that word until the following spring, by which time the press had appropriated it and gone wild, sprinkling the 'h' word liberally through all their derogatory copy.

It is generally agreed that 'The International Poetry Incarnation' at the Royal Albert Hall the previous summer launched our own sixties underground movement. Although, at 13, I was too young to have attended, I believe that it was less a starting point than a confluence of different streams of London's young intellectuals – the Campaign for Nuclear Disarmament, Beats, jazz fans, Situationists, art students and literary types including, of course, representatives from the international poetry scene. Peter Whitehead's film of the event, called *Wholly Communion*, shows that the still-legal drug LSD contributed much to that evening.

However, no one has suggested a date for the end of London's Flower Power proper. If I were trying to pin down the un-pin-downable, I would suggest that the movement had three phases, each associated with an event. In my personal version of the counterculture, Phase 1 is from 11 June 1965 to 15 October 1966. I would describe this as the 'gentsia' stage – starting with the Albert Hall poetry event and ending with the first issue of the underground newspaper *International Times*. Phase 2, which I call the 'euphoric' stage, seeped freely into its neighbouring stages. This was the time when our approach to life was developed and spread more widely among young Londoners and, to a lesser degree, further afield. At this point, nothing had crept in to shake our view that love and peace would triumph. People went around proclaiming that it was all over, that we had won. For a moment, even class barriers seemed to have disappeared.

The beginning of Phase 3, which I call the 'appropriation', can be pinpointed precisely to Wednesday 17 May 1967. This is the date when a documentary was broadcast on the BBC about 'The 14-Hour Technicolor Dream' at Alexandra Palace in North London. Since there were only three television channels, the telly-viewing public could choose between the police drama *Softly Softly*, a murder mystery starring Raymond Francis and Sean Caffrey or Desmond Wilcox's documentary *What is a Happening?* After that evening, talk of the hippies spread like wildfire. We became a national obsession. There was then an asset-stripping of our treasured component parts. Commerce – especially the fashion industry – appropriated our paisleys and our beads and our psychedelic swirls, and those of us who preached peace and love were ridiculed. Coinciding with this was the realisation within the movement that not all those who posed as 'beautiful people' were nice. From that moment on, there was a slow fragmentation.

It was, in fact, the summer of 1966 that transformed me from a schoolgirl into a member of the underground. I looked down from my bedroom window on to the garden fences separating all my near neighbours in their 'little boxes' and imagined the fences gone and the citizen suburb-dwellers enjoying and nurturing the whole space in a spirit of cooperation. By night, curtains drawn open, I would stare up at the Pleiades. I took it as an excellent omen that, in that one year, I had witnessed no fewer than three shooting stars from my Putney bedroom.

These were not just the musings of a 14-year-old. Similar thoughts were expressed by the grown-ups. Graham Stevens remembers that, at around the same time, he had a conversation with the Brazilian artist Sérgio de Camargo about ridding ourselves of national borders since we were all on the same planet. Camargo had replied that this was impossible.

At the centre of our alternative world was the idea that everything was going to be integrated, in harmony and honourable. It was going to be dominated neither by economics nor by corporate greed. It was about freedom and expanding our consciousness. We were filled with compassionate idealism and we knew that absolutely everything was possible.

Liliane Lijn had participated in earlier happenings in Paris such as Jean-Jacques Lebel's *Pour conjurer l'esprit de catastrophe,* in 1963,[1] described as 'a parody of contemporary colonial Cold War tensions'.[2] Some four years later, she expressed a universally shared idealism when she wrote about her idea for 'Art Industry':

> There are artists who speak of art in industry. I am talking of Art Industry. A new industrial complex completely devoted to art. It should have top priority, even over the war materials industry. There should be a strong connection with NASA. It should be able to appropriate materials from all other sections of industry. The practical and social functions of artists will emerge in time. Art Industry will be entirely for the benefit and welfare of the population.[3]

It is this period of hope that is remembered so fondly. There was something in the air. We knew that we were on the verge of something almighty, something that would overwhelm us all and transform the world.

This kind of optimism was widespread among young and creative people in 1966 and 1967, and it is poignant that the demise of Signals Gallery in the autumn of 1966 coincided exactly with this growing feeling of euphoria within the underground.

The end of the gallery was, by contrast, a picture of total devastation. Guy Brett, then art critic of *The Times*, has described it as a very painful moment for everyone involved. Both the gallery's director, Paul Keeler, and its artistic adviser, David Medalla, were in a state of deep distress. They were not the only ones. Frantic artists were wiring them for news of their pieces. Guy fielded many of the calls and did his best to follow up anxious queries with the liquidators. The Mira Schendel exhibition had been cut short. Other exhibitions in the pipeline had to be cancelled. Guy stored the works of the Brazilian artist Hélio Oiticica in the hope that an alternative venue could be arranged at a later date.

Bankruptcy was not seen as a dignified option in the early sixties, nor a positive way out. It had a finality about it and came with far more stigma than would be attached now.

Just as the gallery was on its way out, *International Times* was on its way in. In its second issue, the new newspaper gave a fond farewell salute to Signals:

> The liveliest gallery in London, Signals in Wigmore Street has now closed down. Although it had barely been open two years, under its director Paul Keeler and its artistic adviser David Medalla, Signals changed the London art scene. It was the first gallery to show kinetic art and reveal that the most important developments in abstract art are happening now not in the USA but South America, holding one-man shows of major importance like Lygia Clark and Sérgio de Camargo (Brazil) and Jesús-Rafael Soto (Venezuela).[4]

Like *Signals Newsbulletin*, *International Times* showed a determination to look outwards beyond our national boundaries. This move away from the parochial in both papers was startling. However, where the *Newsbulletin* looked towards what was happening in South

America, *International Times* took its lead from the US Beat scene and the Provo movement in Amsterdam.

I must have picked up my first issue of *International Times* at a poetry reading or folk music venue. The paper was passed from person to person and, like others in the underground, I combed through every article and every small ad. In this way, I read about Allen Ginsberg and William Burroughs, names that were new to me at the age of 15 but were to become landmarks in a whole new world of cultural references.

It is hard to imagine now, in our internet-dominated world, just how important a fortnightly printed publication could be. *International Times*, known subsequently as *IT*, was our rallying point and the touchpaper that lit up London's underground scene. With the arrival of *IT* in October 1966 came the sense that there were a lot of like-minded people out there. Like lone survivors in a film about the end of the world, we delighted in realising that we were not alone after all. The free listings section allowed us to congregate. Through this, I visited the Indica Bookshop and bought a copy of *Last Exit to Brooklyn*, saw an exhibition by Yoko Ono and witnessed Mark Boyle projecting all his bodily fluids on to a large screen. In this sense, *IT* had more in common with the pamphlets of the late 18th century than it did with present-day mass rallying media online.

The editorial team at *IT* wanted their newspaper to be unlike any other. The established Fleet Street standard had always been to take a political stand and project this to the readership. The approach at *IT* differed in that it aimed to be receptive. It was to be a collective, not just in its organisation but also in its selection of content. Barry Miles, known as Miles, was at the heart of things at both Indica and *IT*. In an interview for the BBC in 1967, he said:

> We wanted to get the ideas of the readers to flow in so that the paper was really a mirror of the scene, and after about 20 issues the observer could sit down and look through the paper and crystalise out a sort of mass philosophy and a mass psychology of what was happening.[5]

The *IT* launch party was held on 15 October 1966 at the Roundhouse in Camden, north London, which had been for many years a store for Gilbey's Gin. Its initial role as a railway turning shed had been short-lived, owing to the rapidly increasing size of locomotives. The playwright Arnold Wesker took over its lease in 1964 with an ambitious plan to convert the building into a vast permanent cultural centre. The aim was to find a popular audience for the arts, 'not an audience for popular art'. He named the project Centre 42, after a resolution passed by the Trades Union Congress in 1961 calling for the arts to be more inclusive. My schoolfriend and neighbour Josephine Ranken accompanied me to many underground events. She describes the newly opened Roundhouse in the following way:

> It was a truly wonderful venue. Built by great men for a great purpose, it is magnificent by anyone's standards. It wasn't properly lit, which made it perfect for a concert. When we went there to those early concerts and parties, it was still very crude and primitive with a cobbled floor and no weather-proofing. I remember there were leaves blowing about and this faintly sinister but rugged industrial air about the place.

The Roundhouse was truly underground. In his book *London Calling*, Miles describes the place as it was on the night of the *IT* launch party:

> The building was fundamentally unsafe: there was no proper floor, and great jagged pieces of metal stuck up from a thick layer of grime. There were only two toilets, and the electricity supply was... powerful enough only to light the building. There were several large doors opening out onto the railway freight yards, but the entrance staircase from Chalk Farm Road was so narrow that only one person at a time could enter or leave.[6]

Miles goes on to describe the conditions that faced the 2,000 or so present that evening. People were obliged to keep moving because of the freezing temperatures, and the toilet doors had to be taken off to use as duck boards since both lavatories had flooded. The payoff, as with so many underground events to come, was the excitement and originality of the evening. Miles continues:

> Marianne Faithfull, there with Mick Jagger, won the shortest/barest contest for an extremely abbreviated nun's outfit (these were pre-PC days, though there were several men who were in the running). People wore refraction lenses to indicate their third eye; they wore silver headdresses and long robes, spaceman outfits and rubber bondage wear.[7]

There were other celebrities present, including Paul McCartney, who was dressed as a sheikh, and the actress Monica Vitti, who arrived on the arm of the film-maker Michelangelo Antonioni.

The artist Biddy Peppin made, with a substantial donation from Rowntrees, a giant jelly, working until five in the morning with the Roundhouse single electric kettle that kept giving shocks. The aim was to make the thing rise up like Ayers Rock, and since she wanted it to be an edible sculpture, she flavoured it with peppermint and almond and added purple and green food dye. One reveller bravely stripped in the near-zero temperature to splash about in the sticky mess. Conflicting press cuttings place the giant jelly at both the *IT* launch in October of 1966 and at the Uncommon Market in the spring of 1967. Whatever the true date, the jelly was both tasted and bathed in, and is remembered as an auto-destructive event to promote *IT* in its early days.

Poet and member of The Soft Machine Daevid Allen describes his experience of the launch evening:

> That was our first gig as a quartet. Yoko Ono came onstage and created a giant happening by getting everybody to touch each other in the dark, right in the middle of the set. We also had a motorcycle brought onto stage and would put a microphone against the cylinder head for a good noise.[8]

The evening was punctuated by other disturbing noises. There was the sound of breaking glass, not from a fight but from the recitation of a poem. The poet, also known as 'The Density Man', was at the time living in Hessel Street in the East End, and at night he would regularly hear a drunken old woman pass by, effing and blinding. She would pick up empty milk bottles from the doorsteps and smash them as she went. The poem was an exact repetition of her curses and breakages.

Hot on the heels of the *IT* launch party came the club called UFO. Advertised in issue three as the 'Night Tripper', for those of us in the know that winter this was guaranteed to be our flagship happening. The DJ Jeff Dexter, when talking about UFO, helpfully supplies its pronunciation for the uninitiated: 'UFO as in yooo-foe, or as in you-faux, or as in Yoof-oh.'

Josephine Ranken recalls the Blarney Club, the Irish ballroom that became UFO's home between 23 December 1966 and 28 July 1967:

> The trouble was that, although there was a splendid ambience, the building was cramped, with extremely low ceilings. As a building, it was devoid of atmosphere and didn't add to the sense of occasion. It was a dreary little dungeon. We all loved going there for the music and the dancing, which was jolly good. It was an exciting space despite the building's lack of charm.

On a good night at UFO, you might meet Martin Sharp, the Australian Day-Glo collagist; Pete Brown, the poet and writer of lyrics for The Cream; or Yoko Ono, trying to recruit large numbers of naked buttocks for her film *No. 4*. If you were into music in a big way (who wasn't?), you could dance to one of the two house bands, Pink Floyd or The Soft Machine, or, for a visual treat, sit and watch a film like *The Incredible Shrinking Man* or Akira Kurosawa's *Rashomon*. Most memorable of all, you would be covered, head to toe, in pulsating colour from a lightshow. Often this was the work of Mark Boyle and Joan Hills, working under the name of the 'Sensual Laboratory', or Peter Wynne Willson, the Floyd's own lighting engineer. Lightshows were previously unknown to most of us. For me, a Putney High girl, studying for her O levels, this was the most exciting place in the universe.

UFO-goers have eventually come to be known as UFOrians. This is a suitable title, since our strangeness was viewed with growing fear by the general public, as if we were not true earthlings. We were the children of the damned, with our funny stares. Where was Professor Bernard Quatermass when you needed him, to help stop us from multiplying grotesquely and exponentially? Instead, our swollen pods burst forth their load of deviant spores. The extraterrestrials had landed and were beginning to multiply.

NOTES

1. From closing monologue of *The Incredible Shrinking Man*, 1957, directed by Jack Arnold and written by Richard Matheson
2. Sarah Wilson, *Body, Line, Fire* (exhibition catalogue for 'Liliane Liljn: Selected works 1959–2005'), Austin Desmond Fine Art, 2006.
3. *Signals Newsbulletin*, boxed edition (Iniva, 1995).
4. *International Times*, 31 October 1966.
5. From the BBC documentary *The Impresarios: Transport by Underground*, 23 October 1967 (BBC Archives).
6. Barry Miles, *London Calling: A Countercultural History of London Since 1945* (Atlantic Books, 2011).
7. Miles, *London Calling.*
8. Miles, *London Calling.*1

3

The Uforian Manifesto

You can protect yourself and your family by building a fall-out shelter within your home. Choose a space farthest from the roof and from the outside walls. Make arrangements now. In your safe room you can build a lean-to using doors, which you should secure with rope or string. Fill backpacks, bags and boxes with sand or earth to pack around your refuge. After the warnings have sounded, turn off your gas and electricity supplies and draw all curtains. In your refuge you should have a radio, food for 14 days, an opener, water, a sanitary bucket with a lid, plastic bags, warm clothing, bedding, a clock and a calendar.

The fall-out warning consists of three bangs, maroons or whistles in short succession. A continuous, steady sound will signify all the clear.

PROTECT AND SURVIVE [1]

ALTHOUGH I HAD not yet spent a weekend at No. 99 Balls Pond Road, I have been told just how grim it was during that winter of 1966/67. The house was freezing cold at night. Daytime meals were bought on tick at the local greasy spoon, and supper often consisted of chapatis with no accompaniment.

Paul was still embroiled in the Signals liquidation, with frequent visits to his parents in Windsor and meetings with the accountants. For David, things were slightly different. He was less involved with the insolvency, and he also had an extraordinary capacity to bounce back in times of trouble. The French film-maker Christian Ledoux was now living in the house, and he and David participated in a performance at the Royal College of Art of a play by Tristan Tzara. Needless to say, the Dadaists were adored by the counterculture for their interest in chance, cut-ups, insulting the audience and the absurd. The plays of Alfred Jarry were also great favourites.

After only a few issues of *IT*, a mass philosophy was already emerging. Its themes and preoccupations were our intellectual glue, sticking together an assortment of views into one common ground. Aside from the obvious issues – the Vietnam War, race, miscarriages of justice and the legalisation of pot – on which everyone agreed, there were more problematic ones. While there was agreement that censorship was a bad thing, an early article on Ezra Pound, which conveyed his antisemitic views, did not go down well with everyone. We were a movement that was feeling its way, defining ourselves as we went along.

UFO-goers did not have a manifesto as such, but a number of key issues had begun to crystallise. These determined our outlook, and although one might ask, 'Why on earth attach a manifesto to a dance club?', the answer from someone who was there is: 'Why not?' UFO was never 'just a club' and manifestos were tumbling out from all directions. According to the BBC, Yoko Ono had even suggested that a pretty woman having her clothes snipped off in front of a crowd was a manifesto.

Had our opinions been formulated into numbered resolutions, our own UFOrian manifesto might have been expressed as follows:

RESOLUTION I: ABANDON ALL CONVENTION

Foremost was the issue of compliance. Our parents' generation had done what they were told and where had that landed them? The Cuban missile crisis had just given Planet Earth the closest near miss of its 4.54-billion-year history. Denial eased in the great nuclear lie like a giant shoehorn. Surely we all really knew that anyone living in a major conurbation would be instantly dry-roasted, but the government did not want us jamming the roads with our motorcars. To keep us compliant, they presented mass obliteration as something survivable. They superimposed onto the unimaginable terror the coping strategies that had helped us through the Blitz, which, after all, was still fairly fresh in the public consciousness.

We, the youngsters, were therefore not going to be compliant. We set about challenging conventions wherever they appeared. It wasn't so much a breaking of the rules as a wholesale abandonment of them. Although this applied right across the board, the clearest example can be seen in dress code and appearance, which had previously always followed a strict set of rules. Even after the arrival of the Beatle mop-top, men continued to wear their hair with a parting on the left. Then came non-compliance. Toplessness made a very brief appearance in 1964, and hemlines gradually moved up, the convention having been to keep them below the knee. Once a critical mass of change was reached, however, the whole population shifted to follow suit.

Had I been born some years earlier, I would have done my best at 15 to look like a woman of 45. My accessories would have matched and I would not have been seen dead in a jacket buttoned left over right. But I was born in the generation that liked to describe itself as 'strange'. At Putney High School from 1966, we girls were on occasion made to kneel in lines after assembly. Those of us whose hemlines were higher than two inches off the floor were given a detention. In the hemline check of spring 1967, mine was eight inches off the floor. When the check took place that autumn, the hemline of my pre-war flannel gored skirt had dropped to six inches *below* the knee. This was a personal triumph since the school staff could not object, and because, to my knowledge, I had not yet seen a soul in a maxi skirt.

The fashion expert Jo Johnston remembers that, between 1967 and 1969, she did a roaring trade altering hemlines to two inches above the knee. This was almost entirely for the age group 25 to 40, with only a few members of the Mothers' Union baulking at the exposed knees. This meant that the skirts of every woman from Margaret Thatcher to Margaret Rutherford were harmonised at above the knee. The straight world was doing its best to turn 'the new' into a convention, but we were always one step ahead, blissfully unaware of our own strictly enforced rules.

In the autumn of 1966, a few people had begun to walk around London in fancy dress. By the summer of 1967, members of the Exploding Galaxy could be seen trooping into an tube carriage, each in a different-sized cardboard box, or striding through Oxford Circus in pyjamas and bedroom slippers. This description has little impact post-2000 since virtually all dress conventions have broken down. To understand what a shocking effect the underground dress code had, you would have to have been there. The flower children were considered an appalling affront to decent society.

Add up the same kind of rebellions in other areas and it is clear that youth culture had become a serious threat to established norms. We laughed at 'Norman Normal'.[2] We called ourselves 'freaks'. We chose to be strange.

RESOLUTION 2: IDEAS ARE EVERYTHING

The human brain had been cluttered with conventions that, once abandoned, would leave a great void into which ideas could flow. To the underground mind, invention was given pride of place. Anything was possible. Our culture could be compared to a fertile growing medium; our ideas were like so many thousands of shoots or little mushrooms pushing up through the manure. They say that mushrooms need muck in order to get going, and muck there was, in abundance – the hypocrisy, the warmongering and the unabashed materialism that accompanied our growing affluence. This was the faecal medium which fed the rebellious imagination.

One example of how ideas flourished was the development of inflatables, which had only existed before as Zeppelins and anti-aircraft training tents. They surfaced in the sixties as art forms with recreational potential. These in turn spawned bouncy castles, bean bags and waterbeds.

Territorial concerns about who had created what idea first were not meant to be part of the picture. We shared a collective unconscious through which any number of people spawned similar ideas. This was brought home to me most forcefully with one Exploding Galaxy costume: two people, unknown to each other, created the exact same garment seven years apart. In 1967, Exploding Galaxy member Andrew Forrest found the material for his costume for our performance at the Palais des Sports. It was a reel of 35mm film, which he cut into strips and fastened at his neck. This was never photographed nor described at the time. However, going through the archives at the Centro Hélio Oiticica in Rio de Janeiro recently, I found the drawing for an identical garment – one of Hélio's *parangolés* – his capes. He had drawn it in 1974.

RESOLUTION 3: RAISED CONSCIOUSNESS

We knew that the new materialism of the straight world was gaining too much of a foothold. Galaxy member Simon Shirley explains how many of us saw it:

> The fifties have been described as the world's most boring decade, but actually, when you ask people, they say that they were just relieved after all the killing that had gone before. They just felt incredibly lucky to get through it alive.
>
> One of the great political slogans of the fifties was: 'You have never had it so good,' and that's just another way of saying, 'Shut up and get on with it.' When it came to our generation, we wanted something different – we didn't know what exactly, but we didn't want that.

While for many an altered state of consciousness meant skinning up a joint and breathing in, or dropping an acid tab, for others the religious path beckoned. Popular faiths for hippies were Buddhism and Hinduism. Josephine Ranken, art student and UFO-goer, describes the relative merits of different religions according to hippies:

> My impression was that there was suspicion towards Christianity – the Anglican church was seen as fuddy-duddy and Catholicism as hopelessly prescriptive. Islam was seen in a similar way, with stern rules of conduct which went against the grain of free love. Hinduism and Buddhism offered an exciting, glamorous and exotic kind of mysticism. There wasn't enough contact for many Westerners to have direct encounters with Hinduism. We knew very little about the constraints. We met people coming back from India with attractive artefacts, but we didn't really understand the intricacies.

Few people had researched Eastern mysticism in any great depth. One exception was Amanda Fielding, who had travelled widely in the Middle East and studied comparative religion and classical Arabic at Oxford. She was one among a small group of informed people who believed in trepanation, a great talking point in the late sixties. Was it possible that the fusion of the skull cramped brain tissue and reduced the quality of consciousness? And if so, surely drilling a new permanent hole would free the pulse in the brain? Trepanning dates back to Neolithic times, and was depicted by Hieronymus Bosch in the 15th century. Those who carried out the procedure on themselves in the sixties – always self-administered, sometimes with an electric drill – claimed to be living with a permanent high. Many found the arguments convincing but few had the courage to try. Amanda was later recorded carrying out her own trepanation in a blood-spattered film called *Heartbeat in the Brain*.

There was also renewed interest in the Western occult tradition. Chris Malcolm became an interested onlooker:

> I think it was because people wanted to find some system of thought which would make sense of the experiences they had on an acid trip. The Eastern worldview seemed to fit this well, but some people said, 'What we want is Western mysticism. We want to dig up our own medieval roots and the ancient traditions that have been suppressed for all these centuries'.

The search for answers in Eastern and Western spirituality is best shown by interest in a heavenly book, called the Akashic records, where all knowledge is said to have been written down. And if you get into the right state of mind and you are prepared in the right way, you can get to see this book, open it and read it and be in touch with God or the source of all knowledge. This resonated with people's experience of LSD, which was so vivid and so convincing yet could not be carried back into normal life.

RESOLUTION 4: WE CAN HAVE SEX FREELY

One great lie of the time was to treat sexual acts between consenting males as criminal. There may have been a relaxation of attitudes, but the law did not change until July 1967. Even then, this was only a partial relaxation of the rules, relating just to consenting men over 21.

The thriving but still semi-clandestine gay scene blended seamlessly with the underground world. There was still plenty of prejudice, but this was not expressed openly. Many UFO-goers had been educated at boarding school, which meant that the early sexual experiences of many had been same-sex. Besides, key figures we admired in our movement, such as Allen Ginsberg and Jack Henry Moore, were openly gay, so if you were a homophobe, you kept it to yourself.

For heterosexuals, while there was a fair helping of the Christian in our thinking – we were obliged to turn the other cheek and to spurn greed – coveting another man's wife did not present a moral problem.

For a whole generation of young intellectual men, many of whom had been confined in all-male institutions, there was now plentiful access to vaginas. Women, now freed by the pill from the danger of conceiving, could choose to have sex when and with whom they wanted. At last they were publicly permitted to proclaim this out loud and in print: marriage and babies were no longer an automatic consequence of sexual pleasure. The problem was that, in countercultural circles, women were not free *not* to want sex. While many maidenheads were offered up willingly, delightedly and passionately, many others were prised off women through coercion or worse.

The word *sex*, while used constantly by the press in relation to the flower children, was not a word we chose. We preferred the term 'free love' to 'free sex'. Said poet Heathcote Williams:

> I really believe in love and not sex. I think that *sex* is rather a sinister word... I think there is a division between sex and love. I think there are all kinds of things embroiled in those words, in that language. I would like to investigate language along these lines. I think that *sex* is the separation of physical energy from love, which is physical... Sexual jealousy is not worth the candle. We must get away from the idea of owning people. When we make love to someone, we are not stealing someone else's property.[3]

Sex came to be disassociated from relationships, which worked well for some but caused confusion to those who were happily settled with a steady partner. Fidelity was now seen as uncool.

Jim Haynes proclaimed that, while an apple a day kept the doctor away, an orgasm a day kept the psychiatrist away. There developed in underground thinking a very close association between sexual refusal and mental instability, perfectly shown in Polanski's film *Repulsion*. This view had come directly from Wilhelm Reich, who had been influential in Europe before the war. His theories on orgastic potency led him to be nicknamed the 'prophet of the better orgasm'. Reich had a major influence on sexual permissiveness in the sixties, and his theories about touching and the damage caused by sexual repression were accepted currency among the young and hip.

Acceptance of his views on sexual repression and neurosis compelled some in the underground to go to extremes. One sexual manifesto (written by an adult male) suggested that schoolchildren rise up and demand a sexual relationship with their teachers, 'to get information sparking the gap purely'. Free love, as some of the 'beautiful people' interpreted it, was a groomer's and an abuser's charter – all done under the banner of innocence.

RESOLUTION 5: RANDOM IS IN THE DRIVER'S SEAT

The use of the random had been developed by the Dadaists and later had been taken up in earnest by a number of people, including John Cage with his aleatoric, or 'chance controlled', music. This somehow was absorbed into pop songs. Anything was now possible – from the modal chords of traditional music and the quarter tones of the Indian tradition to the musings of Captain Beefheart. Music was recorded backwards or distorted, with random sounds creeping in as early versions of sampling. Pop music played a central role in the lives of young people, and the most successful musicians of the early to mid-sixties were largely responsible for spreading these ideas of the random and breaking down the rigid conventions of the time.

In the visual arts, Mark Boyle and Joan Hills were to me the most remarkable proponents of the random. For their exhibition at the Indica Gallery, a flyer was produced with a square cut out of the centre, so that wherever it was placed, a small part of whatever was behind was displayed in a frame.

The use of the I Ching to guide decision-making was widely accepted, whether we were Buddhists or atheists. It was an antidote to the accepted approaches of our parents. The logic, good planning and common sense of previous generations had brought us nothing but destruction, bloodshed and despair, so why not try the whimsy of placing stones or turning tarot cards? This became part and parcel of the way the counterculture approached artistic decision-making. Of course, acceptance of the random turned out to be extremely convenient for the underground movement: with so many cock-ups and organisational mishaps, believing that anything was possible and enjoyable made people tolerant of even the most badly conceived aspects of a happening.

RESOLUTION 6: EVERYONE IS AN ARTIST

The key thing about UFOrian thinking was that creativity was not considered to be the property of specialists. It belonged to all of us.

Boundaries were there for the trespassing – in particular, between one form of expression and another. It seemed obvious that a painter could also be a poet and a poet a singer, and if performances could comprise mixed media, then surely it followed that single-minded dedication to perfecting one skill had become redundant. This meant you did not have to be any good in order to have the right to express yourself in a chosen field. As this fitted very nicely with the British love of the amateur, it was readily adopted by the London underground.

I have always been told that true proficiency in anything, from gymnastics to marquetry, required 10,000 hours of serious application.[4] This is demoralising, since most people can probably only boast 10,000 hours at the driver's wheel or sitting in front of some kind of screen. Since the UFOrian manifesto stated that you did not need 10,000 hours of practice to be a bona fide creator, this meant that everyone could be included in the aesthetic process. Poets abounded in the 1960s. We were all at it.

Stan Seigel wrote poetry prolifically at this time and remembers how virtually everyone was a poet. He joined a group of writers who met regularly at the British Museum canteen. He describes how he was walking with his poems one windy day and a sudden gust blew the lot out of his hands. He just thought, 'That's interesting, they're all gone.' Along with the right to express yourself artistically came the delicious understanding of the ephemeral and the pleasure of knowing that creative expression could be unencumbered by the need for permanence.

During my time at Balls Pond Road I was lucky enough to follow this same path as a non-artist artist. I fancied myself as a poet–sculptor–dancer all rolled into one, without the slightest concern about skill. My two teachers were to be David Medalla and Gerald Fitzgerald, both talented, expressive forces. It was the spring of 1967, and they were about to meet for the first time.

In mid-sixties London, Gerald Fitzgerald – otherwise known as the 'Density Man' – was a familiar figure in the alternative art world. In the summer of 1966, he had his own one-man show at the Indica Gallery called 'Sense Activation'. Known in the Exploding Galaxy as 'Fitz', he was one of the most original thinkers at UFO. He was his own walking manifesto, talking at length about his theory of the 'Quaquaversal F' to anybody who cared to listen. To me, he seemed to be particularly preoccupied by three notions: density, the unspecific, and the incongruous. When Fitz told me about his ideas on density, he had started categorising the area – for example, 'frozzling density' was transparency made semi-opaque by the fizz of air bubbles.

Chris Malcolm describes Fitz's garb:

> He used to like to walk about in the parks in this kind of dressed-up fashion and he wore lots and lots of clothes in layers, and the thing is, you could see through them in some kind of a way. So some of it would be transparent polythene, and some of it would be tinted which you could see through partially, and some of it would be net-like. The point was, you could always see past one layer to the next.

Edward Pope met him for the first time at the Rising Sun pub at St Pancras. Fitz invited him to a game of darts, but Edward declined on the grounds that he was very short-sighted, did not have his glasses with him and did not know the game. Fitz insisted and Edward immediately scored a double, which he found significant. They later went on a walk together through London.

Edward remembers:

> He was trying to explain to me that what we actually see with our eyes differs from what our mind presumes. I think that what he meant by the *unspecific* was that you don't put anything into a category – you go straight to the sensory basis of it all. With the *incongruous*, I understood him to mean that an aesthetic virtue lies in what is incongruous. It changes your way of looking at things. He took me to Blackfriars Bridge and showed me a work of art. It was a series of European destinations engraved in stone on a wall of the station. This has since been demolished.

It has been said that it was David Medalla who founded and Fitz who found the Exploding Galaxy. As soon as Edward Pope met Fitz, he made it his business to introduce the two artists, and he finally got them together shortly after 'The 14-Hour Technicolor Dream'. They clearly had some mutual respect for each other. After the meeting, Fitz conceded that, for a kinetic artist, David Medalla was pretty impressive, and David had in turn conceded that Fitz was original in his approach.

It is hard to imagine that two such different personalities as David Medalla and Gerald Fitzgerald could not only live together but also work together. However, the two artists were held for a time in a creative tension with us youngsters revolving around them and running off with their ideas to interpret in our own way. It was this not altogether comfortable polarity that made the Exploding Galaxy the powerful peculiarity that it was.

NOTES

1. Instructions adapted from *Protect and Survive*, a public information film (1974)
2. Norman Normal was a fictional character in *Oz* magazine, who represented the straight world. It was also the nickname given by John Lennon to his sound engineer Norman Smith.
3. *Hello I Love You*, orchestrated by Jim Haynes and Jeanne Pasle-Green (under various imprints, 1974).
4. Malcolm Gladwell, *Outliers: The Story of Success* (2008). This refers to a study by Anders Ericsson that focuses on the 10,000 + hours rule.

4

Dance of the Tribe

On with the dance! let joy be unconfined;
No sleep till morn, when Youth and Pleasure meet
To chase the glowing hours with flying feet.

LORD BYRON [1]

IN MOST DANCE halls in the early sixties, there was a point when couples let go of each other and an alternative emerged that was different from the girl being spun round by the man. Pop tunes emerged to go with the oddly named new dances. For the 'mashed potatoes' there was a choice of three dance hits.[2] The routines were fun, but oh so tame, with the instructions embedded in the lyrics. But what was memorable was the repressed body language, evinced by twitching or flailing arms. In Latin America, young men and women did impossibly wonderful things with their hips; but in sixties London, we didn't do anything with our *bunda* or butt or bum. We just let our limbs twist and jerk in spasms.

What was noticeable about the first weeks of UFO was that so few people actually danced. Apart from half a dozen of us, most just sat on the floor. Joe Boyd, who ran the club with John Hopkins, confirms this: 'I remember the UFO crowd sitting on the wooden floor in front of the stage, completely engrossed as The Floyd played those early gigs.'[3]

However, until it got too crowded in the late spring of 1967, some of the younger ones among us treated the ballroom at UFO more like a playground, dashing and leaping across the whole 80-foot length of the hall. Several students from Central College of Art were particularly uninhibited. We would take running jumps into each other's arms and land in a pile on the floor.

Miles identified two separate generations, present at UFO, who represented the underground:

> They would seem to consist of the following: The young kids (under 20) brought up on plastic toys, TV, sweets and rock 'n' roll. They live for enjoyment and love each other, though they seem to have little tolerance for people not of their 'type'.
>
> They are capable of amazing free expression, which is often the envy of the next generation up (over 20) who were brought up on illustrated volumes of 'The Great War in Pictures', Dad's war pictures, rationing and Frankie Laine.[4]

The general inhibition and absence of dancing at UFO was to change dramatically over the coming months as gradually even those people over 20 began to make it their own space, too.

The DJ Jeff Dexter was there most weeks. He wore a long brocade jacket and did a kind of jumpy-pumpy dance. Malcolm Le Maistre, evidently trained in movement, was all grand strides with chest up and powerful leaps. I was invariably just under the stage, in the little gauze jumble-sale number I had shortened during double chemistry. I looked like Alice in Wonderland on acid, oblivious to anything but the music, which would lead to my own personal dance into wonderment or exploration or fear, as if I really were tripping.

UFO-goer Josephine Ranken has described this new form of dance as wild, bacchanalian writhing and as part of an attempt to evoke the images that an acid trip produced – and as a way to show off your very carefully thought-out wardrobe.

Herzmark, one of the first dancers to join the Exploding Galaxy, remembers:

> It was tremendously exciting because people were doing expressive dancing all of a sudden, and what's more, the bands played for long periods of time – they didn't just do a set of 15 minutes, they played for 40 minutes at a go.

The Floyd's early music was strange, not like pop, and it was internalised, along with the bubbles of pulsating colour that transformed the hall and confirmed our understanding that rules were there to be abandoned. As a result, the movements became personally expressive in a way that had not been previously evident.

I was bowled over by The Floyd's music with all those chromatic descents, and remember playing 'Arnold Layne' in the fifth-form prefab classrooms at Putney High School when it first came out. Later, though, I came to see Pink Floyd as a fairly straight jobbing rock band once their psychedelic signature and Syd Barrett were removed. By contrast, The Soft Machine attempted to transform their performances with extraordinary dancers (The Epileptic Flowers) and an inclination towards the theatre of the absurd. I felt they were truly experimental and underground as a group.

Two events are the most frequently mentioned high points at UFO. The first was the first public playing of the Beatles' *Sergeant Pepper* album, before it was released in the shops. Virtually everybody I interviewed, when asked about UFO, has mentioned this as a significant moment. The second was the appearance of Arthur Brown. His hit 'Fire', still frequently played, does not begin to reflect his theatrical presence. He was a true showman in the old-fashioned Edwardian 'daring young man' sense, with a superb understanding of dramatic impact and an ability to delight audiences.

Along with UFO's distinctly different kind of dance, close attention was paid to regalia. Just as with our movements, where all conventions were abandoned, so, too, in clothing almost anything went. Among the range of garb to be seen on the dance floor at UFO were the conventional Mary Quant mini-skirts and Biba jersey tubes, as well as more adventurous outfits such as paper dresses. Retro-wear varied from exotic Katharine Hepburn-like evening gowns with padded shoulders, which swathed and trailed, to more austere utility frocks. Men's garments were becoming more daring, with the wealthier and more confident donning long paisley jackets cut from hand-printed Indian cotton, originally bedspreads bought at Pontin's

Department Store in High Street Kensington. Josephine Ranken describes the importance of clothes at UFO:

> What you wore was pretty significant. It really was totally improvised because the counterculture had not been commercialised yet. To start with, there wasn't anything to buy, and so people had to be very inventive. Most of us managed to put together wardrobes made up almost entirely from jumble sales. In those days, you could still buy soft velvet jackets and those beautiful long printed silk scarves that were fashionable in the thirties. You could also acquire interesting hats and crêpe de Chine dresses for next to nothing. In this way, you could use your imagination and concoct a style entirely your own.
>
> Some of it was particularly severe and some of us wore garments that looked positively Victorian and forbidding, such as high-necked blouses with pin-tucks and lace, with long black skirts and tight little boots. This was not anything approaching high-street fashion. It was a determined attempt to avoid anything commercial or mass-produced. In this way, it was quintessentially counterculture. It was not even subversive – it was just underground.

The overall effect was of a fancy dress party and, with few exceptions, what I noticed was that the fancy dress stayed the same each week, since there was no notion of obsolescence among us in those days. What worked once became permanent attire. I wore my gauze, yoked, pale green wartime frock for all gatherings and dances for ten months, and Galaxy member Leighana's darling stripey dress can be seen snapped in photographs taken six months apart. Galaxy member Rag Doll reckoned that his principal clothing over a two-year period consisted of a single outfit of jeans, a stripey matelot T-shirt and an Arab *shemagh* scarf, bought in Suez on the way over from Oz, plus bare feet.

If there were a time machine to take me back to mid-April 1967, I would visit UFO with a fat wodge of questionnaires. These would not ask about drug habits, sexual preferences or promiscuity, the preoccupations of both the underground and the gutter press at the time. They would instead monitor class background, present occupation, level of wealth and ethnic origin. I feel certain that the findings would bear out what I then noticed-without-noticing – namely, that just like our present Cabinet at least half the UFO crowd had been privately educated at great expense, and that a large proportion were former Oxbridge undergraduates. Of the remaining half, a large chunk were attending art college, and a smaller but substantial section consisted of writers, musicians and/or celebs. Of the remainder, there was a smattering of Grovers and London Free School enthusiasts and a still smaller handful of fifth- and sixth-formers from the Girls' Public Day School Trust (of whom I was one). If you were at UFO in the early spring of 1967 and did not fit into any of those categories, and especially if you were not white, you were exceptional.

By far the smallest group to attend UFO was a spill-over of mod types who had migrated from Tiles and other discotheques. These were hardcore clubbers who came in from the 'Fords' (Romford, Ilford, Catford and Greenford). They swapped their uppers for LSD and their tailored button-down gear for beads and loose-fitting shirts, and they backcombed their hair into faux Afros. Essentially, though, at heart they were as they always had been: used to partying hard.

Two of these UFO mod clubbers, known as the Fuzzy-Gigglies, later moved into 99 Balls Pond Road after it had become a commune, and they stayed until the place became proactively drug-free. At UFO, they hung out to the left of the stage in various states of trip, and if you had downed an acid tab yourself, you needed to avoid them at all costs. This was because if they knew you were tripping they would pull scary faces and do their best to freak you out.

Looking back, there is no mistaking the not-so-invisible barriers that kept the social circles apart. At UFO, you got to dance with Pete Townshend, but you weren't likely to be invited back to his place for a cup of tea. The rule was that you pretended you didn't know who a celebrity was. In this way, I managed not to notice Jimi Hendrix, Eric Clapton, Ginger Baker, Paul McCartney and a host of other stars.

The UFO elite consisted of the following groups: musos, the *Oz* magazine 'mafia', DJs, celebs and their entourages, the drug suppliers, the Cambridge undergraduate commuters, the Chelsea set and anyone involved in the organisation of UFO or the production of *IT* magazine. The rest of us were the 'prole-e-delics'. The only way that a prole-e-delic could penetrate the invisible wall of social superiority and exclusion was to be simultaneously both sexually desirable and sexually available.

If you went to UFO and were not sure whether you were a prole-e-delic or a member of the elite, there were two questions to answer: (1) Did you ever go the Speak (the Speakeasy Club)? and (2) Did you regularly visit the boutique called 'Hung on You'? If you didn't, then you were more than likely a prole.

Despite the egalitarian pronouncements from the politically committed and despite the smug certainty of the flower impresarios, it was just the same old elitism at work, blind to its own double standards. In answer to the question 'Was London's hippie movement farsighted and ahead of its time, or misogynous and old school?', the answer has to be 'It was both.'

NOTES

1. Lord Byron, 'The Eve of Waterloo', from *Childe Harold's Pilgrimage.*
2. These were by: Nat Kendrick and the Swans; James Brown; Dee Dee Sharp.
3. Joe Boyd, *White Bicycles: making music in the 1960s* (Serpent's Tail, 2006).
4. *International Times,* issue 7, 30 January 1967.
5. 'Grovers' were those members of the underground who lived in the area of Ladbroke Grove and Notting Hill Gate.

5

Blarney Stoned

It is hard now to entertain the possibility of a night club – the most popular in London, possibly even in Europe – where you could not buy an alcoholic beverage. We all queued up for orange pop.

DRUMBEAT, EX-EXPLODER, OUTER GALAXY

THE FLOYD'S MANAGER at the time, Peter Jenner, has said that there was a middle-class do-gooding feel to the London Free School.[1] UFO was also strikingly reminiscent of a community social in a church hall. Since dance partners were not obligatory and because we all shared a cause, it was very easy to get to know others at those early UFOs. Josephine and I, in the spirit of giving and sharing, used to bake cakes and chocolate-coated cornflakes and buy olives on Fridays, to distribute in the club. These would be devoured within seconds by surprised clubbers, but it meant that we got to know practically everyone there. The quiet between sets meant that you didn't have to shout introductions. You could exchange ideas. In these moments, we developed the notion that what we, the underground, were doing was enormously significant.

Of the many UFO-goers I met weekly, several stood out and soon became friends and part of my crowd. Edward Pope was the most notable. He had cut off the sleeves of his white denim jacket and painted across the back 'Coming, Bliss & Freak', as though these three words made up the name of an accountancy partnership. He was there for every UFO, although I didn't meet him until three weeks in. Nowadays, he would be described as a facilitator, making it his business to share his discoveries with his acquaintances and enable others in various ways. It was through him that I came to visit The Process in a lavish Regency building off Park Lane, an offshoot of

Scientology where they wore polo necks and medallions and, as far as I could make out, believed that Jehovah and Lucifer were engaged in some sort of temporary truce. It was there that I first clapped eyes on Marianne Faithfull as she looked down at us from a gallery above the sweeping stairway – an exquisitely beautiful apparition. This confirmed to me that I was going to all the most interesting places.

There was nothing Edward liked better than to introduce one freak to another and to take a new acquaintance to an unusual venue. For me, he was the person who joined up the dots, connecting one cell or quirky idea to another, to reveal sense in the whole. Through him, I got a glimpse of just how eclectic and crazy the freak movement really was, with any number of different or even contradictory sub-movements, united only by the fact that they were determinedly breaking new ground and going against the old ways. Some believed in ley lines, others in tepees. Still others were committed anarchists. The straight world saw one subculture. We saw a myriad of mini-subcultures that scraped and scuffed around each other and were, despite appearances, not mutually exclusive. It was Edward who took me to the macrobiotic restaurant Seed and brought me to the house in Balls Pond Road where I broke the Soto sculpture.

Other memorable people at UFO were Kevin Ayers of The Soft Machine, with whom I often danced; and the red-haired giant Michael Chapman, whose vast presence trapped a captive audience on the stairs as they waited to be let in. There was also the wealthy Edinburgh eccentric Alisdair Burke who wore a fedora and carried about a placard reading: 'Alisdair Burke is an acid head'; and Syd Barrett of Pink Floyd, who was quite simply the most beautiful man I had ever laid eyes on. When, mid-set, Syd asked me if I could get hold of a plectrum, I rushed off and produced one within four minutes. I suppose I was, like Edward, one of the many unnoticed counterculture worker bees.

The women at UFO tended to be more imaginative than the men, both in what they wore and in the way they danced. For example, one regular called Sue Hall had cut her fringe into a sci-fi point. Despite their quirky glamour, women were generally absent from the lists of UFO performers for most of the club's life, and formed a kind of sub-strata there. They took the entrance fee of ten shillings (50 pence) until Joe Boyd decided that they were 'in over their heads'.

The business of drugs was also a male preserve. Josephine Ranken remembers that it was customary for the men to do both the supplying and the scoring. The ladies seemed to be, on the whole, either excluded from the process or intimidated by it.

The women club members I remember most were all plummy and public school and a number were under the crucial age of 16, including me. I remember meeting a girl from the year above me at Putney High in the UFO ladies. She took me to one side and confessed that she had taken methedrine. I looked at her blankly, not having a clue what she was talking about. Then there were the two Putney High muses. Emily Young, later known for her fabulous work in stone, is credited by some with inspiring Syd Barrett's song 'See Emily Play'. As for the other muse, the rumour at school was that Donovan's lyrics about a girl named Fourteen were inspired not only by a real person, but one who was in my year.

The two organisers of UFO were John (Hoppy) Hopkins and Joe Boyd. Hoppy had a wistful, haunted look about him. I now realise this was because he had a court case pending for possession of cannabis, although he later admitted to being in total denial about the impending court appearance. He was popular with everyone, having the ability to unify the very different sub-strands of freakdom, from the strutting and politicised working-class heroes to the Chelsea fops. I particularly liked the way that he would let me in free every week if he happened to be on the door.

Joe Boyd would stand there with what has been described as his 'Harvard graduate's smile', and it was difficult to know if he was one stage beyond being a smooth operator or just a really nice guy. Some of us remember how attentive he was when it came to setting up a makeshift changing room for the Exploding Galaxy women, consisting of strung-up sheets. Others recalled how he paid UFO-goer Chris Holmes to stand guard, to stop men going into the ladies toilet, since couples had taken to sneaking in there for a quick knee-trembler.

Because Joe Boyd was American, a fair amount of bitching envy was directed at him at the time. In fact, all the people in key positions in our underground world seemed to be either American or Australian. Jim Haynes has explained this by saying that it takes an outsider to see the possibilities in a place. I think that English amateurism had a role to play, too. We didn't have the same focus or professional push or perhaps the confidence these expats brought with them when they came to London. I'm also certain that sour grapes were partly why the comments were made.

The difficulty for both Hoppy and Joe was that they had to enforce rules in accordance with the freak rule book, which stated that rules were there for the breaking. To look like bouncers or school caretakers or any other kind of authority figure would have been unthinkable – one of the greatest crimes in our alternative world – and so they had to stand by, smiling benignly. This meant that they, along with other entrepreneurs, were often faced with avoidable losses, simply because they didn't feel they could mimic establishment behaviour in any way. For instance, according to Miles, Indica Books' liquidation was due in part to the scale of theft that went on there. He describes how numerous people 'liberated' books, safe in the knowledge that the police would never be contacted even if the thieves were caught red-handed.[2]

By the end of March 1967, there had been a dozen UFOs, with just one Friday meeting unbooked due to Paddy's Night. On that particular Friday, the Blarney club reverted to its identity as Irish dance hall. That evening is marked 'St Patrick's' in fountain pen in my diary. By the beginning of April, I had met virtually everyone in the club and realised that London hippies numbered no more than a few hundred familiar faces. At the end of July, when the *News of the World* estimated there were 300 hippies, I would have multiplied that number by 20 or 30.

The only demographic analysis of freaks carried out in 1967 was done by staff at *IT*. Using the addresses of the paper's subscribers, they identified one common feature – the No. 31 bus route, which took in Camden, Notting Hill Gate and Chelsea.

So there we were, turned-on flower children, minding our own provocative business, avidly reading our copies of *IT* every fortnight. Titillation came in the form of the exposed breasts displayed by not very confident 'readers' wives' who obligingly gave proof of the new sexual openness and who probably increased the circulation figures, too. This was all harmless enough in relation to the law. Where the paper diced with danger was in some of its copy. In issue 4, American comedian and black activist Dick Gregory was interviewed. He started off all fluffy, saying how he's a vegetarian and thoroughly non-violent, and how he likes to read his five children bedtime stories. The next moment he goes into a ballistic rant. The following was not deleted or modified before publication:

> A hundred years we worried about what white folks think. I say fuck white folks. A hundred years of worrying about that bastard and he ain't got off my back. I say fuck him up his ass. I got five black kids and I couldn't give a fuck what a white man thought of them from now to the day I die... Five white kids burn their draft cards and in two weeks' time we got an anti-draft card burning bill. But we can't get an anti-lynching bill in a hundred years. So this man just told me that he thinks more of a piece of cardboard than he do of my five black babies. I say fuck him up the ass, man, and I might have to kill him myself.[3]

Chosen for its violent sexual content rather than its blatent racism, the 'fuck him up his ass' phrase was now going to cause big trouble for the white folks back at *IT* headquarters in Southampton Row.

In his book *London Calling*, Miles describes how, on 9 March, the Obscene Publications Squad carried out their raid on the *IT* office. Using a rare search-and-seizure warrant, they removed absolutely everything essential to the running of the paper in a three-ton truck. According to Miles, 'They seemed more interested in disrupting the running of the paper than in actually taking away something that might be obscene.'[4]

The fact that the police had taken over two months to act following publication of the Dick Gregory interview indicates that the decision to nobble the paper came before an offending piece had been chosen. They must have sat there reading through the lot, drooling over the readers' wives and looking for something in the content that could be deemed 'obscene'.

Apart from word of mouth, *IT* was our only means of communication and there was no doubt in anyone's mind that, by singling out the paper, our whole movement was being cynically targeted, with the aim of finishing off the flower children. The plot thickens when you consider the information that has since emerged about the Rolling Stones' Redlands drugs bust a few weeks previously – namely, that the FBI's counter-intelligence division and our own MI5 were both bent on discrediting representative figures of youth culture.

At UFO, people rallied round. It was not just tea and sympathy. Within 24 hours of the *IT* raid, £100 had been raised – no mean sum in sixties monetary terms. Those attending the second 'Uncommon Market' at the Roundhouse were urged to pay double at the door for the defence appeal. Dave Howson and Hoppy had been hatching something altogether grander – bigger, in fact, than anything that had happened before – and this was now intended to raise money to pay the *IT*'s likely legal bills. It was to be called 'The 14-Hour Technicolor Dream'. Viv Stanshall, songwriter and lead singer of the Bonzo Dog Doo-Dah Band, appealed to the public to 'Make this happen – make this reverberate into the daffodil mellow yellow summer of the armpit that lies ahead'. UFO was also used to gather support and contributions. It was time for some do-gooding and some Dunkirk spirit, which we had in abundance, although we would never have described it as such.

A familiar face at UFO was David Medalla, whom most people knew as a sculptor at that time. Yoko Ono has since attracted much more attention than either David or Gerald Fitzgerald, both of whom, if not better known than Yoko in 1966, were certainly more visibly eccentric then – Medalla with his striking Oriental good looks, use of *mudras* and Indian dance poses during Pink Floyd solos and irresistible and very un-English playfulness and lack of reserve.

In quieter moments in the second half of April, I heard talk that David was planning to set up a dance theatre group with Larry Smart. Larry was one of the few London artists at the time attempting to express psychedelic experience through the medium of paint. His most famous work was a portrait of Jimi Hendrix in saturated colours with a motif of flames along the base and a number of startlingly beautiful giant mandalas. David and Larry were hanging out together in Notting Hill a lot, hatching some ideas about turning happenings into something involving dance – something that would be crazy and amazing.

The first members of the group were David Medalla, Larry Smart and his wife Carol, Christian Ledoux and Malcolm Le Maistre, Malcolm having been approached by David the week after Paddy's Night. Edward Pope and I were invited to join at around the same time, and our first appearance was as an anonymous accompaniment to The Soft Machine who, with Mark Boyle, were top of the bill at the Theatre Royal Stratford East on 16 April. Daevid Allen opened the set with an anti-censorship 'Lord's Prayer'. Then, as soon as The Soft Machine struck up their opening bars, the stage filled with dancers. There were several of us – David, Malcolm, Josephine and Herzmark, Larry and me. Each individual did their usual UFO dance, but within the confines of the spaces between the instrumentalists and their amplifiers. This was the first performance of the as yet unnamed Exploding Galaxy.

The 'Dream' was fixed for 29 April. Although there was no sense of urgency about the impending performance at Ally Pally, there were 'rehearsals'. Edward remembers the first of these:

> It was at Larry Smart's pad in Notting Hill. I remember seeking the address – it was a sunny day. I hadn't been there before and was impressed by the multi-coloured peeling paint on the houses. I bought a pineapple to share around, and did so at several meetings thereafter, putting it on my orange shawl to slice it. As I remember, nothing actually got rehearsed – there was just general discussion.

I was there on the same occasion. Larry's wife Carol was heavily pregnant. It turned out she was a singer with a powerful, earthy voice who later changed her name to Carol Grimes. Now she was busy being the skivvy, clearing plates and making tea for everybody, while Larry was the welcoming host. Their tomcat Mustapha was cringing on top of the wardrobe. Someone explained that he had somehow consumed a tab and was undergoing a feline acid trip.

Although we were performing that Saturday at the 'Technicolor Dream', we still had no name. For this reason, neither the poster nor the ticket for that great event bore the words 'Exploding' or 'Galaxy'. If the name we eventually came up with was anyone's idea, it was Larry Smart's. We were all sitting round dumbly when someone piped up, 'What's that painting called?', pointing to a picture propped up against the wall. Larry replied, '*The Exploding Galaxy*.' When I recently asked Carol what became of the painting, she said it had been given to the saxophonist and single dad, Lol Coxhill, for one of his children.

An Exploding Galaxy launch party was held at 99 Balls Pond Road later in the week. Since there was no electricity, the main room was candlelit and the sound system comprised pots-and-pans-style percussion in the basement. It was at this party that Christian announced the start of 'kinetic drama', taking art to its next stage in a progression from kinetic sculpture and bio-kinetics to sculpture via humano-kinetics using living people.

Another rehearsal followed at All Saints Hall in Notting Hill, followed by a final one in Kensington Gardens on 28 April (described in my diary as a 'picnic at the Round Pond'), where again nothing much got done. There were at least ten of us there, with the Frensham

Heights School contingent consisting of Malcolm and his girlfriend Annabel Rutter. This was the first time that I met Christian Ledoux, a charismatic young French film-maker with cinematic bone structure. There was also the saxophonist Dave Tomlin, who played in The Giant Sun Trolley, a band that often performed in the early hours at UFO and whose wild improvisations were for serious musos only – they were said to be able to clear the hall in under two minutes.

After this last gathering in the park, which concluded with very few actual decisions and only the vaguest idea for a plot, we all felt entirely ready for our performance in front of the 10,000 people expected at Alexandra Palace.

NOTES

1. Credited with being key to the start of UFO, *International Times* and the Notting Hill Carnival, the London Free School was started by John Hopkins, Rhaune Laslett and others to provide alternative, free, local education for adults.
2. Barry Miles, *London Calling: A Countercultural History of London since 1945* (Atlantic Books, 2010).
3. *International Times*, issue 4, 28 November 1966.
4. Miles, *London Calling.*

6

The 14-Hour Technicolor Dream

When daffodils begin to peer,
With heigh! the doxy over the dale,
Why, then comes in the sweet o' the year;
For the red blood reigns in the winter's pale.

WILLIAM SHAKESPEARE, *A WINTER'S TALE*

ALEXANDRA PALACE IS an absurdity and a relic, yet it commands great affection. If Ally Pally were a person, it would be described either as a national treasure or a bloody-minded eccentric, loved in part for its sheer awkwardness in a conformist world. Like Battersea Power Station, its monstrous impracticality fires fierce debate over its viability as a glorified leisure palace. Unlike Battersea Power Station, this was, in fact, its original role. Ally Pally's first sobriquet back in 1873 was 'The People's Palace'.

My father had worked there in 1952, in the early days of BBC Television, when announcers talked as if they had been chewing on lemons. The BBC presenter John Snagge asked him to do a couple of months in production, and every afternoon a coach took the team up from the West End so that they would be ready for the opening of transmission at 7.30pm. Dad had use of what was called the 'telecine' studio and a continuity studio. His job was to brief the announcer, fill in any gaps, choose props and deal appropriately with the many emergencies. If there was some kind of blip, he would keep the kettle boiling by showing films like the one of the potter's wheel or the windmill's sails slowly turning. When I was born in 1951, we already had a television set, probably the only one in the Hurlingham Court mansion block where we lived, but this was replaced with a bigger screen in time for the Coronation. I remember being called to the TV on the occasions when Dad came on as continuity announcer, but have an even stronger memory of the menacing picture of the Alexandra Palace mast, and its nasty sci-fi spikes.

Ally Pally has always been a problematic building. It is too big and cold for the average function and too antiquated to suit larger events. It just sits there like one grand lump, with no specific role. The West Hall is known for its snooker, darts and ping-pong championships, and the Great Hall seems to work at its best when used for business expos, antiques fairs and the like.

My companion through most of the underground events of 1967 was Josephine Ranken and she has always been of the opinion that there was something 'definitely inauspicious' about the place:

> I think it was burnt twice or three times. And it has never been successful as a venue. It has got a sort of miserable kind of feel about it. It is a great big ugly building and it should be wonderful but it isn't. There is something wrong with the place. Some years after the 'Technicolor Dream', I remember seeing an extraordinary photograph on the front of *The Times* which showed a group of geomancers standing in a circle apparently doing something very like praying. They went on their knees and they were trying to invoke spirits to improve the fortunes of the place. They were aware that there something was badly wrong with it.

If there was one thing that underground London liked, it was quirky architecture in which to house its playgrounds, so in this sense Ally Pally was the perfect setting. Hoppy had taken pictures there of the Rolling Stones and John Lee Hooker, among others, and he immediately thought of the Great Hall for the 'Dream'. However, the photos he took in 1964 give an idea of just how difficult the building was for rock music events. The vastness of the space alters perception so that even large crowds are reduced to just a scattering of individuals. More importantly, the acoustics are poor, allowing sound to get sucked up into the great vaulted roof.

I have noticed a fair amount of bragging going on in the business of counterculture nostalgia. Impresarios or would-be impresarios out there are claiming ownership of ideas – everything from the concept of a listing magazine to the term 'world music'. 'The 14-hour Technicolor Dream' is no exception – several people claim to have been instrumental in launching it. My understanding of its origins is that Dave Howson and Hoppy first developed the idea, but after the *IT* bust, many more people became involved, either selflessly or as jostlers, making and taking out of self-interest.

Several people have described the 'streams of people' converging on the Palace on the evening of 29 April. This was my first experience of the excitement of a mass rally, and as I approached Ally Pally I felt an overwhelming sense of common purpose, which was shared with all those alighting at Wood Green tube station. Most sources say there were 10,000 present, compared with the modest numbers who came to UFO nights. Whether or not there were actually that many, this event certainly did feel different. The numbers lent us validity. The straight world would at last have to sit up and pay attention.

The Great Hall was done out like a freak's fairground, with helter-skelter, candyfloss stand and the less conventional 'banana-skin-smoking igloo'. Other oddities were a dot-matrix light-bulb screen for displaying messages like 'Vietnam is a sad trip', and inflatable sculptures, new to most people in 1967. Graham Stevens produced what seemed like infinitely long tubing that, when filled with air, shot about the hall as if animated. Anthony (Scottie) Scott's contribution was his inflatable Swizprick, a giant transparent phallus, complete with air-filled polythene testicles, which he displayed proudly off the scaffolding that encased the Henry Willis pipe organ. All this activity in the Great Hall was coated with globules of colour from several lightshows, by now standard accessories to partying.

One feature of the evening was the sheer number of acts. Anybody who did anything vaguely performable had offered their services, and since there was a strong ethic in our underground movement of non-selection and 'whatever happens, happens', no one was turned down. The only way to handle the 40 or so acts was to double up, using the two stages at the same time. I seem to remember that there was a space allocated for poetry readings, and it was here that I watched the six-foot-four poet Michael Chapman spewing out sounds in his own private dialogue with his inner muse, and announcing matter-of-factly to anyone watching, including the TV cameras, that he was on an LSD trip. Although he was not then part of the Exploding Galaxy, it was shortly after this that Mike began to join in our performances, and although he did not give up gigging in his own right, he became a committed explorer-exploder and an integral part of Galactic investigation and performance for the next 18 months or so.

The impact of amplified sound coming from two directions depended very much on your viewpoint. John Lennon did eventually arrive and, with his fondness for the random, clearly liked the sound clash. Fashion designer Karen Moller, one of the few women memoir-writers of our counterculture, has given her account of the moment during the Dream, when she was standing within earshot of the Beatle:

> Suddenly John Lennon appeared among the crowd and headed in our direction with John Dunbar from the Indica Gallery. 'Hi, man!' my friend shouted to them. 'Great to see you again. Glad you guys could make it.' 'Yeah, far out,' Dunbar said, tugging at his jacket as if it made him uncomfortable. 'We seen them filming this "Technicolor Dream" on TV and said: "Let's go."' Lennon stopped and put his hand up as if to say wait. He moved back and then slowly forward, looking quite pensive. 'Did you hear that?' he asked. He turned and again walked back through the audio fusion zone created by the sounds of the two bands at opposite ends of that great hall. He appeared to be listening to the sounds; then he returned, smiled and, perhaps in imitation of Hoppy's much used phrase, said 'Far-fucking-out!'[1]

Sue Hall, of the sci-fi haircut, was never afraid to speak her mind, and she complained to the organisers about the competing sound sources:

> The thing I couldn't stand, and philosophically I had arguments with this both before and after that evening, was the idea that it was good to hear two bands at once. It does depend on what you like, but for me it was the sound of chaos, which is interesting for a few seconds but if it goes on longer, you really want to get away from it. It made me feel ill.

While I was wandering around the Great Hall, other Galaxy members were getting ready for our performance in a nearby house. Somebody's parents were away and so this was the unofficial 'green room'.

Herzmark, who had joined our first performance in Stratford, played the Prostitute. She put on a trench coat, belted tightly at the waist, with a French beret perched at a slant on her head. Under the mac, one leg was stockinged and the other, bare one was painted with alluring swirls.

David Medalla wore a leotard and white bandana, and on his legs he had painted large circles like the Guaica Indians of Venezuela, to represent the doors into and out of the soul. We were called on to one of the stages sometime before midnight and announced as the Exploding Galaxy. This was our second appearance as a dance troupe and our first booking under the name that was to make us notorious.

I remember seeing a film in the early 1970s called the *Red Detachment of Women*, in which Chinese dancers executed with breathtaking balletic mastery the thinnest of plots, in which good, in the form of extremely attractive Revolutionary Guards, overcame the reactionary forces of evil. As in all these sorts of didactic performances, the characters were pure cardboard, totally subservient to their symbolic value. The performances were all delivered with athletic ease – the best that a national government could finance.

The Exploding Galaxy's performance for the 'Dream' was called *Fuzzdeath*. It had the same sort of inane plot, but in this case, executed without any dramatic or balletic mastery. This was not the point for us – it was about being, experiencing, expressing and exploring. It was essential to our success on the night that we would be performing to an audience that had already been won over.

Malcolm Le Maistre was key to the production, having recently danced and choreographed in Switzerland a piece about the Berlin Wall. He was the one who chose a Bartók piece to be played full blast at the exact moment when the fuzz forces of repression burst on to the stage.

The plot of *Fuzzdeath* was roughly as follows: Once upon a time, the beautiful people were all living happily together under the Magic Mushroom.[2] Peace and harmony were torn apart by the forces of evil in the form of the (masked) secret police. Following the flower children's capture and imprisonment, the chief oppressor – the Archbishop – interrogated the Prostitute, who failed in her attempt to seduce him. The beautiful people then rose up chanting 'Turn on, turn on, turn on' and, by doing this, overpowered the oppressors with the force of their love. Peace and harmony were finally restored. The audience seemed to appreciate both the performance and its message.

The storyline might now be described as flimsy, but what we were expressing was the widely held belief among freaks in the spring of 1967 that the power of our love could change the world and that, by turning straight people on, we could somehow transform humanity. Daevid Allen has described the oneness we all felt on that night:

> I was part of a tribe, a movement, a gigantic soul. We looked around and saw ourselves reflected in multiples and we felt our power to change the world. This was the beginning of the peaceful revolution.[3]

Joe Boyd voiced similar views:

> I think my senses were a little elevated, but I do remember seeing these crowds stream out of the hall and down the hill and I remember thinking, 'This is it. We won. It's all over, we are in charge now. This is so big.'[4]

'The 14-Hour Technicolor Dream' has been described as one of the 100 best gigs of all time, but I wonder how much of this is due to fairy dust, blown over the thing you adore because of what it represents now rather than how it actually felt at the time. Perhaps we are all a little in love with that night because of what it symbolised, especially in the light of subsequent world events that dashed all our hopes so thoroughly.

The truth is, though, that it was an organisational shambles that resulted in a good deal of waiting around and the kind of discomfort you might feel after long hours in a terminal building during an airport strike. To manage to sustain yourself for that length of time without anywhere comfortable to sit was a tall order. At least at the Blarney Club there was a sprung dance floor to crash out on at 3am; but here, by the early hours, sleeping people were lining the walls in shivering rows like Londoners on Tube platforms during the Blitz two and a half decades earlier.

Despite our feeling that this really was the 'defining moment', many people just got tired and bored. An hour or two after the Galaxy performance, we Putney High girls showed moderate enterprise by finding an unlocked storage cupboard directly under the vast organ and, switching on the light, settled down to some serious revision. The rest of the night was passed learning off by heart key lines from *A Winter's Tale*, which was on the A level syllabus, as was *The Waste Land and Other Poems*. I fell asleep under my grandmother's musquash coat to the strains of T S Eliot.

Many people took LSD that evening – John Lennon and John Hopkins, for sure, as well as, by all accounts, Syd Barrett and Pete Jenner. It is also known that a new version of LSD, called STP, was being launched and was handed out free to any takers. However, I believe that there was far less consumed than contemporary accounts would have us believe. My impression is that numbers were inflated by our desire for that evening to represent more than it did. If the Exploding Galaxy was anything to go by, the take-up of hallucinogens that evening was low. None of the members who performed that night had yet dropped acid, although this was soon to change. By the summer and autumn, LSD-induced performance by some, but not all, members of the troupe was to become part of Exploding Galaxy explorations.

Documentary footage of that evening shows the element of menace provided by mods. Peter Daltrey, of the band Kaleidoscope, confirms this:

> As the evening wore on, the shimmering gloss that had dazzled and beguiled began to wear off. One 50-minute wait to use the over-subscribed loo saw to that. As Wilson Pickett's hour approached, the detritus began to accumulate in dead piles across the floor: fag boxes and fag ends, empty Rizla packets, glistening pools of vomit, apple cores, condoms, crisp packets, odd shoes, handbags, watches, beads, the corpses of flattened chips, ketchup and a fair old crop of discarded Wrigleys. Rather foolishly we wandered hand in hand into the shadowy extremities of the hall, away from the brilliant heart. And there we came across a guy who had just been glassed in the face. He honestly looked like a ketchup accident in a trucker's café: blood all over his face, bits of flesh hanging off like used Elastoplasts. It would have taken more than a sticky strip to put him back together again. We went back towards the light. Back to the dream.[5]

Perhaps because I was in the walk-in cupboard for so long, I was oblivious to the menace. On the Tube home, groups of young people were evaluating the experience with John Peel, who was travelling back in the same carriage. Only Josephine was outspoken enough to say, 'Quite honestly, I think it was a technicolor yawn.'

The event had not been a success for the organisers. It had all the hallmarks of flower power ineptitude. Nowadays festivals are synchronised with military precision, with every change-over programmed and every hiccup anticipated. Slickness trumps all. Our special evening belonged to us. Slickness seemed an irrelevance and 'against art'. Instead, we had community spirit. We had accepted that no one had decided who was going to perform or where or in what order, and this held its own charm for us. Crucially though, nobody had kept tabs on the ticket sales and takings either.

If anything symbolises the chasm between wishful thinking and badly behaved commercial reality, it is the double-page spread in the next issue of *IT* – issue 13. Pages 2 and 3 evaluate the evening in two columns, one on each side of a photo in negative of the pipe organ. The column on the left confidently claims that the aims of the evening have been largely achieved and states that, in the streets, young people are even starting to behave differently towards each other. The evening is described as a beautiful scene 'where one became aware, through the collecting of all these people, of just how much beauty and force there is here'. Thanks are also given to the numerous 'beautiful' volunteers.

In the right-hand column, the denial of reality continues, with claims that profits of upwards of £3,000 were due immediately, with a possible £20,000 likely for the *IT* film rights. However, the column contains a list of those who still, weeks after the evening, had not paid for the tickets that they had been advanced. This added up to no mean sum, since sale or return tickets had been handed out in wads to more or less anyone who asked. The 'naming and shaming' list of those who, by the time of publication, had not yet paid for their bulk-buy tickets, makes interesting reading.

Linking the two columns in the article is a thread of text that seems to be LSD-induced rambling:

> dear peoples who wander on the shores of planet earth, go back to the earth because it is from the earth that you come! you have lost your humanity because you have seen yourself as outside nature. You will never suck the rich goodness of life. Back into the rich jungle! Now! Now! Set yourselves the task of leading mankind back to the earth because this is the only way you can proceed into the reality of multi-dimensionality. This is my message I give you... take heed... For I see and know all things from the outer limits of the galaxies, even to the tiniest amoeba that swims under a raindrop!

There was no way that this acid-induced drivel could survive cut-throat reality. After the 'Dream' was over, Hoppy was unable to pay the Alexandra Palace owners for the hire of the hall. The bill remains unpaid to this day.

For many in the underground movement, especially those who had been at the first Albert Hall readings, there was a growing sense that the end was in sight. The writing was on the wall for psychedelic culture. It was now being usurped by avarice and commerce and was visibly turning sour. This was a view I had occasionally heard from as early as the spring of 1967. At the time, I did not begin to understand the implications. Malcolm Le Maistre later described it as the whining and blustering of the counterculture old school, who were no longer going to get things their own way. It was now *our* time. We were going to start our own mental revolution and, for me and for other Galaxy members, the phase of freedom and experimentation was only just beginning.

NOTES

1. Karen Moller, *Techicolor Dreamin': The 1960s Rainbow and Beyond* (Trafford Publishing, 2006).
2. This pre-dates the first listed mention of 'magic mushroom' in the *Oxford English Dictionary*.
3. Daevid Allen, quoted in *Shindig Annual*, no. 3 (Volcano Publishing).
4. From *A Technicolor Dream*, a film documentary, directed by Stephen Gammond and co-produced by White Crow Productions and Eagle Rock Entertainment Ltd, 2008.
5. Peter Daltrey, *Tambourine Days* (Blurb Books, 2011).

7

Playscape London

...Art galleries had such a specific atmosphere that only very solemn people could want to attend them. Funeral parlours have a similar effect. Object worship is self-evidently materialistic and is a poor way of relating to people. The morgue-like environment was the inevitable result, and art, if it was to breathe, had to evolve outside of it.

GERALD FITZGERALD

IF THE 14-HOUR Technicolor Dream had been the defining moment of the English flower children, then stepping out on to the grassy slopes of the grounds of Alexandra Palace and into the April dawn of the morning after was the defining moment of the defining moment.

For me, the morning of 30 April 1967 meant more than just moving out of the confines of that particular interior. We were shaking off the fear that had so gripped the nation in the decades before. The Blitz had sent our parents' generation scurrying into the Anderson shelters and down on to the platforms of London underground stations. Now we, their children, were emerging, rubbing our eyes, looking around and gulping in the fresh air.

For us post-war babies, there was no ignoring the lingering traces of devastation in London – the ominous gaps in residential terraces, the buddleia cheerfully poking out of mounds of rubble, the occasional supporting wall now bearing no more than a lone art nouveau fireplace suspended halfway up. Even in the mid-1960s, the evidence was still there for all to see.

Aside from the flattened infrastructure and the ruined churches, the Blitz and the later 'V rockets' damaged or destroyed one million London homes and took upwards of 20,000 Londoners' lives. In fact, it was not until well into the war that mortality figures of the British troops caught up with the number of deaths of men, women and children due to the Blitz.

The government's answer to the craters and the damaged dwellings was to level everything and start again. This was the beginning of the high-rise and office block bonanza that took hold in the 1960s. London was being transformed at breakneck speed, and in the hurry to house the population and to 'chuck out the chintz', countless concrete boxes were built. Few buildings from that post-war era were spared that have since been thought worth listing.

If the straight world's answer was to flatten and rebuild, our generation's solution was to transform and convert, starting with warehouses, which were now seen as potential working, living and gathering spaces. It was also after the war that the first adventure playgrounds appeared in the centre of London's dereliction, offering something more challenging than the tamer 'four Ss' – swings, seesaw, slide and sandbox. I remember that the bombsites themselves had provided unofficial adventure playgrounds, unencumbered by supervising grown-ups and health and safety regulations. It was here that post-war kids from both crumbling terraces and sleek new high-rises skilfully leapt across deep drops onto rubble and negotiated hazardous planks pierced with rusty nails.

Our generation was beginning to envisage new possibilities for the built environment and to see post-war planning as part of the problem. To us, concrete as a material was repressive. We saw bombsites as something to jump about on, like The Beatles on the cover of their *Twist and Shout* EP.

In the spring of 1967, our way of thinking coincided with the improving weather, which meant that we could dispense with buildings altogether. *IT* called for action with the headline 'Play in the parks. You must. You will.' London's flower children took to the streets at the drop of a hat. The continual niggling by the police made it abundantly clear that we did not have society's blessing, yet we knew, with a heady sense of our own power, that the streets and parks belonged to us now. One afternoon, we all went to Piccadilly Circus to smoke cabbage leaf cigarettes or cunningly disguised joints and blow on flutes. Later, when Mick Jagger and Keith Richards were given prison sentences for drug possession, we went en masse to protest outside the *News of the World* offices in Bouverie Street. The numerous times we took to the streets to create manifestations and happenings between these two events have merged in my mind. We all felt incredibly sorry for the misguided police officers, and looked on them with patronising pity as they attempted to intervene. The demonstration that took place after the police raid on *IT* took the form of a mock funeral procession. Despite a prior agreement to hand flowers to police officers, some demonstrators could not contain their feelings and, instead, started throwing bouquets, like grenades – a premonition of that famous Banksy image.

For artists at that time, used to the constraints of galleries, the move to parks and open spaces was liberating. It freed them from the tyranny of big business and all its repressiveness and provided more exciting opportunities for engagement with the spectator.

For the two ex-Signals Gallery directors, David Medalla and Paul Keeler, there were obvious advantages to freeing artistic expression from the world of art as commerce. Their support for sculptors like Camargo, Soto and Clark had produced virtually non-existent sales. In the London market of 1966, you could hardly give away works by these artists; but by leaving the art business out of the equation, you could follow your passion in new ways, with a minimum of overheads.

David, in particular, was drawn to this notion of artworks being taken down off the walls and the art event leaving the gallery.

At this point, the Exploding Galaxy was known purely as a dance troupe and our performances were called 'ballets'. It took some time for our sense of ourselves to evolve beyond the purely theatrical event into becoming something more akin to humanoid sculptures. This came about through the scavenging we did, which became increasingly important as the months went by.

Open-air Galaxy events went on for two years or so alongside the gigs and the life exploration that was our existence at 99 Balls Pond Road. I was at any number of these park events, and however the dramatic themes differed from park to street or from one month to the next, they all shared this quality of immediately engaging the participation of passers-by.

Herzmark's principal memory of the Galaxy was of the outside performances:

> The thing that impressed me and also merged with my own political feelings was that we performed on housing estates. We engaged the children to dance and play silly games. The adults used to join in from their windows and balconies because they were curious as to what was going on. On some of the really fabulous occasions, you had all the adults with their frying pans and saucepans and wooden spoons beating time with the kids down below dancing around in the middle and that was magical. I remember that we used to perform in parks, and since you weren't supposed to perform in parks, the keeper would invariably come to move us on. We used to make great play of it because it is so absurd that you can't dance in a park. Fair enough, if they came along and said you can't perform on this housing estate because it is causing a rumpus. But the dancing in the park we took very seriously. That was completely absurd.

On one such occasion in Regent's Park in June 1967, park regulars turned their deckchairs around to watch a Galaxy rehearsal. By the time the park attendant asked us to move on, a crowd of about 150 had gathered. Having no luck, he went off to seek help. When he returned with the police, the crowd had grown to 250 or more. A theatrical event ensued as we appealed to the crowd: 'These men say we should leave the park because we are creating a disturbance. Are we disturbing you and do you want us to leave?' The crowd answered with a resounding 'No!' 'Leave them alone. It's nice', they shouted at the police. The afternoon ended with an altercation between the general public and the police about who pays for parks and in what way an individual could or could not enjoy public spaces.

Although the Exploding Galaxy did not consist of political activists, we were certainly perceived as a threat by the authorities. As a result, we received copious amounts of police attention, especially on our night-time rambles through central London.

Paul Keeler described one such walk across London in the report *Planted*:

> Fitz, Simon and I were walking back from visiting some friends in Ladbroke Grove. It was about 5 o'clock in the morning. We walked down Wigmore Street, and stopped to look in the window of the Scripture Union Shop. There was a full-sized camel standing in a scene of sand surrounded by Bibles. We found this most incongruous and laughed for several minutes.
>
> At the end of Wigmore Street was a flashing yellow light on one of those heavy wooden pyramid supports, and we looked at it for a short while. I told the others how it related closely to the sculptures of Takis, the Greek artist I had exhibited at Signals…
>
> A few streets further on, outside a large industrial building, we saw some large boxes which had inside them yards of white computer tape. This had been left out for the dustmen. We were very excited at this because we were performing that evening at the Electric Garden and the tape was an excellent attachment for one of the dramas that we were preparing. We began to pick it up in order to take it away. Fitz jumped into one of the boxes and was delighted because it was exactly the right size for a human being to lie in. In fact, it was a metaphorical coffin.

It was at this point that two police officers ran up and asked the Exploders what the hell they thought they were doing. The officers told the three to put the computer paper and cardboard down, and that they had been acting suspiciously. From a passing patrol car police officers called out, 'Been to a hippie love-in?' It was during the search that followed that the officers came across a document called *The Quaquaversal 'F'*. Fitz proceeded to give the policemen a 20-minute explanation of his theories on this and on the work of the Exploding Galaxy. The mood changed from one of hostility to one of amused interest. The encounter ended at sunrise with the police giving them directions to the nearest all-night café in Covent Garden. Such encounters were our kinetic dramas.

The Situationists were ten years old by the time the Galaxy came into being in 1967. They had similar ideas about integrating art and culture into everyday life but were more radical in the way they set about creating situations to jerk us out of our role as spectators. They developed the idea of a 'drifting wander', which came from their theory that geographical settings act directly on the mood and behaviour of the individual and that the effect of modern urban planning is alienating. Out of this came the notion of treating the city as a game. One idea was to navigate Paris using the street plan of Venice. Another involved following a numbers rule – say, 'first right, second left, first right, then repeat'.

Our urban roaming differed from the Situationists' in that it did not spring from a political argument. Our wanderings were not 'insurrectional acts to subvert the controls of a manipulative system'. Our treks had grown out of our quest for costumes and props and our goal in harvesting rubbish came from a preoccupation with artistic investigation. When we came across a large rubbish bin, we would bring out objects or fragments of material that could be admired as artworks. Discussions would then ensue about the foraged object, or about the incongruous alignment of bits of street furniture, so that a walk from A to B could take several hours and was better described with the name we gave it – 'an exploration'.

Although our group walks were Galaxy occasions, nothing was necessarily announced within the household beforehand or even recounted afterwards. There are, therefore, no joint memories or photographs to document many of the Galaxy explorations that took place between 1967 and 1969. Artists now need to record the ephemeral in order to flag it up to the world, with the aid of top-end film equipment and internet skills to match. To us, the idea of documentation was absurd if you really did believe in the importance of taking art off its pedestal, to stop treating it as something separate from everyday life.

An example of this lack of formality and documentation can be seen in the way Michael Chapman went about reading his poems in public, hardly noticed by the rest of us. Christian Ledoux remembers how Mike treated these occasions much as a job, leaving the house punctually, like a dutiful commuter. Says Michael:

> I would often leave Balls Pond Road in the morning. I'd walk around London, picking up anything interesting I found along the way. These were an assortment of discarded objects, like a bamboo stick, the shiny hubcap of a car, a Chinese lantern or piece of rubber lining, a bit of wire netting from the gutter, a potato or some herbs. I would discuss the aesthetical and metaphorical implications of these materials with anyone who happened to be passing by, attaching things together, until they formed a coherent whole... Once I found a length of thick rope, which I hung around my shoulders. I went to town to explore the possibilities of this remarkable object: scaling lampposts, cordoning off the side of tube trains, tying the ends to a bar to create a makeshift swing or hammock. People gathered around and a public meeting would soon develop where I would discuss the issue.

It was only when I saw a documentary about Mike that I saw this street activation for myself. Filmed in January 1968, it shows a crowd standing around him in Trafalgar Square. They are not sniggering at his strangeness as one might expect. In their bouffant hairdos and their left-sided Brylcreemed partings, they are actually listening. Michael is in his fisherman's polo neck – almost bent double with the force of the rant: '*Ah ga snop agrr...*' The rant is loud and Mike is following the lines in his giant handwritten book. He turns the page and continues reading: '*Ggggrrrr ugh ugh...*' The crowd continues to listen, concentrating on the performance. It was by chance that this particular kinetic drama was filmed. Many others remain, as they should be, undocumented and invisible.

These days, we are accustomed to seeing street theatre in all its guises, from silvered statues that move a fraction if you drop a coin to carefully choreographed surprises in formal settings. The ferocious consumption of ideas means that we have seen it all before – if not live, then on YouTube. The freshness has gone, so we are amused for a moment and then we move on. For a small window at the end of the 1960s, the streets of London really were a place of true possibility and the Exploding Galaxy loved nothing more than playing with this concept. In this sense, London really was our magnificent playground.

It was on one of our many wandering street explorations that Edward came across an interesting object. It appeared to be a set of iron springs, joined together as a small rusty construction. It looked as if it had once been part of a child's bed and it may well have come from one of the bombsites we passed on our meanderings. This object was to become an artwork of great significance and gave birth to the term *scrudge*, a term that dominated Galactic thinking for the next 18 months. Mercifully, the object does not reside in some art gallery. Since it has gone for ever, it retains its noble status as truly ephemeral.

8

The Nature of Scrudge

Scrounge, *informal, verb (with obj.) Seek to obtain something (typically food or money) at the expense or through the generosity of others or by stealth. ORIGIN early 20th cent.: varient of dialect scrunge 'steal'.*

Scrunch, *verb (no obj.) Make a loud crunching noise. (with obj. and adverbial) Crush or squeeze something into a compact mass. ORIGIN late 18th cent.: (in the sense eat or bite noisily): probably imitative; compare with crunch.*

Scrump, *verb (with obj.) Brit. informal, steal (fruit) from an orchard or garden. ORIGIN mid 19th cent.: from dialect scrump 'withered apple'.*

OXFORD ENGLISH DICTIONARY

BY THE LATE spring of 1967, the scope of the Exploding Galaxy had widened by several notches. We had broadened from ballet troupe to street exploration to a state of being that addressed every aspect of daily living.

At 99 Balls Pond Road, the constant toing and froing of ideas and counter-ideas, the fact that even such everyday events as brewing up a cuppa came to be something examined and discussed at length by the group (whether you placed the leaves in the pot with a spoon or let them fall from your fingertips, the heating of the pot, and so on) and the ever-present desire to transform what surrounded us – all this led us into a whole new world of terminology, that belonged to the Exploding Galaxy and not the wider counterculture and was quite separate from expressions common to freakdom.

Underground terminology had its own etymology (often from American jazz and black culture) and a number of these words gradually became absorbed into wider parlance. The words *hip* and *cool* survived, whereas the widely used *bread*, meaning money, did not. *Breadhead*, employed to describe someone who was only interested in money, is not common now, but the suffix *-head* remains, to denote a person with an unhealthy interest in something, for example, *petrolhead*.

The Exploding Galaxy lexis was entirely different. For example, the adjective *straight* was used by hippies to mean conventional or establishment. Its connotation was fixed and derogatory, so that a 'straight chick', even if she were gorgeous, would still be flawed by being straight because she would not truly understand the values of the flower children. In the Galaxy, we used two words taken from geology to describe degrees of 'straightness': *centroclinal* and *quaquaversal.*

Fitz explained the terms in the following way:

> QUAQUAVERSAL – pointing in every direction – is a geological term, but is used here to denote an open and unspecific approach to art and people, not governed by the laws observed by the professionals of any art medium. CENTROCLINAL is the opposite.[1]

Other words frequently used within the Galaxy were *linear* (which was negative, as in 'linear thinking') and *evolved* (which was positive because it implied a moving beyond the obvious and the unthinking). We also frequently used the words *possibility* (since we would not limit ourselves to the predictable option) and *activate* because we felt it our duty to re-educate the centroclinal world. Our rehearsals could not be described as such. From as early as the *Fuzzdeath* ballet at Ally Pally in April 1967, I hardly ever heard the word 'rehearsal' used in relation to the Exploding Galaxy. Our work-in-progress meetings were eventually called *explorations* where work was 'evolved'; these could be part-rehearsal and part-exhibition since we had dispensed with the world of art galleries. Explorations were seen as more kinetic than exhibitions and more inclusive than art usually is. A kinetegram was part play, part document, part artwork. In the kinetegram *Orange and Blue*, Orange attempts to explain these words to the very square Blue.

Of all the words in the Exploding Galaxy lexicon, it was the term *scrudge* that delighted us the most.

Being a country girl, Audrey Vipond thought that scrudge was closely associated with the verb *scrump*. She also thought that the sound of the word described exactly that of snow being crunched underfoot. The word was certainly flexible – both in its onomatopoeic associations and in its meaning.

Galaxy member Judith Pertz thought that the term was incongruous:

> I always found it to be a funny word because it reminds me of 'scrounge' and 'sludge', which aren't very positive things when you think about it. And I remember it was supposed to be something very special and transcendental and I thought it was funny to have a transcendental word that sounds like sludge and scrounge mixed together. As far as I am concerned, they were these objects that were unused and were put together in unusual ways and made into something different.

Edward describes the story of how scrudge came into being:

> It was thanks to this metal spring of a scrunched-up sprung mattress. It was lots of spirals of wire, as you had in these sprung mattresses, and they were all joined together, but all the fabric had gone and it had rusted. It was quite small, not like a double bed or anything. It was a smallish piece of rusty bed innards.
>
> I had found it in the street and I took it back to a flat in Islington High Street where Fitz and some other people were – and I was saying, 'Isn't it beautiful?' Fitz got on to it. He found it quite an enjoyable object and he was maybe sitting on it and moving it round and making sounds with it.
>
> I am pretty sure it was Fitz who used the word to describe the sound that you were getting – the sound and the feel of sitting or standing on this mattress and it was also in his mind and he went on to say, 'It's scrudging – that's what it is and that's what those two bits of tissue paper are doing.'
>
> He was referring to two pieces of coloured tissue paper which were flapping against each other.

Lizzie described scrudge as *objets trouvés*, but this was not my understanding of the term at all. An objet trouvé, once obtained and placed in a gallery, challenged the established view. Scrudges were closely related yet almost the opposite of this. Why would they need to be put on show along with other artworks? Surely we should consider everything around and about as artworks, without the need to be placed in a gallery. If scrudge were considered to be 'an artwork' and sold through an art dealer, that would take it out of the realm of everyday metaphorical experience and back into the world of the centrocline and art-as-business. At this point, scrudge would cease to be authentic and genuinely revolutionary. In this sense, scrudge was a true challenge to the established art world.

Edward continues:

> Scrudges were usually just materials rather than an object that was a concept in itself or a found object, although they were related to that. A scrudge came to mean anything you found that you made into an artwork. It's different from the traditional modern art idea of a surrealist thing. They were materials which could go towards making costumes or decorating your walls or whatever.

A further difference can be seen in comparing the way that scrudges and 'readymades' were selected. Readymades were everyday manufactured objects that were given new status as artworks, the most famous being Marcel Duchamp's upturned urinal to which he gave the title *Fountain*. Duchamp described the need to remove notions of taste when choosing a readymade; he had to be sufficiently indifferent in order to make the selection. A scrudge, by comparison, was selected on the basis of the aesthetic emotion it engendered, and the object's attraction was therefore closely bound up with the chooser's personal taste. For example, Fitz loved small bits of chiffon in many colours – he especially liked anything that was partially transparent.

I would say that our search for scrudges was more like the selection made by magpies, driven by attraction for some quality that might be its sheen or its absence of sheen or its metaphorical qualities.

Although most of the scrudges that we worked with were moveable and often used as costumes, a scrudge could equally be an industrial process or a fixed piece of debris or street furniture.

Edward describes two scrudges that were fixed:

> I had one scrudge that I discovered that I didn't attempt to move. It was somewhere down the back of Liverpool Road in Islington, in what was quite a derelict area, and there was this whole piece of rubbish that had become a sort of organism in itself. It had kind of melded together and had become one thing. I don't know how the thing came into being before I discovered it. It was extraordinarily unified in its structure. Most of the pieces of it you couldn't detach even if you wanted to, and you couldn't quite determine what they were. They weren't utterly revolting sorts of rubbish. They were a mixture of building rubble, and moss and stuff had grown it together. It was very difficult to describe. It was in a little corner between two buildings that had just ended up being used for dumping things. I did take one piece away from it.
>
> There was also an actual paving stone in the Pentonville Road. Most paving stones were fairly smooth and flat but this one just had hundreds of indentations on it and it was very like one of Fitz's density paintings. He walked me half a mile to show me this particular thing – 'It's a scrudge!' It had obviously been done that way by the people when they were concreting it – for some reason. It had this very dense grid of lines on it.

Generally speaking, though, scrudges were items scavenged from the roads that lay in the triangle between Dalston Junction, the Angel and Highbury Corner. Hugo Williams remembers the Dalston/Islington area well then and its plentiful supply of varied rubbish:

> The great thing about Islington in those days was that it was full of little workshops and lots of foundries, small factories making souvenirs – and there was waste product from there. They have all gone. They have all been turned into back extensions and garages and tiny maisonettes at the backs of houses. But I can point them out on every street. Each had its little factory or foundry that had its rubbish which spewed out on to the pavement.

Another favourite hunting ground was the area called Fitzrovia. The principal scrudged items here comprised computer paper and a ready supply of cardboard tubes of varying lengths. There were also bins filled with fabric offcuts in the area north of Oxford Street. I remember, in particular, large sheets of simulated leather with circles punched out. We hung these down like banners on Parliament Hill. Since Soho was a centre for film and theatre, this area provided a much coveted supply of spotlight gels that had the added benefit of making a wonderful clattering sound when strung together.

Dalston Market in the Kingsland Road provided a vast array of materials – sheets of fake grass, delicate squares of tissue with intricate printed designs in which fruit had been individually wrapped, and quantities of plastic crates that, when piled high, could be used to subdivide a room. Of particular interest were the sheets of stiff blue indented cellophane, which were used to divide layers of fruit within a crate. These crackled when moved and caught the light enticingly when pinned to a wall.

Jumble sales provided extraordinary scrudges – items that were a complete surprise, often created out of odd-shaped lengths of garter or stocking-stitch and stuffed by the knitter. These could be worn as headdresses. Blankets made of knitted rectangles were a delight because of the random juxtaposition of colours. Audrey found one garter-stitch blanket, where the blocks of colour were almost, but not quite, the same hue, mainly silver greys and maroons, with a single random splodge of turquoise in one corner. Whoever had constructed this thing had done so without any interest in its look – its sole purpose was to provide warmth.

Every item purchased or found was valued for its own imagined story, becoming an aesthetic talking point in its own right, and brought back to Balls Pond Road to adorn our spaces. Going to a jumble sale in Islington or Hackney at the end of the 1960s was an extraordinary experience, perhaps more like a quest for treasure. Each church hall or community centre was an emporium, with the trestle tables piled high with what would now be called 'vintage' garments so gorgeous that they would make you draw in your breath. But to get to the real trove, you had to struggle and fight your way past

Hackney battleaxes, local women who would think nothing of giving you bruising jabs with their elbows to get to the tables first or of allowing a silk shirt to tear rather than relinquish their half.

I got my entire range of scrudges from jumbles, and by the autumn of 1967, they had become part of my everyday attire, an array of quirky objects that were accessories without a purpose. For example, I would hang a child-sized hot-water bottle that looked as if it were made of embossed pewter from my waist like a sporran, and I would carry about scrudges of interest in a deep 1930s pram. I did not, in fact, buy my first proper handbag until I was in my late twenties.

There were two great scrudge coups. The first was the discovery of a derelict baker's factory south of Balls Pond Road, between Essex and Kingland roads. It had been boarded up, but some Galaxy members broke in and found a wealth of abandoned catering items. I did not join in on the raid. I already had a horror of foraging from bins in the street in case I was accused of stealing, and my aversion to trespassing deprived me of a wonderful adventure. The others returned with armloads of doilies, glittery cake bases and paper garlands, which provided enormous scope for discussion, creativity and scrudge discovery over the following days and weeks.

The other great scrudge coup occurred further afield. A number of students from Camberwell Art College, living in a large Victorian villa in the Upper Richmond Road, had purchased two trunkfuls of clothing from a defunct collection of oriental clothing. There was a complete range of costumes from many countries from the Near to the Far East. Many had been made without darts or even gathers so that they could be laid out flat in extraordinary shapes, like the drawings in Max Tilke's book *Costume Patterns and Designs*.[2] For instance, there was a pair of what seemed like drainpipe trousers, the legs alone being as long as an adult is tall, the better to form hundreds of tiny folds down at the ankle. Eve Ridoux found a pair of pom-pom trousers that looked almost like a giant puffball, which she can be seen wearing in the film *Acéphale*. I acquired two Rajasthani cotton skirts which, given my dark complexion, made me look like a Roma girl.

Although most scrudges were acquired through recycling, it would be wrong to conclude that they could not be bought new. Electrical suppliers provided a range of goods that worked well as scrudges. According to Edward:

> We certainly went to shops as well as to rubbish bins, but we tended to buy things not for the purpose they were meant for. In particular, we frequented shops with electrical wiring. We went for the ones where there were lots of coloured wires and little functional bits that we didn't know what they were meant for, and some of these shops had these old guys and they were quite happy to sell you stuff. They knew everything about electrical parts.

For me, the concept of scrudge was the direct result of two separate paths crossing. LSD brought a change in consciousness. It totally transformed the way you looked at your surroundings, and with this came an absorption in surfaces and textures and the 'otherness' of everyday objects. You didn't actually have to have taken LSD to see the world in this way – just looking at the objects and textures around you and giving your full attention to them would do it, so those of us who had not yet taken acid were not left out. It's just that LSD was the shortcut.

Combine this with the Signals Gallery connection and, in particular, the attention paid in the Balls Pond Road house to the work of conceptual artists and the kinetic artworks that surrounded us there, with their emphasis on transformation, on light and on process, and it was inevitable that the notion of marketable artwork would become redundant.

The most telling evidence for this is Mike Chapman's description of a scrudge. In November 1967, while travelling to perform at the 'Flight to Lowlands Paradise' event in the Netherlands, a very large amount of LSD was consumed. Some of the group took several acid trips in one go. Here is Michael's description of watching a dredger at work:

While in Amsterdam some of us would observe dredger boats cleaning the canals for what seemed like hours, commenting enthusiastically about the aesthetics of the operation (chain sequence of buckets full of watery mud rising up from the bottom of the canals, doing a little jolt at the top just before emptying their loads, continue around until they hit the water again). This was so fascinating to us.

Except for the functional purpose of the dredger, this could be a description of one of the kinetic artworks in Signals Gallery. In this sense, the word scrudge had come to mean just a way of looking – with new eyes.

The Exploding Galaxy did not have a manifesto as such, but there were certain themes and preoccupations that dominated the way we spent our days and helped to define us.

1 THE DOMINANCE OF SCRUDGE.

It is true to say that each of us defined the word in our own way and that this gave scrudge several layers of meaning. After the photographer Mitja Hinderks visited us at Balls Pond Road, he described the house as epitomising our de-materialist philosophy through scrudge:

> Partly out of necessity, but mainly out of principle, they recycled or re-adapted just about everything. They took consumer and commercial waste – which they called scrudge – and made personal clothing and decoration with it as well as serious, playful, temporary and less temporary artworks… within their world they could eliminate materialism almost entirely.

2 THE CENTRAL ROLE OF METAPHOR…

Nothing was to be taken at face value. Edward Pope explained this in the following way:

> Every one of us became a walking justification of his own life, and honesty became a necessity for those who wished to inspire others with the creative way of life. You might see one of us on a bus, wearing clothes that could neither be called respectable nor bohemian, but you might call them bizarre were it not for the sense in them, or you might call them

> jokes were they not also full of inventive imagination and poetry. People ask, 'Why do you wear that?', 'What is that?', 'How do you live?', and we explain, in a simple way, how, by treating things in one's life with fresh imagination, by changing their purpose, like wearing a cushion for a hat, turning an umbrella into a newspaper or a bus into a church, one penetrates the pretence that life is humdrum and comes to see one's own life transformed into part of the life of the imagination, the life that gives meaning and makes history.

3 DOING THINGS DIFFERENTLY

Since the Exploding Galaxy concerned themselves with transforming every aspect of life into an artistic experience, the notion of evolving behaviour was more appealing than repeated behaviour, even – or perhaps especially – in relation to everyday routine. Edward absorbed this fairly fully into his approach to daily events. When called one day by David to join a meeting down in the garden, he and Leighana (who had created a living space for themselves in the bathroom) resolved to go downstairs via the outside of the house rather than the staircase. Leighana wore her stripey dress, but no underwear and Edward wore trousers with a gaping hole at the crotch with no underwear, so it is not surprising that the neighbour two doors down started pelting the two of them with bricks as they climbed down the drainpipe onto the outhouse roof.

Later, a short time after we had all split up, I remember a reading a novel in which the protagonist led his life entirely according to the throw of a die.[3] If he threw, say a six or a four, he would 'become' a veteran from the Detroit Tigers or an escaped convict for an evening or Jesus Christ for a day. His life suddenly took on new meaning. This was faintly reminiscent of how the notion of possibility was taken to extremes by some members of the group.

Mike Chapman describes these 'What should I do now?' moments:

> I would just stay glued to the pavement and start debating with myself about what my next action in life should be, and its reason, with me literally struggling with myself.

4 THE IMPORTANCE PLACED ON FOUND TEXTS

The Exploding Galaxy were just some of the people exploring found text as poetry. While we were busy scavenging for meaning in texts discovered in the dustbins of Soho, Tom Phillips had begun his long engagement with a Victorian novel he'd found in a furniture repository in Peckham Rye, painstakingly altering the book, blotting out words, painting in sections and so forth, using a number of procedures, some determined by chance. Several years prior to this, Brion Gysin had revived the cut-up when his Stanley knife slipped and sliced into some newsprint. In May 1962, Joe Orton and Kenneth Halliwell were each given a six-month prison sentence for defacing library books with surrealistic collages. All of this experimentation could be seen as dating back to Dada, but it was only in the sixties that it erupted into a mass cultural awareness – an outpouring from all directions. These techniques with texts were suddenly available to us all. In this way, without knowing how it related to the creative whole, the 15-year-old me sat in my school uniform with a group of friends in my bedroom in Putney, typing out whatever I could from the discussion taking place around me, knowing that I could capture no more than snippets of dialogue. The text, when read out as a coherent whole, delighted us all. We had all been given permission to investigate the nature of creativity and it wasn't just the well known or the avant-garde elite who were at it.

This sense that we were all entitled to make art was everywhere. John Taylor, a musician and ocarina maker, was fairly typical of artists at the time in the way he allowed his creativity to spill out in all directions. Galaxy flautist Judith Pertz often visited him and remembers that, sometime during that year, he and his flatmates decided that there were too many words and set about reducing the English language into three phrases, which happened to be: 'That's about the size of it', 'When I want your bloody opinion I'll ask for it' and 'Nothing like a nice cup of tea.' They then reduced this further. Says Judith:

> The next time I came, everywhere in the house was written 'opinion' and 'size' – a little word stuck to the piano, the wall or the floor – and they sitting around and only saying one word: 'Opinion', 'Size', 'Size', 'Opinion'... The funny thing was the next time I came to their house these words were appearing on the fence and written in the middle of the street. It didn't get further than the corner.

5 INCORPORATION OF EASTERN MYSTICISM

It was David Medalla's influence that brought tales from Buddhism and Hinduism into the explorations of the Exploding Galaxy. In his book about David Medalla, Guy Brett describes the reaction to *The Buddha Ballet* initiated by David and John Dugger for Galactic exploration:

> Some admirers of Medalla's kinetic work had mixed feelings about the Exploding Galaxy. The French critic Jean Clay, for example, praised the Galaxy as an audacious break with the institutions of art, but disapproved of its orientalising tendency. This was seen as a retreat into an exotic past, a failure to confront contemporary problems. For Medalla and Dugger the Buddhist stories were of 'universal value'. I see Medalla's involvement with Buddhism as a search for another set of human relations in art.[3]

My favourite story of all was the explanation of the Sanskrit word *kalpa*, from Indian cosmology, which was told and retold in the Galaxy household:

> A disciple once asked for an explanation of the word *kalpa* (an Indian measurement of time comprising the creation and destruction of a cosmic system). The disciple wanted to know how long a *kalpa* lasts. The Buddha replied in the following way: 'Imagine a large piece of Benares stone four cubic leagues in size. Imagine further that every one hundred

years a man would come and wipe the surface of the stone with a piece of the finest Benares muslin. The stone would be worn away long before the *kalpa* had come to an end.[4]

Such stories and teachings were excellent ways of reminding us of our insignificance, and just in case we got too big for our avant-garde boots, they acted a as a reality check, taking us down a peg or two by also reminding us that, in not so many decades' time, we would all be dust.

These tales provided a means by which all of us could perform in our own way, and I was at my happiest in the Exploding Galaxy when trying to interpret in dance, tales from the *Mahabharata*, under the direction of David Medalla. These sessions were utterly bound up with the intuitive and therefore, to me, infinitely superior to anything else I was invited to work on. The most exciting of the Galaxy's productions was without question *The Bird Ballet*. This in itself can be described as combining epic storytelling with kinetic artwork, with people, not foam, extruding out their individual shapes from the collective imagination.

I have never gone for matching accessories, and David's tales from Eastern mysticism provided a healthy eclecticism in the Exploding Galaxy, a human balance to counter and complement the abstract intellectual elements provided by our preoccupation with conceptual art. If our eclecticism had given way to a single set of rules, the group might have become vulnerable to a single personality, theory or doctrine.

6 ACTIVATION

At around this time, David Medalla said:

> I believe it is the duty of every architect and artist to renew people's sensory awareness and use the technology available to make people active participants in their immediate surroundings rather than passive and inhibited spectators.[5]

Whenever we were out and about, the extended Galaxy tried to live up to these ideals by engaging artistically with our surroundings. As we travelled around London on foot, dressed in our scrap finery, we would stop at commercial rubbish bins in search of scrudges, look for metaphors in the street furniture and produce kinetic drama out of everyday street life, engaging with and 'activating' those people we encountered.

NOTES

1. *Planted*, a report compiled by Paul Keeler, London, 1968.
2. Max Tilke, *Costume Patterns and Designs* (London: A. Zwemmer Ltd, 1956).
3. Luke Rhinehart, *The Dice Man* (William Morrow, 1971).
4. Guy Brett, *Exploding Galaxies: The Art of David Medalla* (London: Kala Press, 1995).
5. *Planted*.

9

LSD Anyone?

Taking LSD is like climbing the Matterhorn – very dangerous, but with its own rewards. I would never prevent anyone who wanted to from climbing the Matterhorn.

R D LAING

IN THE LATE sixties, the roundabout just south of Waterloo Bridge was known as the Bull Ring. The concrete undercroft of this space was strangely empty, for this was the South Bank that pre-dated the bash-dwellings of Cardboard City and pre-dated the *trundle* and *flip* of skateboards. The only 'skyscraper' in the vicinity was the Shell Centre, which, at 351 feet, had been the tallest building in the United Kingdom for one brief year until 1962.

On 30 May 1967, it was here at the Bull Ring that Edward chose to hold his 19th birthday party – a Galaxy-style happening. Among those present were the artists Li Yuan-Chia, David Medalla and Gerald Fitzgerald. Of the younger ones, there was my friend Josephine, Edward's brother and an art student friend called Ruy, whom I regarded as the best dancer at UFO. We had with us a number of five-foot cardboard carpet tubes taken from Soho bins and my Edwardian parasol from the shop Granny Takes a Trip. We were standing approximately where the foyer of the Imax Cinema now is, the idea being to provide some interest for the drivers negotiating the roundabout. One cardboard tube was inserted into another, and with the parasol placed on top it looked like a caber-tossing exercise. The construction peeped above the parapet so that it was visible to the circling traffic. This was a fairly typical Galaxy outing, activating the centroclinal world. Being out in the street allowed for interaction with the general public and made possible all kinds of kinetic dramas.

Another guest was Dave, whom Edward had met at The Process. He arrived with a birthday present for Edward: a small number of acid tabs. The kinetic drama that was to unfold that evening following this act of generosity left one person permanently traumatised, and the rest of us who witnessed the event shamed and with a healthy fear of lysergic acid diethylamide.

It is interesting that 'they' did not own up. By 'they', I mean a number of counterculture bigwigs who failed to broadcast the fact that they had *never* taken LSD and had no desire to do so. Jim Haynes has stated that he never intentionally took LSD, but found to his horror that his drink had been spiked one night at John Lennon's birthday party. I do not know whether UFO impresario Joe Boyd did eventually touch the stuff, but rumour has it that he had not done so by the end of those turned-on years 1967–1968. By 1967, songwriter and poet Pete Brown, after a period of excess, was against all drugs. His one and only experience of a hallucinogen had come about through a horrific DMT (dimethyltryptamine) spiking. When The Cream's album *Disraeli Gears* came out, I had assumed that Pete's lyrics were the result of his LSD experiences. In fact, during our interview, he described being appalled by what he called 'acid fascism', which assumed that somehow you were contemptible and not much of a man if you did not partake. He went further by suggesting that the counterculture was disabled as a political movement by its love of drugs:

> As far as I could see, it destroyed consciousness rather than opening it, and it made people vulnerable. It damaged some good brains. My paranoid theory at the time was that the people who were supplying the stuff were like the enemy. They had dodgy connections and were working with the government. Acid was presented to us as something highly desirable, but in fact it was actually fed to the underground in order to destroy it. A part of me still does subscribe to that idea. I still have very big doubts about LSD and I think that it subverted the underground rather than doing us any good.

Contrary to his outspoken views, most of us believed that acid had the power to alter consciousness and herald a new era. Although we had no idea of the true scope of the CIA's Project MKUltra mind control programme, we had heard about experiments on soldiers in which, once under the influence, they would lose all sense of urgency and be incapable of carrying out orders. Radio operators and soldiers carrying rocket launchers put down their gear and just giggled or climbed trees to talk to the birds. In 1967, many, from both extremes of the political divide, thought that LSD could change not just behaviour but also outlook, and therefore could transform the world.

The issue was not whether you believed, as many of us did, that LSD was a good thing globally, but whether you had dared to take it yourself. Some folk, like the Fuzzy-Gigglies, downed tabs like Rowntree's Jelly Tots. Others among us were afraid.

The fear came from several directions. First, the press claimed not only that LSD broke down chromosomes and caused birth defects, but also that it might trigger leukaemia. Then there was the publicity about extremely frightening 'trips gone wrong', like the six students who had gone into the countryside to commune with nature and had become blind from staring directly at the sun for hours on end. There was also the Guinness heir, Tara Browne, immortalised in a Beatles song, whom most people still believe was killed while driving on an acid trip.[1] Chinese whispers abounded about friends of friends who had fought with a petrol pump or jumped off a bridge. Everyone who had taken acid had a tale to tell about their rogue moments. These often contained common themes, like the ability to see behind and beyond. Edward Pope remembers:

> I could see inside my head – all the veins in my head – and behind that, exactly that kind of crinkly shape that you see in medical drawings, when they go digging into the brain. When I realised I could see inside my head, I suddenly thought that it was like seeing death and I didn't want to look.

Carol Grimes recalls:

> I had my baby son in my arms, and I watched his head become transparent, almost as if I could see the blood going through his veins. It scared the hell out of me, and I said, 'Never again.'

Yet another shared hallucination was the speeding up or slowing down of time, or even arrival at the very end of time. Edward Pope again:

> I wasn't in any part of what I could describe as the earthly physical universe. I was in something like outer space, but it was an infinite void and I was travelling through it very fast. In the distance, I saw this little figure and it came closer to me. I saw that it was a seated Buddha in meditation posture and so I felt that I was going to learn something really amazing or wonderful. Then I realised that the Buddha was a Buddha of hate, disseminating pure hatred towards me.

Chris Malcolm says:

> The first experience I had was shattering, and what is interesting is that I shared the exact same visions as a friend of mine. We took our trips at different times and in different places, but she, like me, experienced lifting off into a sort of dark cold part of the universe where time had stopped and where ashes were slowly falling like snow. It was the end of everything and I thought to myself, 'Oh my god, I've blown my brains. I'm going to spend the rest of my days in a mental institution.' I thought I had gone mad and this was it, and my mind had just gone out so far it would never return.
>
> Afterwards, my friend's attitude was: 'I'm never going to touch that stuff again! That was absolutely horrible! It was a bad trip!' My attitude was:'Wow! You come back! That *is* interesting!'

My friend Josephine and I were extremely cautious. Although news about Syd Barrett's breakdown had not filtered through to us yet, we had met a number of people who were taking real chances with the drug and one or two who had gone to pieces. We did not want to fry our brains. Josephine remembers:

> To take LSD is to go on an adventure, and of course, young people want to have adventures, especially young men. In a real adventure you would do something dangerous, like going on a sailing expedition in a small boat. This kind of danger is character forming. Taking recreational drugs, by contrast, is character damaging. It is certainly not for the faint-hearted.

In the case of Ruy's trip at the Bull Ring, it was disastrous. He was a talented student at Central School of Art who had a superb sense of the surreal and he was producing some extraordinary and very inventive work. One LSD trip was enough to wreck his life.

Nevertheless, despite the frightening anecdotes, many of us were either extremely curious about 'the experience' or felt duty bound to try it, due to the immense peer pressure exerted within the counterculture. Once Paul McCartney came out on telly, it became very unhip to have never turned on. It is therefore not surprising that, where LSD was concerned, there was a lot of faking going on. It was easy to pretend you were on an acid trip. Many of us were walking around with benign smiles anyway, and in the dark of a club, who was to notice whether your pupils were dilated? If someone asked whether you were tripping, it was easy enough to say, 'Yes.' For young women, it was not a million miles from answering the question, 'Did you come?'

What made the LSD story so very different from that of other drugs available at the time was that its discovery could be pinpointed to a specific time – April 1943 – and to a specific place: the town of Sandoz, in Switzerland. The research biochemist Albert Hofmann had been working on a fungus called ergot when he accidentally ingested the substance and immediately realised its therapeutic potential. It soon came into use in psychotherapy as a 'sympathetic and effective' treatment of seemingly untreatable disorders. By the 1950s, it was being used in the United Kingdom, most notably by pioneer Dr Ronald Sandison at Powick Hospital in Worcestershire. By the early 1960s, hundreds of patients had been treated with courses of LSD on the National Health. Medical practitioners, curious to try this extraordinary substance, turned to self-experimentation, and this led to LSD's spread sideways into the wider population as a recreational drug. By the mid-sixties, it was increasingly used in intellectual circles. It was because of this social use that Albert Hofmann came to describe the drug as his 'problem child'. LSD was added to the list of prohibited drugs in the UK in 1966, by which time general anxiety and bad publicity had jeopardised its use in medicine.

Both Hofmann and Sandison were lifelong believers in the benefits of LSD, but were horrified at its popularity as a party drug with young people and disappointed by the impact this had on its development as a medical therapy. Hofmann saw the careless and irresponsible taking of LSD as the tragic result of misunderstanding the nature and meaning of the substance. According to him, it should be taken only by centred people, later in life, or used within an established cultural ritual in a spiritual context. He most certainly believed in its power to open the mind:

> Through my LSD experience and my new picture of reality, I became aware of the wonder of creation, the magnificence of creation and of the animal and plant kingdom. I became very sensitive to what will happen to all of this and all of us. [2]

He believed that the drug could be used as a tool to give us the awareness we needed to connect with our environment and stop us from laying waste the natural world.

Of course, not all hippie use of LSD was cavalier. There were plenty of young people with a mature approach who had a mindful and cautious attitude towards the drug and its effects. They were able to benefit from the all-encompassing sense of reality that came with an acid trip. Insights during this rare and mystical state include feeling at one with the whole of existence, experiencing the intense beauty of all things and understanding the nature of God. According to Chris Malcolm:

> During an acid trip it's very common to feel that you've been brought face to face with the supreme source of all knowledge but it's all just too much for your little, ordinary, everyday, mortal mind. You can see and grasp bits of it, but you can't hold onto it. You're like a child in a toy shop. I think Ali Baba's cave is a nice metaphor for this. In the version of the story I heard as a child, Ali Baba went to this cave and it was absolutely full of all these jewels. He filled his pockets with them, and when he came out of the cave, they turned to ashes. And that's one of these things that can happen on a trip. You go to this wonderful place and you have all this fantastic insights and maybe you can even write them down so that you can read them later, but when you come back to a normal state of mind,

it's all slipped away. Somehow you can't hold it. What you've written down is nonsense.

Simon Shirley remembers:

My own first experience of acid was with my girlfriend down in Claygate. We walked over the railway tracks and into some woodland and made love while tripping. A horse and rider came by on the bridle track. I could feel the approaching horse and reverberating hooves coming up through the ground to me and feel this connection to the world beyond my body.

Acid was powerful because it was something I was *experiencing* and not something I was reading about. Just to *experience* breath – the wall would breathe and you would breathe and you would start to realise that we are one and the truth of what a friend of mine said, 'The greatest lie in this world is that you end at your fingertips.'

If you took acid, you couldn't really go back, and once you had experienced this oneness, you couldn't pretend that it didn't exist. You'd see people in their cars going about their business and you could see how absurd and ridiculous it all was.

Sue Hall concurs:

A good trip is determined by your inner view, which colours everything. If acid taught me anything, it taught me that beauty is in the eye of the beholder. I can remember taking acid in my squat in 1972. The décor was in a state of decay and the architrave around the door damaged, and for the first time on this acid trip, I noticed that there were 17 layers of wallpaper between the top layer and the lath-and-plaster underneath. It looked fantastic – utterly beautiful.

LSD as a drug was extremely well suited to counterculture thinking, because it allowed us to see the world differently. We had come through the fifties, a time of extreme conformity. We were in a state of shock that our parents' generation, for all their niceties, had got us all into yet another 'fine mess', a mess that could not be put right. We didn't agree with our parents or the system and, what is more, we knew we were right.

LSD, like nothing else, helped to accentuate the absurdity and the hypocrisy of the straight world. Edward Pope remembers:

> I was walking along past the suburban houses quite near the Margriethal in Utrecht, where people often don't draw their curtains. It was teatime and I went past three houses, and in each house, one after the other, an almost identical family was sitting down to tea at the same time, and it totally did my head in. It was like the whole world was exactly the same.

Fitz remembers:

> Going to the post office suddenly seemed strange, seeing people in a queue and getting these little bits of paper. The business of financial transactions seemed to me to be completely bizarre. Suddenly, coins didn't seem to be coins anymore; they were just round pieces of metal. And it seemed to be completely mad to see people putting them carefully on the counter and somebody counting more little bits of metal. I thought: 'What's going on?'

At Edward Pope's birthday party in the Bull Ring, Ruy put a piece of blotting paper in his mouth. The older members – the 'grown-ups': David, Fitz, Li Yuan Chia and Paul Keeler – had long gone, and the youngsters, including Edward Pope, Malcolm Le Maistre, Ruy and me – hung around a bit longer before making our way back to Balls Pond Road. This meant taking the Northern Line from Waterloo to the Angel and then a No. 38 bus to the house.

Halfway to the platform at Waterloo, Ruy went wild, dashing up one escalator and down another, flinging off his shirt, revealing a torso flushed an unusual shade of bright red. Once in the train, he bounced off the sides of the carriage like a pinball thrown off the flippers. Wherever he was, it was not a good place, and it seems extraordinary to me that he did not end up on the live rail. Somehow we got him out of the station at the Angel and on to the bus. However, once we had coaxed him into the house at Balls Pond Road, nothing could put things right.

Edward, who was also tripping, then became frightened himself, retreating to the bathroom, which became, as a result, the place in the house where he always felt most at home.

Christian, one of the grown-ups, came downstairs to calm Ruy, but that only made things worse. I had not taken any drugs, but I was definitely breaking my family's rules. The agreement was that I, being only 15, had to ring my parents, no matter how late, to put their minds at rest. There was a phone box outside in the street, but Ruy would not let me out of his sight long enough for me to walk the few yards to make the call.

A taxi was eventually called to take me back to Putney and I drove off, leaving Ruy to his terror. The next morning he was found by police in the street outside the house eating something unsavoury off the pavement. To complicate matters further, he had borrowed Malcolm's coat, containing Malcolm's identity, so it was Malcolm's father who anxiously rushed across London to the Dalston police cells to rescue his 'son'. It was only later that Ruy's distressed mother flew in from Lisbon to take *her* son home. Fitz, who as an art therapist had experience of the use of LSD in psychiatric practice, had gone straight to the police station to try to persuade them of the need for Ruy to get medical attention.

We soon felt the fallout from that dreadful evening. It briefly divided the generations in the house. The older ones, acutely aware of the possible consequences, were alarmed by what had happened and condemned our actions as irresponsible. David Medalla was livid with Edward and told him so.

Ruy did eventually return to London. Although he went on to study at the Slade and make a career for himself as an extremely talented artist, it is my belief that he never fully recovered, and that this experience contributed to his early death under tragic circumstances.

A natural consequence of the events of that evening was to make the house a regular blip on police radar. From that moment on, 99 Balls Pond Road became a legitimate target for police interest. The Ruy incident gave individuals among the local constabulary and the Drugs Squad the permission and moral authority to harass us and then, when they failed to find any illegal substances, to plant them.

NOTES

1. This accident was referred to in the lyics of the Beatles song 'A Day in the Life'.
2. From 'Stanislav Grof interviews Dr Albert Hofmann' , Esalen Institute, Big Sur, California, 1984, *maps*. vol. XI, no. 2, Fall 2001.

10

99 Balls Pond Road

In my ten-foot bamboo hut this spring,
There is nothing: there is everything.

FROM *A NET OF FIREFLIES* [1]

CERTAIN PLACE NAMES inspire comic writing. Balham is one ('Gateway to the South'), and Tooting another ('Home rule for Tooting!'). Balls Pond Road has inspired several references from some of our best comedy writers. Marty Feldman and Barry Tooke gave 'Radio Balls Pond' a regular slot in *Around the Horne* and Peter Sellers immortalised the place in his recording about 'Auntie Rotter's Home for Orphaned Children'. I also seem to remember Balls Pond Road being a cue for laughter in either *Porridge* or *Steptoe and Son*, or both. There is certainly a widely perceived lack of sophistication in the name that raises a laugh. Even though now gentrified and most of it part of the listed De Beauvoir conservation area, the road could never sound genteel. The Balls Pond Road, like 'the Old Kent Road' at the cheap end of the Monopoly board, was usually preceded by a definite article.

It is recorded that a certain John Ball owned a tavern – and, with it, a pond – which was located at the Newington Green end of the road. Here, in the 18th century, drinkers would derive great entertainment and mirth from baiting bulls and shooting at ducks.

There is no record of when No. 99 itself was built, but on a map dated 1821, the terrace is clearly visible. Originally known as Elizabeth Place, the parade, which included the Duke of Wellington pub, was renamed in 1865, along with all the other terraces on that thoroughfare, and given the single name of Balls Pond Road.

In the mid-19th century, the houses on this terrace were inhabited principally by single families or by small families with perhaps a boarder or two. This changed when the North London Railway was extended to Broad Street and when Dalston Junction station opened in 1865, and the area became distinctly more crowded. By the census of 1901, the four storeys of No. 99 were occupied by two large families with nine children between them. The head of the household was a journeyman tailor, originally from Dublin, who was followed in the next census by a widow from Cork. Typical occupations in the terrace before the First World War were those of gasfitters, greengrocers, market porters, butchers, dressmakers, boot shop workers and canned goods inspectors.

With the advent of the Second World War, widespread bombing in Islington and Hackney had, by the end of 1940, resulted in 1,871 buildings damaged beyond repair and 16,061 damaged but repairable.[2] This did nothing to subdue 'Oswald Mosley's Blackshirts', and the local area became known for its post-war fascist sympathies, with questions being asked in the House as to why it was that police turned a blind eye to Nazi salutes in Dalston.

My impression of the area in the mid-sixties was of a sizeable Turkish community running restaurants and shops nearby. Despite our wild appearance they were consistently polite to us, which made a welcome change from the attitudes of other locals. Another impression I had at the time was of the whole area being full to the brim with businesses. These did not just provide services. There was also an abundance of small workshops producing a wide range of manufactured goods.

My memory of the house when I first visited was of a down-at-heel but still smartly decorated interior that was elegant in a minimalist, arty kind of way. The rooms lacked furniture, but had dark blue fitted carpet on the floor – an absolute luxury and the ultimate in cool for me at that time. The halls and stairway were papered with neutral vertical stripes, in keeping with the regency origins of the house. Like so many houses built in the early 19th century, it felt slightly too small for us big-boned post-war baby boomers as we walked around inside. In fact, the basement reception room was only six-and-a-half-feet high from floor to ceiling, well under the permitted height for a modern dwelling place.

In the early sixties, people who could afford to decorate still had a 'pre-makeover' mentality. I can remember almost no one then knocking rooms through or moving bathrooms, and I can think of no one at all who would have thought of opening out a side return. The only architectural savagery I remember at the time was a fad for installing spiral staircases, a space-saving device that allowed four-storey houses to be turned into two self-contained flats. This was, in fact, the fate that was to befall 99 Balls Pond Road five years after its sale in 1969. Generally speaking, however, the massive transformation of dwellings would have to wait until the boom in borrowing associated with the 'Loadsamoney' mentality of the eighties. So, in 1967, 99 Balls Pond Road maintained its pre-war layout, with a hatchway through from kitchen to reception room and a lean-to out at the back. The lack of kitchen utensils indicated that this was a house where people ate out, and what crockery there was came from Habitat – turned earthenware that made scratchy, scraping noises when you ate off it.

When I visited the house for the Exploding Galaxy launch in April, it was crowded, but this being a party and a special occasion, that was to be expected. When I returned two months later, the place had already been divided into mini-'plots' of living space and was surprisingly busy, with numbers of residents topping the previous record in 1901 of 18. The household population that summer was to exceed even this, with the building as crowded as a bus station. At one point, Paul Keeler was so amazed by the throng that he did a head count and found over 60 people present.

A majority of those present would have been living elsewhere, and of those who slept at Balls Pond Road, there were several categories of house guest. There were the 'weekenders' like me, who lived with family out in the suburbs and were regular attenders at Galaxy events. Other weekenders were Malcolm Le Maistre and Rakis, neither of whom liked staying at the house much but loved the performances. There were also the 'short-stretchers', who appeared at the house and stayed for certain lengths of time – say, a week or ten days or so – but had other places to go or, like Simon Shirley, who had a partner to return to. These people kept returning and showed up regularly for performances. Another group were those who made Balls Pond Road their home for a couple of months or so before spinning off on another quite different trajectory. These were Rag Doll, Leighana Morris, and Shelagh Cluett, who left the Galaxy for art college in the autumn of 1967 to start a career as a sculptor. The final category were the 'stalwarts'. These were Eve Ridoux, Audrey Vipond, Christian Ledoux, Andrew Forrest and, of course, David and Fitz. Paul was frequently absent, presumably in Windsor picking up the pieces of the failed gallery business, but all the while presiding over the chaos as a kind of benevolent uncle figure.

The organisation of the house was definitely tribal, with the upper-ground and first-floor rooms divided into a number of small plots. The arrangement could best be described as stack-a-tribe rather than spread-a-tribe as the house was on four floors. These spaces might be inhabited long term – say, over a period of weeks or months, such as by Fitz's density tent or Judith Pertz's shining mobile corner – or for just a couple of nights at a time. In the latter case, the space was marked by some kind of bedding – a sleeping bag if you were lucky. As a weekender, I would bed down wherever there was space, which was usually either on the first or upper-ground floor. I always slept on carpet and under coats since blankets were kept carefully by those who had them. At times, the place appeared to be a series of houses within a house, with symbolic walls built out of milk crates sectioning off parts of a room like towels on a lounger by a pool. Ensuring a comfortable night became a priority. Rakis recalls:

> During the week, probably because there was no electricity, there were a lot of early nights. I remember it being rather like animal bedtime at the zoo at dusk. There was not enough bedding to go around, and as darkness settled, there was this shuffling around, as people made sure of their blankets and floor space.

As with other tribes, location of dwelling was related to one's importance in the group. What became clear from the many interviews I did was that your position above ground level related to your importance. Rakis remembers that top-floor rooms were 'out of bounds'. You would knock before entering, and access was 'by invitation only'.

This was most tellingly seen in the case of Audrey Vipond and Jane Ellis, who had shared a bedsit in Notting Hill and, having been chucked out, then moved into Balls Pond Road, arriving at the house on the same evening. Audrey, through her relationship with Christian, had immediate top-room status and soon after gained 'penthouse' privileges – for example, people could not sleep on her floor unless invited to do so. Jane, on other hand, was relegated to the basement in the cubby hole under the stairs. She shared her area with Colin Colclough and John Cox – the Fuzzy-Gigglies – to start with, although later, when they became known as the Acid Islanders, they moved to the upper-ground level. Jane noticed that there was a tendency for the working-class kids to live on the lower floors and the more confident, privately educated Exploders to move swiftly upstairs – a kind of hippie version of *Upstairs Downstairs*.

Not everyone agrees with this assessment, and some people did move in the opposite direction. For instance, Judith Pertz, who started at upper ground, eventually settled happily in the basement.

Without any discussions of rules or structure, the community naturally formed itself into a hierarchy. Our leaders were two strong, confident and intensely creative personalities, both older than most of the residents and both established artists: David Medalla and Gerald Fitzgerald. David had the edge, since this had been his home prior to its transformation into communal living and it was he who determined whether someone could come and join the household. It is interesting to note that, once David left for India, Fitz soon replaced him as top dweller.

I recently asked two ex-Galaxy associates how they would have studied the Exploding Galaxy as anthropological observers. Rakis unerringly said, 'By putting a fixed camera on the front door. It would have been interesting to see people coming and going. The house was never the same. A day or two days was a long time in that house.'

Lesley Forrest's answer was influenced by her work as an anthropologist during the 1970s, living as a participant/observer in a cluster of huts in a coastal Carib community in Surinam. She lived in the village as a member of one of the families, and this formed part of the research she did for her doctorate in anthropology:[3]

> My interest was in the economical, social organisation of labour, about 'the pool' and who shares what with whom. Who eats the fish? Who gets which bit of the fish? If I were going into 99 Balls Pond Road as an anthropologist, I would have looked at how people were organised financially, how they made a living, who brought what in and who was in control of the distribution. I would be interested in what is shared and what isn't, and why.

The Galaxy would have posed two major difficulties for such a participant/observer. The first was that we were not a single culture with a single tradition. We were, in fact, a number of microcultures, each with its own set of rules and its own allegiances. The second problem was that, due to these differing parallel moralities, some members of the commune were remarkably secretive about money. This, in itself, would have made an interesting area of study, but it would have been problematic to fathom or record. The fact is that those residing at 99 Balls Pond Road each perceived quite differently what living there with the group meant. What united us was what we were rejecting.

Bernard Levin, in his book *The Pendulum Years: Britain in the Sixties*, commented on the large-scale rejection by the young of what he calls 'mock-life'. By this, he meant appalling manifestations of affluence, particularly those fed to the nation weekly via advertising in the Sunday papers. He described this as 'turn-over worship' and wryly quoted from an *Observer* supplement which, in its feature on Lorenzo de' Medici, described him as 'an inspiration to our affluent society'.

The reaction against this insatiable materialism was an understandable rejection of possessions. Levin wrote:

> For some the search took the form of a new kind of apostolic poverty, and a new tribe of wandering holy men (and women) appeared, some of them being the children of wealthy and aristocratic families, who went from place to place on foot, or with a horse and cart, living as best they might, free from the fetters of place and possession.[4]

The simplicity of lifestyle he pointed to is an accurate account of our commune. Although only two people I knew actually did take to the road with a horse and cart,[5] the full-scale rejection of the trappings of modern living was very much in evidence at 99 Balls Pond Road. Edward remembers how his UFO friends usually owned, at the very least, a record player and a handful of LPs. With no electricity, we had neither sound system nor white goods. How far this was a deliberate rejection of consumer living is debatable, since we had no money with which to buy mod cons, but the outcome was that the Exploding Galaxy as a commune lived a contented life without electricity.

Audrey describes her enjoyment of visits to public baths:

> I just made do. I went to the wonderful baths on Essex Road and did my laundry there. You could do a hand wash for 1/6d or you could do a machine wash. They had one of those copper-mounted machines. The racks were different colours – red, blue and yellow. It was utterly beautiful, like a Van Gogh. You pulled the racks out of the wall and put the sheets and clothing over the racks and then you pushed them back in, so that warm air circulated behind and dried it all. While it was drying, you could go and have a bath upstairs and wash your hair, safe in the knowledge that no one was going to rip your stuff off – it all came from jumble sales.

I remember visiting the Hackney Baths – the vast tubs, the abundance of hot water – and the sense that this was a real treat has remained with me. Others remember making use of several Galaxy sympathisers – such as Hermine Demoriane and Hugo Williams – who were frequently called on to provide a civilised sitting room with comfortable lounging space and a blast of quality pop music or a much prized hot soak in a normal bath. The photographer Mitja Hinderks recalls our camping in his garden in Swiss Cottage and how taken we were with the cooker in the kitchen and his bathtub.

The usual Galactic way of life was utterly uncomplicated, and so experiences like these 'annexe visits' brought home the sense that we were living the right way.

It is interesting that, just when technology offered the promise of freedom from drudgery to large sections of the population for the first time, some members of the counterculture were seeking just that kind of simplicity. In the year 1966, over 45 per cent of dwellings in Hackney's De Beauvoir ward had no exclusive access to a WC and more than 41 per cent of the population lived without a bath or shower.[6]

All around us in the East End, families were doing their utmost to rid themselves of their outside toilets, and there was a marked increase in the purchase of washing machines, bought on the never-never, to replace visits to the launderette. However, at Balls Pond Road, it seemed that the posher the background, the more wholeheartedly a back-to-basics approach was embraced. For these privileged people, this kind of toil was 'exotic' – until, that is, they took the next step and moved out to a smallholding in Wales, where they would be in for a big shock.

Life in the house was perhaps influenced by class conditioning in another way. Several Galaxy members had been to boarding school, and prep schools certainly trained eight-year-olds to take frugal conditions in their stride and even, possibly, enjoy the challenge. When interviewed, Paul Keeler described this stoicism in relation to British prisoners of war and how there were two different castes in the POW community:

> The Germans captured the officer class who generally coped well, because the whole thing was like being back at school. The officer prisoners used to organise theatre clubs and skate clubs and the food wasn't any worse than boarding school, since food in prep school was a phenomenon. For

the non-privately educated soldiers it was another matter. They had never been away from home before. They missed mum and were in a terrible state by comparison.

Physical conditions were certainly tough at Balls Pond Road. There was nearly always a shortage of blankets at night and 'Kingsland soup' [7] was frequently on the menu.Yet scarcity was met with cheerful resilience, and for me this is not unconnected to the fact that so many of the residents had been educated in a system designed to toughen up youngsters in readiness for administering the empire.

In choosing to spend our time at Balls Pond Road, we had opted for destitution and harsh conditions. We had also chosen squalor, and the filth built up and solidified over the months – like the layers of greyish candle wax that caked the carpets, our coats and even our hair. The change was gradual, so went unnoticed, as when someone you love changes physically as the days pass. It is only those who leave and then return who are startled by the change.

As time went by, living in the house became more of a challenge, with the pungent smell of cat pervading the place. For some, it all became too much and they attempted to address the problem. Lynn Darnton was concerned about the health aspect. He tried many times to get everyone to clean up as a team effort, but as he said, 'There was so much work to do and no one seemed to care about the house itself.'

Eventually, the infrastructure of the house began to give way.

First to go was the lower bathroom, which soon after became a scrudge store. By the autumn of the following year, we had no kitchen sink. Someone had placed a lighted candle there and it had burned right through, leaving a dripping hole. After that, the only way we could carry on as a functioning household was to set up our kitchen in the bathroom upstairs – the one remaining place in the house where there was running water. A board was placed across the bath, and from then on, the bathroom functioned as both kitchen and toilet.

To outsiders and to some insiders, the place was intolerably squalid. Some Galaxy members created their own sense of order, sweeping the wax-encrusted carpet, moving scrudges and artworks to the corners and washing teacups with scalding water, but the shipshape brigade were outnumbered and the decay continued.

I saw none of the squalor. I did not notice the stench. Nor did I feel the cold, nor the bruising hard floor beneath me at night. For me, the house was a magical place, where my companions understood what really mattered in life. I felt privileged to spend time in the company of these intellects, to join scrudgehunts and to have the chance to create my own artworks. Within this chaos lay absolute freedom.

NOTES

1. *A Net of Fireflies*, trans. Harold Stewart (Charles E. Tuttle Publishing, 1993).
2. *London County Council Bomb Damage Maps 1935–1945*, ed. Ann Saunders (London Topographical Society, 2005).
3. Forrest, L. (1987) *Economics and the Social Organisation of Labour: A Case Study of a Coastal carib Community in Surinam* (PhD thesis) London School of Economics.
4. Bernard Levin, *The Pendulum Years: Britain in the Sixties* (Pan, 1970).
5. One was the songwriter Vashti Bunyan, whose recordings of her wayward years have since been bought up by big business for marketing purposes, and the other was Galaxy member Rakis, who bought a wagon and mare from a traveller in Cambridge and took to the roads in Ireland for a time.
6. Borough of Hackney, Social Statistics by Wards, 1966 local census.
7. Kingsland soup (named after the nearly market in Kingsland Road) consisted of a stock cube, vegetables scavenged from the market pavements and lots of water. This was enjoyed with slices of the round Turkish loaves bought a few doors down.

11

The Legalise Pot Rally and Other Happenings

We have been told by the fuzz that we can't use our loudspeaking equipment. You don't need to worry about that because this is not a rally, it's a picnic. We are not going to have lots of speeches. We are going to have lots of poets, lots of musicians.

STEVE ABRAMS [1]

I WAS STANDING on Primrose Hill at the beginning of June with the two Bobs, both of whom had strong connections with *Oz* magazine and were high-caste counterculture. One was the art critic Robert Hughes and the other was Robert Whitaker, the photographer whom I had got to know at UFO. He had been Brian Epstein's own in-house photographer after they met in Australia and had witnessed some of the most shocking extremes of Beatlemania. His pictures often reflected his opinion of the wild and mindless adulation of the fans. I had recently gone with Whitaker to see the newly released film *Blow-Up*, directed by Antonioni, and it did later cross my mind just how cool it was to have seen that particular film with the man responsible for snapping most of the Beatles album covers, including the banned and extremely rare 'Baby Butcher' cover for *Yesterday and Today.*

Early one morning, a crowd of us had gone back to Bob's place, where tripped-out painter Martin Sharp was his house guest. We were there for a dawn cuppa after being turfed out of UFO. As was the custom once the Tube opened, we would make our way to a friendly pad, white moustached from the milk stolen from doorsteps and with our ears still ringing from UFO's blast. Bob lived in a wood-panelled artist's studio off Jubilee Place, just behind The Pheasantry in the Kings Road. Not many years after this visit, the whole of that picturesque little lane was demolished and turned into the back end of a bookshop.

I hung around with Bob sometimes, although I did not like him enough to go all the way. He was, after all, in his late twenties, which was way too old for my taste, and his white nylon polo necks didn't help. However, it was he who introduced me to haiku and Edith Sitwell's sound poems, something for which I am still grateful. He had a ferocious interest in art and owned some production-line Takis works – the ones that stood out on stalks and flashed randomly.

That morning, we all danced around his studio *à la* UFO and blew soap bubbles until it was time to go home.

The occasion on Primrose Hill was a 'be-in' organised by Yoko Ono – a kite flying event, as I remember, with participants exhorted to 'make the trees laugh, colour the clouds and find an imaginary snail'. The two Bobs were discussing Martin Sharp and whether he was safe to drive a car during an acid trip. They concluded that he probably was. The Flower Power movement was over – of that they were certain. This was June 1967. We had hardly reached what was later to be called the 'Summer of Love' and they, like quite a few others, were saying it had all gone sour. Neither of them gave the impression that they had given up on materialism – both appeared to be highly successful and competent – and neither seemed to resemble my idea of 'beautiful people', so what did they know?

We went to Robert Hughes' place nearby. It was a lovely sixties 'clone flat' – they all seemed the same: in mansion blocks and virtually empty except for artworks or unusual designer seating, rooms were minimalist cubes with no clutter and no furniture to speak of, with whitewashed walls, large paper lampshades, neutral fitted carpets and low or floor-level beds. This interior design gave a room a magnificent sense of space, especially if it had high ceilings, as this one did.

Hughes was preoccupied by the fact that his cat had deposited a large wet turd behind his op art canvas. It was a Bridget Riley, gently tilted against the wall, but too heavy to move in order to get at the cat, which was cowering beside the poo.

I was out of my depth with these people and had nothing much to say, an empty head except for a good knowledge of folk music, sailors' knots and *Ready Steady Go!*, but I had never been shy of showing off my ignorance. I launched into a debate with Robert Hughes about the painting that took pride of place above the fireplace, arguing that it was hideous. With unblinking ease, Hughes salami-sliced my words into a miserable mess on the floor with his explanation of the juxtaposition of the colours around the nipples. I was suitably chastised but unrepentant: I knew I was right.

That summer was punctuated with afternoons like this – balmy outdoor events in public parks, where the same core of people gathered. We all knew each other from UFO and were full of love and peace, so we would smile, wave, hug or do whatever beautiful people did. There was an incredible feeling of togetherness, which strengthened whenever the park keepers came to see what was up. Somehow, though, things were changing. At each happening, the crowd grew slightly bigger, and this was what the two Bobs had been complaining about.

Similar changes were also apparent at UFO. News had got out about Pink Floyd and The Soft Machine being the bands to see, and after the BBC's Ally Pally documentary, the club had become dangerously crowded, to the point where it was a long, laborious process to negotiate through bodies from one side of the hall to the other. By June, it took a good ten minutes to squeeze through past the light-show tower to the bar area, and any meaningful dancing extravagance became impossible.

For many of the originals, the spirit of UFO disappeared around the time Hoppy entered prison to start his nine-month sentence in June 1967. Regarded by many as king of the counterculture, he spent the key moments of that seminal year in a state of deep trauma behind bars in Brixton.

The 'Legalise Pot' rally at Hyde Park Corner was timely. It was held on the afternoon of Sunday 16 July 1967, not long after Hoppy's conviction and some ten days after Mick Jagger, Keith Richards and Robert Fraser had all been found guilty of possession at Chichester Crown Court. This combined incarceration was an outrage to us all, and so that afternoon was also a protest about them. It was not the only demonstration. After the Chichester conviction, there had been several marches down to the *News of the World* offices in Bouverie Street – we all knew the police were in cahoots with the scummy journalists. When I went down to Fleet Street one Saturday after UFO, I knew everyone protesting there – it had the same cosy atmosphere as all those early gatherings. But the Hyde Park rally was to be something entirely different. A full-page advertisement was being planned for *The Times*, and there had been extensive publicity beforehand, including TV interviews with Steve Abrams, the campaigner for cannabis law reform.

Of course, large numbers were welcomed in order to make our point to the world, but it seemed that the movement had lost its intimacy. It had become a great big institution that no longer belonged to the originators. It was somehow now too democratic, too available, and it could no longer support the footfall. The snobby relics among the hippies were revealed as whinging old fuddy-duddies.

The mainstream press called the afternoon the 'March of the flower pot men' while *The Sun* led with its own poll that claimed that a majority of people aged between 21 and 34 thought Jagger should have received more than three months in jail. The *News of the World* continued to protest that it was a 'monstrous charge' to suggest that they had set up the Rolling Stones. Meanwhile, our lot distributed thousands of 'No search without warrant' buttons.

I was walking towards Speakers' Corner with Bob Whitaker. It was hot – somewhere in the mid-80s – and the ice creams we had bought were melting faster than we could consume them. Sticky dribbles were running down our wrists. We bumped into Larry and Carol Smart. They were my idea of the ultimate hip romantic couple, proudly parading their newborn. Their son had had a lucky escape: Larry had wanted to name him 'Frodo', from *The Lord of the Rings*, but 'Sam' had been chosen instead. This was a time when wacky names were chosen for babies – Astra Space, Burgundy Sky, Trickle Rain and Moondance Moon.

Baby Sam had been dressed in mauve garments and tinsel instead of the uniform baby colours of blue, pink and canary yellow. Nowadays, there are no style rules to break any more, but in 1967, every time a fashion commandment was transgressed, it was truly surprising and utterly miraculous.

In the crowd, I recognised William Burroughs, who as usual looked like a high street solicitor. Allen Ginsberg was up a ladder, playing his harmonium. Other sounds filling the air were directionless and untrained attempts at the bongos and the ocarina – a kind of 'sound wallpaper' throughout that summer. The parks police were out in force, wanting to damp down the abandon but not quite sure how. Pettiness reduced their actions to picking on a byelaw prohibiting music in parks. Ginsberg's harmonium was silenced, as was Rag Doll's music box.

Bob seemed particularly interested in the fact that it had been my birthday that week and that I was now 16. I knew why he was interested, but it was water off a duck's back. He was wary of my Exploding Galaxy friends. Like other high-ranking counterculture codgers, he was fascinated by our sexual promise, but also put off by our scruffiness, our strange ways and our unpredictability.

Wherever there was a crowd, David Medalla could always be found surrounded by an audience, and today was no exception. There he was at the centre of the action, in full *mudra*. If one photograph sums up London's flower child summer, it is surely the one of David, his torso bedaubed with swirls and painted flowers, at the Hyde Park rally, his arms raised and holding up a placard saying 'flower power'.

Six days after this gathering, David was also the central figure in the troupe of Exploders who made their way down the Kings Road to publicise our kinetic ballets at a new club that had recently opened in Covent Garden. The Electric Garden in King Street was by now a regular venue for Galaxy performances, although our first outing there with Yoko Ono had coincided with a nasty scene. Bouncers and alcohol were unknown in many underground circles, but at this club, both were present. The organisers, who obviously wanted to cash in on the psychedelic pound, clearly had no clue about *IT* or the nature of a Yoko Ono performance. Barry Miles, of *IT*, having been given prior permission to set up a stall, was told once there, 'Get out. We don't want that bloody newspaper in here.'[2] Yoko's performance with the Exploding Galaxy – involving a floor strewn with balloons and shreds of cloth – was cut short. What set off the trouble were some of Yoko's vocalisations. Someone involved in the running of the club agreed to sabotage her microphone and she was left on stage, silenced and tied to a chair with bandages. A scuffle ensued and the performers left unpaid. Judy Gemes was driven to put her thoughts down the next morning:

> What the fuck is happening on this scene? Where do the real threats emerge from? The establishment and fuzz? No, baby, that was yesterday's naivety… There are bad, evil vibrations within the scene, which if not blocked may blow the whole thing apart.[3]

From then on, even after its official name change in August 1967 to the gentler sounding Middle Earth, the club continued to be known by derisory nicknames such as the 'Defective Garden' or the 'Garden of Poisoned Fruit'. Galaxy members renamed it the 'Electric Reject'. Despite this name, the Reject became one of our regular and favourite gigs.

On Saturday 22 July, the Exploding Galaxy divided into two groups to publicise some new kinetic dramas to be performed at the Reject the next day. One went to the Portobello Road and the other to the Kings Road. The Kings Road party consisted of Audrey, Judith, Leighana, Chrissie, Gwendolyn, David, Edward, Rakis, Brian, Rag Doll and Fitz. Other Galaxy members tagged along. I was not present on this occasion since I was in Darmstadt, staying with my German penfriend, so I missed out on being arrested.

The idea was to hand out leaflets for *The Birdcage Ballet* and *The Toy Ballet*. The arrangement was to meet up at the Chelsea Town Hall and then move along the road as a colourful parade and, through dancing and our free approach, 'activate' the pedestrians by talking to them and telling them about the Sunday event. Edward remembers:

> We drew a lot of attention, simply because of the way we were dressed. We were hemmed in by a crowd and followed by photographers. Judith started playing the flute and the rest of us began hand dances and then we festooned a tree with pieces of chiffon of various colours. Then PC381B appeared and said, 'Come on, break it up!' We stopped dancing and squatted against the wall, softly chanting, and after the remaining Galaxy members arrived, we moved on.[4]

A police van later came down the road, and even though the group had by now broken up and was moving on in ones and twos, Exploders – easy to spot because of their bare feet – were picked up and put into the vehicle. In all, nine were arrested for obstruction and each was fined £2 in what was later remembered as the 'Kinetic Ballet of Marylebone Magistrates Court'.

This was just one of several police actions against us during the next month. When taken to a police station in August, Fitz complained to the desk sergeant that he objected to being searched in the street and that this was the fourth time in the previous two weeks that he had been stopped by a police officer for no good reason. Anyone in any doubt about the inappropriateness of police treatment of the Exploding Galaxy should see the footage in the documentary *Transport by Underground,* in which a policeman can be seen shouting at Galaxy members as they walked up the steps to the front door at 99 Balls Pond Road after a Sunday night Electric Reject performance.

Back at Balls Pond Road, life was busy. The place had changed from being an offshoot of a defunct art gallery, inhabited by a few highly educated people, to a crowded commune. When asked what life meant for those living at the house, Malcolm Le Maistre has said that it represented whatever people wanted it to represent. In other words, if you sought physical pleasure, it was the house of the lotus eaters, or if you were caught by the spell of the psychedelic, you could join the Acid Islanders on the upper-ground floor, or if you saw the house as a place of learning, it was your very own monastery, dedicated to the pursuit of the intellectual. People saw precisely what they wanted to see, although one thing that was totally absent at this time was any discussion of politics. Instead, talk was of Hindu myths and legends or of the aesthetic merit of some scrap of corrugated cardboard found in a gutter.

At Balls Pond Road, there were two generations living under one roof. The 'parental' generation – the established artists – did little to control the excesses of the younger ones. Some of those who were in their teens or very early twenties were like wild children disguised in adult bodies. Few of the boys had ever lived away from the confines of family life. The kind of nuisance that would usually occur in first student digs was tolerated because no one felt able to set any boundaries. The poet Hugo Williams has said that he found the atmosphere in the house unpleasant because it reminded him so much of the tensions in the boys' corridors at Eton. Rakis has said that there was rarely a sense of tranquillity in the house; rather, there was too much overexcited posturing. Jane Ellis – who had no wish to stay on at Balls Pond Road because 'it was so squalid and no one would take responsibility' – found the 'private school' atmosphere intimidating. She was gone from the house before long.

I noticed none of this. I gradually sought the company of the Galaxy more frequently, preferring the Galactic bubble, where conversations revolved about the nature of scrudge, to the relentless materialism to be had outside. My friends came from different strata in the counterculture hierarchy, and it never seemed odd to me that they crossed paths only superficially. I never questioned being totally excluded from Bob Whitaker's crowd: Jeff Dexter, Germaine Greer, Martin Sharp, Eric Clapton, George Harrison, Salvador Dali – these were all famous-name dots. What would be the point of joining up those dots? The celebrity elite operated at least as efficiently as the class structure. I would no more have considered myself able to belong to this group than a scullery maid in a big house would have contemplated a pre-supper sherry upstairs in the drawing room.

Little hypocrisies and larger ones within our movement were at last being revealed for what they were. Equality came in the form of grand statements, but with no thinking of what lay closer to home. Sharks in sheep's clothing (i.e. kaftans) made a killing by ripping off the unsuspecting in various business scams. Their patsies were us, the beautiful people. Some were too stoned to take action, and others were forced to turn the other cheek because, as Galaxy member Lizzie said, 'The greatest injustice of the counterculture was that you were obliged at all times not to mind.'

The next time I heard from Bob Whitaker was in 1969. He was in a private hospital somewhere in Kensington and asked me to visit him. In a glass jar next to his bed was a vicious-looking scrap of metal. He had just done a photo-shoot for *Life* magazine in Cambodia, which is how he got the shrapnel souvenir.

The next I heard of Robert Hughes, he was busy saving a sinking Venice.

NOTES

1. Steve Abrams, Hyde Park, 16 July 1967.
2. *International Times*, issue 14, 2 June 1967.
3. *International Times*, issue 14, 2 June 1967.
4. *Planted*, a report compiled by Paul Keeler, 1968.

12

Wallpaper with Ears

Even as feminism took hold, and women were allowed into men's fora (music, politics, art), feminists felt that, although they could now be present, they were expected to be wallpaper with ears.

MONICA THRELFALL

I WAS AT a Yoko Ono happening at the Jeannetta Cochrane Theatre. Yoko sat in a chair with her back to the audience, doing what she did so well – screaming an unpleasant piercing scream. It went on for a very long time. After that finished, she asked participants from the audience up on to the stage to work with a scaffolding pole which was suspended from the flies above. Unfortunately one of the volunteers was an obnoxious youth at the lower end of his teens called Randy Fields.[1] He adored the Galaxy and was mothered by all of us females at Balls Pond Road, but was liked rather less by the men. Later, as a student, he took his college lecturers to court for going on strike, and then went on to start an airline with Richard Branson. Now, Randy wasn't having any of what Yoko was offering. When she said A, he did B – his own teenaged sabotage. I saw his point. This was supposed to be a happening and she was treating us as though this were a schoolroom and we should do things her way. The performance ended with everyone being told they could contribute something red to her red picture. People tentatively walked forward with sweet papers and the like. I was outraged. As far as I was concerned this was definitely not an artistic experience.

Despite not liking Yoko's creations much, I do have to take my hat off to her and to Germaine Greer and to Caroline Coon. The thing is, they were actually visible. If it hadn't been for the likes of a handful of outspoken and often derided individuals, you might believe that there were no women at all gracing the underground movement between 1965 and 1969.

If you look at underground sources from the late sixties, you can see clearly the way in which women were ignored. The best starting point would be the film *Wholly Communion*, a documentary about the International Poetry Incarnation at the Albert Hall in June 1965. This is generally regarded as the 'launching event' of London's counterculture and the footage comes courtesy of the super-bright underground film-maker Peter Whitehead. His editing choices could not be described as anything other than anti-establishment, yet through the fog of a thousand cigarettes, you can see that he filmed only male poets. This is because not one female poet was invited onto the stage that night. Approximately 3,000 people in the hall were women, but their role was confined to responding to the men's words and to the men's *angst*-y moments. In the film, the camera dwells on only two women for any length of time. One with baby-doll Twiggy eyes, dressed in a spotted coat and hat, watches the proceedings attentively. She is cute and decorative. The other, whose abandon is consistent with an acid trip, interprets the words with her dancing arms as they flow and writes things down on scraps of paper. If these are poems, she is not going to be invited to read them. These two women are supposed to be in tune with the men, which really sums up the role of women in counterculture of the late sixties: to appreciate and empathise with their menfolk.

Eighteen months after this event, at 'The 14-Hour Technicolor Dream', documentary film-makers repeated the pattern. With virtually no women's names on the bill, they were hard pushed to find female performers to film. Instead, women were designated roles that were sexy, like the go-go girls in frilly bloomers and a model on a stepladder, having her clothes snipped off, or, in the case of Suzy Creamcheese, downright wacky. Since much of the footage that night came from the BBC's *Man Alive* crew, this could be put down to the preoccupations of the straight world to some degree. Not so the editorial choices of *IT*, which was tirelessly sexist in its early issues.

In an issue in January 1967, the magazine's readers are coyly asked to find women prepared to take their tops off for the camera: 'If you feel you qualify as an *IT* girl (or if you know someone who does), send a photograph (or other documentation) to the fantasy editor.' In issue 12, we can see the kind of personal ads people felt suitable to post: 'Wanted: two dollies, twentyish, to look after two undomesticated blokes. Call after six.'[2] If you look at all the issues of *IT* in its first year and exclude anything about Yoko, there is a depressing scarcity of women as subjects of feature articles or women with their own bylines or women fully clothed in photographs.

Many scraggy and unpolished notions issued forth from the counterculture. Although frequently muddled, these were basically along the right lines, morally speaking. But on the issue of gender equality, things were different, as though the counterculture had a kind of colour blindness. The same men who could see the justice of the civil rights movement in the United States, who marched against the bomb from Aldermaston to Trafalgar Square, who demonstrated against the Vietnam War and who crusaded for women's right to choose abortion, would send their girlfriends scurrying out to the kitchen to make the tea.

Sue Hall remembers how it went without question that a woman always made the tea at Young CND gatherings. The same was true at *IT*. Here is Sue Miles' account of how it got its name:

> My job was to make the tea and the sandwiches, and whenever they were going to actually make decisions, I was asked to go out of the room. And I did. There were lots of conversations about what the name should be and we talked about the 'IT girl', and being from a journalistic background, I said, 'Well, call it IT. We've got IT!' And they said, 'What's IT? It's got to stand for something.' And I said, 'Well, *International Times*, I suppose,' and they said, 'Fine!'[3]

The young intellectuals of the counterculture found fault with absolutely everything their parents stood for – everything except, that is, the relegation of women to the role of unpaid co-worker, scivvy, waitress, listener, ego-massager, blow-job giver and sperm receptacle.

These same men spread their seed liberally, thinking nothing of the colossal emotional consequences for the woman of possibly facing one of three choices: parting with a newborn for adoption, snuffing out the life growing inside her or spending decades as a lone parent.[4]

Carol Grimes, who had her first baby in the spring of 1967, provides an example of the way in which young women were overshadowed in the late sixties. Then known as Carol Smart, she and her husband Larry were two of the original members of the Exploding Galaxy and had been present at the founding gathering at the Theatre Royal Stratford East on 16 April 1967. I knew that Larry was a popular psychedelic artist whose paintings were selling well, but had no idea that Carol was already well established as a singer. At their flat, everything revolved around Larry, and I simply knew her as 'Larry's old lady' because, in those days, wives and girlfriends were introduced as 'my old lady'. Carol remembers:

> Larry was *mein host* – all the paintings on the walls, the music, the pipe, the dope and the acid... it was very much that I was the 'hippie-chicky mummy' putting on the food – the brown rice and vegetables – and it was all focused on Larry. It was only later on that the penny dropped. I was watching a friend. This lovely gentle woman was constantly cooking food for all these men sitting on the floor in the lotus position. The women were cooking the brown rice on some makeshift stove in some shithole in Ladbroke Grove. That's all they ever did.

It was in this way that some highly creative women within the counterculture were diddled out of opportunities by their menfolk, especially once they were compromised by their own biology.

I suppose this set-up differed from Balls Pond Road because we lived as a large group. I cannot remember being expected to make tea or to cook, unlike my post-Galaxy experience in Paris where I clearly remember asking a group of men to lift their legs so that I could hoover underneath while they discussed Marxism and the abolition of exclusive spheres of activity. At 99 Balls Pond Road, most of the food consumed was 'bread and spreads' or take-aways, but in 1968, after John Dugger's arrival, we were treated to wonderful food cooked by two men, John and David. These were giant curries, enough to serve the whole household. I can honestly say that I never noticed a division of labour similar to the blatantly sexist one in the outside world.

However, kinetic dramas were a slightly different matter. Although I never felt that my potential for self-expression was cramped by my gender, I never put myself forward to name or choreograph a drama or propose an idea for an exploration. Looking back, I've realised that, apart from Herzmark, Galaxy women were generally not initiators of kinetic explorations, whereas ideas for performances were constantly proposed by the Galaxy men, including Rag Doll, Simon, Edward and Mike, Malcolm, the two Johns and, of course, David and Fitz. Plenty of the Galaxy men had no artistic credentials to speak of, but this did not stop them from seeing themselves as *auteurs* of their own works.

I did not notice this at the time, and I believe that none of the Galaxy women would have considered themselves to be secondary Exploders. Experimental theatre and performance art tended to be led by men – for example, Jack Henry Moore of The Human Family – and it seems that, in this area, we saw ourselves in a supporting role. One Galaxy member has described the female contribution as 'the mortar holding together the Galactic brickwork' and another as the work of 'Exploder-handmaidens'.

In relation to the women's own production of paintings, sculptures costumes and artifacts and in the exploration of scrudge, Galaxy culture felt 100 per cent inclusive – I do not think any of us ever felt cheated. In this arena, we did have plenty of female examples to inspire us. Some of us were familiar with the work of Lygia Clark, Liliane Lijn, Niki de Saint Phalle and Pauline Boty, and there were highly successful women artists out there like Bridget Riley and Barbara Hepworth, so in this area at least, there were obvious role models.

Felt-tipped pens were new on the market and could be bought from Woolworths in long packets of a multitude of colours. Eve Ridoux specialised in producing works using these, and Audrey Vipond produced small ink paintings which she sold off a stall in Portobello Road market. Outer Galaxy artist Drumbeat was prolific, at that time concentrating on making illustrated booklets, and Shelagh Cluett, in her life as an artist after leaving the Galaxy, continued to produce scrudge-like sculptures. My particular interest was to build up scrudge artifacts, which I turned into garments. I saw these as my own sculptures.

There was a powerful mechanism at work throughout London's counterculture that conspired to make women invisible. It related primarily to what was noticed and, after that, to what was recorded for public consumption. Those reporting events consistently sought out men as mouthpieces and women as decoration. Caroline Coon comments:

> Every time there have been vanguard women – and there have been vanguard women going back to the 12th century – they were buried from us. The women that we could have seen as our examples were hidden, were taken out of the canon. It's the moment it gets written up. The women are working side by side with the men, and if you look at the German avant-garde, if you look at the Russian avant-garde, if you look at the French avant-garde, the women are always there, shoulder to shoulder with the men. They are active as artists, but they haven't got access to employment in the critical magazines and in the cultural newspapers. These are in the hands of the men, so the minute it gets written up, the women are excluded. I don't call it a forgivable lapse. I call it a wilful exclusion.

When these men came to write their memoirs, it was easy for them to absorb the contributions of their girlfriends into their own lives. Richard Neville is well known as the editor of *Oz* magazine. His autobiography tells the story of his development as writer and editor, and although his long-term girlfriend in London, Louise Ferrier, makes any number of appearances in his book, he only ever seems to give her credit for her wardrobe. She is like a footballer's wife, seen going off to shop at Kensington Market and at Biba; she is a clothes horse, looking gorgeous in white jeans and a sloppy joe, a silver lurex micro-mini, iridescent Thai silk or lolly-pink shift or jeans with a cowboy shirt. And when Richard is taken ill, there she is mopping his brow. Above all, Louise brews up a great deal of tea.[5] This version of Louise differs from the account by Marsha Rowe, who was witness to enough of what went on at *Oz* headquarters in Palace Gardens Terrace to tell us another story. According to Marsha, Richard could not operate without Louise. 'Without Louise,' says Marsha, '*Oz* would never have happened.'[6]

Feature writers would frequently magic away women's contributions. An example of this in the Galaxy was the way our music was featured in the press. One strong and consistent presence at the centre of most of our performances was Judith Pertz. Her flute music pervaded and surrounded most of what we did, which gave a strong female element to our scheduled performances. Yet the only published reference to music within the Galaxy came from *Unit Magazine*:

> Another side to the Galaxy's commitment to art and culture came when their musical director, Richard Topp, performed Eric Satie's rarely played *Vexations* at the Arts Lab shortly after it opened; it consists of the same musical piece repeated 840 times. A support team fed him sandwiches and drinks through the night and someone was on hand to substitute for him when he had to make unavoidable breaks.[7]

I remember this event, but not the person mentioned, who, although on the bill with us that particular evening, was not known at the house or at our other performances. We would not have had a musical director, but if we had, it would surely have been Judith Pertz.

Since researchers largely work from what is already in print, the erasure of women from arts history is inadvertently repeated and made more complete. The story of the fictitious musical director has since been retold in print. Generally speaking, the following names are associated in print with the Exploding Galaxy: David Medalla, John Dugger, Gerald Fitzgerald, Simon Shirley, Edward Pope and Larry Smart. In addition, the film-maker Derek Jarman, who did no more than brush against our fringes, and the performance artist Genesis P-Orridge, who was never part of the original Exploding Galaxy, are both frequently credited with Galaxy membership.

The Exploding Galaxy themselves were not guilt-free in contributing to this selective erasure. In the document *Planted*, much is made of the Galaxy poets, but there was one poet member not mentioned, although she had been in print as a poet for far longer than the others and had long given readings on the poetry circuits of her heroes, Tom Gunn and Ted Hughes. Like many young women at the time, Lizzie could type at speed and so she volunteered to type the proofs for *Planted*. It therefore fell to the extraordinary poet Lizzie to type the following names as being the Galaxy poets: Edward Pope, Michael Chapman, Gerald Fitzgerald and Simon Shirley. She did this without so much as a raised eyebrow. The only time she was publicly given credit was in Yugoslavia, when Michael Chapman, caked entirely in mud for his speech at the Struga Poetry festival, declared her 'the Galaxy's greatest poet'.

It wasn't that we women all colluded in our own deletion. In 1967, many of us were so lacking in consciousness that it did not occur to us that anything was amiss. One or two women in the underground may have had read Betty Friedan's *The Feminine Mystique,* but most of us females had to wait until 1970 and the appearance of 'that book' to wake us up. It was only then that feminist consciousness really did rock the nation.

Interestingly, Germaine Greer herself is evidence of the degree to which we women colluded in the male version of events. In 1968, the Beatles' photographer Bob Whitaker first showed his film *Darling, do you love me?*, based on a Martin Sharp cartoon, which almost immediately won several prizes. In the four-minute film, UFO-goer Alisdair Burke is seen attempting to walk down a tree-lined avenue. His path is blocked at every turn by Germaine, who hectors and suffocates him, and finally destroys him with her demands and her clawing hands. My memory of that time tells me that it was not the women but the men who were the possessive ones.

Perhaps, after all those male 'I did it my way' memoirs from the period, the 'supergroupie' Germaine Greer has had the last laugh. Within five months of the publication of *The Female Eunuch*, it had almost sold out its second printing and had been translated into 11 languages. Under the imprints Paladin and Flamingo Modern Classics, the book went into a total of 36 editions and has become a multi-million seller worldwide.

NOTES

1. Randy's mother Nancy Gayer, an American lecturer in education, was a leading figure in conceptual analysis. Her Cambridge PhD was on the notion of permission and the negative consequences of not understanding what the notion really means.
2. *International Times*, issue 12.
3. Robert Harris, article on the Exploding Galaxy, *Unit Magazine*, issue 9.
4. Jonathon Green, *Days in the Life: Voices from the English Underground, 1961–1971* (Pimlico, 1988).
5. During interviews for this book, I was curious to know how many abortions male interviewees were each responsible for. The maximum number was six.
6. Richard Neville, *Hippie Hippie Shake* (Duckworth Overlook, 2009).
7. Green, *Days in the Life.*
8. Robert Harris, article on the Exploding Galaxy, *Unit Magazine*, issue 9.

13

The Bumping Bodies Ballet

To be sure a European woman would blush to her fingers' ends at the very idea of appearing publicly stark naked; but education and prejudice are everything, since it is an axiom that where there is no feeling of self-reproach, there can assuredly be no shame.

CAPTAIN J G STEDMAN [1]

FLOWER CHILDREN LIKED the idea of nakedness. This was connected to our feeling that we were going back to a state of innocence in the Garden of Eden. Many of us went barefoot through the city streets, which took some getting used to. You started gingerly, but then, over a period of months, your soles became as tough as leather and you were fine, apart from the occasional encounter with a pair of stilettos in the bus queue. Rag Doll, a Galaxy member from Down Under, remembers going unshod except in the coldest weather for around two years.

We were a vast and growing tribe who now walked the Earth with the dignity of the Ashanti or the Orinoco Yanomami or the Sepik River tribes of New Guinea. We needed nothing more than beaded adornments, simple woven loin cloths or our bare skin to face the world. Caroline Coon says:

> The first contact I had with the hippie counterculture and that youth revolution was when I was 21. I was excited by the anti-war politics and the incredible outbreak of optimism and peace and love. Our generation vowed to break down the bigotry and hypocrisy in relation to sexuality and love. One of the reasons we took our clothes off and performed nude so often was because we thought the nude body was beautiful, organic and not obscene. Until 1968 the Lord Chamberlain's office still had the power to censor nudity as obscene! At the time, none of my women

friends and to my knowledge – maybe that was a naivety – none of the men I knew had actually seen hardcore pornography. Vanguard women considered nudity natural and we wanted to understand our bodies better. When we frolicked in nature naked, it was anti-obscenity. We wanted to banish our body 'shame'.

Early Exploding Galaxy performances may have had an amateur feel but were riveting viewing, given our frequent nakedness and the striking good looks of so many in the troupe. Our first programmed performance to involve a strip was in early June of 1967 at UFO and it was called *Mellow Yellow*. At this, Mike and Fitz read out a poem while Edward as the corrupt politician (he was fast becoming typecast) gesticulated wildly. Provocatively writhing Galaxy girls removed his garments one by one until he was down to a jock strap made entirely out of Monopoly money. We then all danced to the Donovan song of the same title.

There followed a number of ideas coming from different group members. In *The Bird Cage Ballet*, topless Exploders moved from pose to pose within the confines of a frame, and in Simon Shirley's piece *The Buddha and the Embryo*, also known as *Birth of a Flower Child*, naked torsos moved up and out, like an opening bud, for the audience at the Electric Garden. Rag Doll was key to this choreography:

> Leighana was the foetus curled up on the floor, and I went around to everybody getting them to hold hands and move and form a flower arrangement so that, when they all leaned backwards, they were like a flower opening up, and while we all lay back, Leighana crawled over the top and then across through the crowd along the floor.

Arthur Brown was already well known for his crown of flames and flying entrances, and his song 'Fire', with its Hammond organ riff, was fleetingly a No. 1 hit. He frequently performed with the Galaxy. Some thought this was because his manager, Kit Lambert, had been to public school at Lancing with Paul Keeler, or more likely, it could have been simply because our acts were so often side by side on a bill. Whatever the reason, we often shared the stage in some kind of dual extravagance. Arthur's most popular trick was his flaming helmet.

This was crudely constructed out of a leather skull cap on to which was bolted a metal dish containing lighter fuel or petrol.[2] Rag Doll recalls:

> One time, I took Arthur Brown aside and I arranged this procession through the Electric Garden. They turned all the lights out and I went to four Galaxy members and gave them a flaming torch each, and they paraded in from outside the building, in the pitch black, on to the centre of the stage and lit his helmet and he started singing 'Fire'. The torches were just bits of a stick with a flame on top. They weren't into health and safety at the Arts Lab or at the Electric Garden.

One of these Exploding Galaxy evenings with Arthur Brown was reported by Jack Henry Moore in *International Times*:

> Last Sunday they gave a performance which must constitute London's most liberated theatrical performance in history. Unfortunately it is impossible to describe the performance without endangering the Galaxy, but let it suffice to say that never have so many been so nude so early and for such good reasons. Arthur Brown gave what looked to me like his best performance to date and inaugurated pornographic pop in London. Singing while wallowing on the floor with four Galaxy nudes, he reached the all-time high in erectile music.[3]

The *People* newspaper reported the same event in a more negative light:

> The 'modern' thinkers, the would-be intellectuals – they're all raving these days about the Hippies and their cult of love and happiness. Well – Arthur Brown is a Hippie... and he looks a pretty sad character to us! He and his expression group kept hundreds of Hippies screaming at a fantastic party in Covent Garden last week. Teenage girls ripped off their clothes and danced topless while others gave bloodcurdling shrieks and writhed on the floor. 'Degrading, decadent, just plain daft,' our reporter calls it...

A 'Hippie' ballet was due to start. 'It will be lovely,' said the Hippie.

> Eventually the dances got more and more uncontrolled. A beautiful teenage blonde sank to the floor, groaning and head between her knees. One girl stripped off the top part of her clothing. Within minutes I counted two other bare-chested girls. … Eventually the 'topless' girls and their young men, now wearing only the scantiest of briefs, went on stage for the 'ballet'. They danced to a plaintive song on the flute, played by a girl squatting on the floor. … What do you think? Would you, as a parent, want your teenage sons and daughters to express themselves in this Hippie way? If your answer is 'no' then this paper gives you ten out of ten marks for common sense. The Hippie cult is degrading, decadent and just plain daft.[4]

Following this report, which used the term 'Hippie' in virtually every sentence, the gutter press were primed and ready. We knew that they would be back the following week for bare breasts to splash on the Sunday front page as an orgy. We had a plan. Biddy Peppin's sewing machine was used to produce a stretchy tube costume for each Galaxy member, covering each of them from crown to toe. This materialised as *The Bumping Bodies Ballet*. The gutter press were wrong-footed. They stood there armed with their lenses, clearly expecting to collect a series of shock pictures. What they got was discreet and subtle moving forms of anonymous people-shapes pushing out against the fabric, first one way and then another. This was equally photogenic but was left unsnapped. Herzmark remembers:

> The previous week we had done what amounted to a virtually nude ballet, but there was just one press photographer in the club. We knew that the next week there would be lots, so we did a ballet where we were completely and utterly covered. We thought this very funny. Imagine a bag made out of flexible white material and you dance within it so that you are like a moving sculpture. Your face can't be seen, but your limbs can because you are pushing out through the material. It shows a completely different aspect of the human form. It was a good idea and I noticed that quite a few years later a famous American ballet company used the same at Covent Garden.

In the basement clubs that summer, the Galaxy was definitely attempting to push the boundaries of what was permissible, but our performances were never just about bare flesh. To have been fixed on one means or message would have run counter to the Exploding Galaxy's creative approach.

Nevertheless, Fitz had become concerned at some elements of excess, both on stage and in the house.

It was at this time that he started on his manuscript for a kinetic drama called *Paranightmare of the Exploding Galaxy*. It was on concertina'd computer paper, which folded down upon itself but was described as a scroll. Umiak, who was to join the Galaxy in the autumn of 1967, says of the *Paranightmare*:

> It was a script that you could look at. In that sense, it was transmedia. You can see the script. It is a painting, but Fitz is using words and then he reads it aloud. He interprets it. It is a document you can look at with the words written on it and it is performed and it is expressing a kind of hell – as in a kind of paranoid nightmare. And he's expressing something about hippie-dom, where everybody is sleeping with everybody but there is no communication going on. It's a critique.

Out there in the counterculture, there was a degree of sexual sophistication and promiscuity not evident to me at Balls Pond Road. In his grotto at the Arts Lab, Jim Haynes was a great fan of 'social sex', which was a renaming of the term *orgy* with all its prudish associations. Others set their sights not on raising but on lowering numbers. By this, I mean age. Certain underground moguls specifically liked girls under the legal age limit. For Polanski-type reasons, this will never appear in anyone's memoirs, but there was the strong stench of paedophilia noticeable around some of the higher-order London hippie cliques. Incidents of abuse bordering on systematic grooming are shockingly similar to recent cases in the news. Attempts by me to find out about these – or the 'Fourteen-year-old Fuck-in' – have met with closed ranks and blank stares.

Maya Sendall describes the experience of losing her virginity to a well-known counterculture high-flyer at the age of 13 as ghastly ('Bloody hell, they were bad at sex those men. Wow, they were awful!). No sooner had he withdrawn than he was giving her a lecture on how this was not a relationship. Around a year later, she was raped:

> It wasn't until my forties that I realised I had been raped. Someone put acid in my drink when I was at the Speakeasy and he dragged me off home with him and decided to have sex with me while I was out of my head. I am surprised I ever came back from that because it was such a horror-trip. I felt like I was burning in hell. I was fourteen. These guys weren't youngsters. They were the ones in control.

Despite these early traumatic experiences, Maya is positive about this time, when looking back:

> We have to remember that any paradigm shift is subject to some blind upheaval and opportunism. Without exonerating my early predators, I chose to take responsibility for overcoming what happened to me. There was so much incredible adventure around me that, once I had worked out a few basic things, I had some truly amazing encounters. These could only have been nurtured by the sixties culture, because we were encouraged to look more deeply into ourselves and into each other. It was a truly amazing time.

Date rape was commonplace among the beautiful people. Caroline Coon remembers that at that time you had to be very careful to have your hand on the doorknob so that you could make a quick exit, otherwise you were at risk of being forced into something you did not want. It was much easier to take the mental step of forcing a woman in a climate where women were seen as misguided for resisting, which was the general view at the time.

The rape took a variety of forms: man on woman, man on man and even woman on man in one instance told to me. In this case, it would have been out of the question to talk about it in anything other than a joking way, so the sense of violation remained hidden.

Maya was one of the participants in the *Buddha Ballet* at Parliament Hill Fields in the summer of 1968. She visited Balls Pond Road on many occasions and found the atmosphere there pleasantly unmenacing. This fits with what I felt at the age of 15. When out and about on my own, I was constantly contending with the accusation that, if I said no, I must be suffering from severe sexual neurosis. It was a constant nagging pressure. While surrounded by members of the Exploding Galaxy, I was entirely free of advances and could simply enjoy being creative and being young. When I did eventually lose my virginity, towards the end of 1968, it was to a fellow Galactician, in a place and at a time I wanted.

By contrast with the outside world, things were fairly tame at Balls Pond Road. From interviews and my own memory, most people were in monogamous or near monogamous relationships or in serially monogamous ones. This is why the *People* article about 'Women as communal property' caused such indignation among the women and led to phone calls to solicitors. However, this was 1967, the year of free love. The house had a substantial population and what may not have applied to the majority certainly did apply to the few. Like the counterculture at large, wildly differing approaches sat side by side, without being seen as mutually exclusive. Promiscuous sex was there alongside the long-term partnerships. This led to a joke by Medalla about fountains of sperm.

For some of the young men involved, the year 1967 represented their first full-on experience of sex. Many were inexperienced, clumsy and keen to try out. The two most available women – the female 'circulators' – also happened to be, in my opinion, the two most vulnerable, although others disagree with this assessment. They were the only ones to participate in the rare public displays of sex, but they are no longer here to sue or counter any attempts to embellish, or any attempts to turn recollections from the depressingly mundane into 'artworks'. From what has been related, and from my own observations, given that sleeping space was shared, sexual encounters usually amounted to nothing more than a few fleeting moments of vigorous penetration. As I lay there trying not to listen, I thought, 'Is that all there is to it?' Encounters between men would have been far more discreet, so I never heard these from my mattress of caked candlewax.

Intimacy was difficult in an overcrowded building. For this reason, the hall and stairs became a place of privacy. In natural history documentaries, copulation is described in a very matter-of-fact way – 'fertilsation takes place on the wing', or 'during the rut, the intensity of activity is at its maximum'. In a natural history documentary about sex in an overcrowded sixties commune, commentary might run something like this: 'Mating takes place in the seclusion of the hallway. The female of the species rarely experiences climax.'

Is it any wonder that the counterculture men look back with misty-eyed nostalgia and the women, by and large, fail to recall any of it?

It was around this time that the term 'Bumping Bodies Ballet' – the title of one of Fitz's dramas – came to be used in the Galaxy as a euphemism for promiscuous sex. Fitz was not the only one concerned about wild behaviour at the house. David had been furious over the Ruy LSD incident, which had brought in the local police. It was he who had named the middle room 'Acid Island' – a place for those stranded in a sea of illusion.

Paul Keeler, although often at his parents' house in Windsor, was extremely worried. The open-door policy made him particularly vulnerable, since his name was the only one on the deeds. He could be charged by the police if drugs were found at the house, even if he knew nothing about them. At one stage, he had counted 60 or so people present in the house. There was no electricity, but even without record players blaring, large numbers like this were an unmissable presence to neighbours, who had become alarmed and would be likely to call the police.

Without serious vetting, anybody could make the place their home, and at that time at least one smack-head had settled in at the house for the free accommodation it provided. I never witnessed anyone shooting up, but Mike Chapman did and was horrified. In the Beat and jazz world, there was a certain admiration for the tragic junkie figure as creative talent, but not so in our crowd. We treated them with kind distance and with great caution when they came to stay. To us, heroin, unlike LSD, was utterly straight in every aspect of its effects and its rituals. As a junkie, you were a slave to commerce and locked into the kind of rigorous timetable of purchasing that even the most boring capitalists would find a challenge. Heroin use was utterly centroclinal from a Galactic point of view.

At the beginning of July, the police broke down the front door of No. 99 in a dawn raid. Some white pills were found on one of the people staying in the house, but the owner was able to show that they were prescription drugs. The police then left, but Galaxy members were very shaken because of the hostility of the officers and because of the way the women were humiliated and made to strip in a place that did not offer any privacy.[5]

Then there was the spiking incident. In 1967, the spiking of drinks was considered by some to be an altruistic act and a way of turning on the world. It was not seen as a crime by many, although, under section 24 of the Offences Against the Person Act, depending on the outcome for the victim, it could carry a maximum sentence of five years. Rag Doll says:

> I remember one day somebody came in with some orange juice on a tray and offered it round. Fitz had a drink, not realising that it had been laced with amphetamine. He was up all night, in a bad way, and he wrote all night on the back of the sports page of a newspaper. At the next UFO event, he read it out as a poem, with the cricket score words mixed with his own words.

Whether it was this incident or the police raid that marked the turning point is unclear, but towards the end of July, Paul put his foot down. He posted a notice in a prominent position near the entrance, making it clear that anyone found with drugs would be expelled from the house. This was the start of the no-drugs rule at Balls Pond Road, and it is a mark of everyone's respect for Paul that it was observed.

On only two further occasions was cannabis known to be on the premises. Lynn Darnton, whose name was later associated with the

Tribe of the Sacred Mushroom, was living at Balls Pond Road. He was horrified by the squalor and wanted to heighten people's awareness sufficiently in order to jolt them into cleaning up. The resulting smoking session did have the desired effect. Barry Miles mentions this incident in his book, *London Calling*, but does not describe what happened as a result. As soon as Paul found out that Lynn had brought cannabis into the house, he told him to leave for good.[6]

The only other occasion was when a group of psychiatrists from a therapeutic community down the road gave us a bottle of legally obtained prescription cannabis tincture and asked Galaxy members to help themselves. They then spent time as visitors to the house, observing us, although I don't remember anyone actually taking notes. It would be interesting to know whether any learned papers or dissertations emerged from this psychiatric research, and if so what the title of the research paper was. Sue Hall (non-Galaxy) has remarked that this must have been the ultimate in performance art – the observation of people going about their daily lives at home. Yet this was not 'our normal daily lives', since taking cannabis was not part of the Galaxy way of life. When I heard about it, I thought it just another example of the abusive behaviour that was so prevalent within the counterculture – this time abusive behaviour from so-called doctors.

My own experience of cannabis at 99 Balls Pond Road was zero. In the 18 months that I frequented the house, I knew of no spliffs being lit up or passed around. It was two years later, when I frequented an art student house-share in Putney, that I saw the degree to which cannabis was in daily recreational use by people of my generation, and I learned to roll a joint.

The no-drugs rule at Balls Pond Road also applied to LSD. Although acid remained important to some, for Galaxy gigs and excursions, its possession and use was banned from the house, particularly after the Ruy incident. Umiak remembers how one young Dutch boy, on stating that he had a number of tabs on him, had been made to get rid of them in order to stay with us. Everyone saw the point. They did not want to be busted and they did not want to be evicted from the house. Gradually, those for whom opiates and tetrahydrocannabinol were a way of life got squeezed out, leaving a pool of people whose sole priority was to explore consciousness as an artistic mission.

NOTES

1. Captain J G Stedman (1744–97), refering to the Indians of Surinam.
2. Polly Marshall, *The God of Hellfire: The Crazy life and Times of Arthur Brown* (SAF Publishing, 2005).
3. *International Times*, issue 17, 28 July 1967.
4. *The People*, 30 July 1967.
5. *Planted*, a report compiled by Paul Keeler, 1968.
6. *Planted.*

14

The College of Gallactic Knowledge

Each second we live is a new and unique moment of the universe, a moment that will never be again, And what do we teach our children? We teach them that two and two make four, and that Paris is the capital of France.

PABLO CASALS

WE IN THE Exploding Galaxy were, for the most part, rough-cut but privileged. The older artists in the house naturally fell into the role of educators, smoothing off our jagged edges and training us into a new way of thinking and behaving. There was nothing deliberate or premeditated about this. It just happened because they were widely read art-world eggheads and we were enthusiastic, impressionable and primed for anti-education.

In the 1960s the prefix *anti-* cropped up a lot: the anti-university, anti-poetry and anti-art, which later spawned anti-anti-art. Perhaps 99 Balls Pond Road could be described as an anti-finishing school – or even a starting school. At the Château Mont-Choisi in Switzerland, young women might learn to attain perfect poise and social etiquette with a smattering of art history thrown in. In the Galaxy household, what we immersed ourselves in was the unravelling of the aesthetic rules we had grown up with and the deconstruction of conventional approaches to living.

A neat little label like 'anti-art history' would not really pin down the process. The term *anti-* has itself become part of 'the spectacle', part of the tyranny of art-as-commodity. Besides, *anti-* implies disapproval and we were anything but disapproving of what lay in London's galleries and museums. A closer description of our engagement with the old masters would be: 'Zen in the art of art appreciation.'

My understanding of Zen in the art of learning came from Eugen Herrigel, whom I read at the time. His evaluation of *kyodo* – traditional Japanese archery – has since been questioned by Zen scholars, but what I understood at the time from Herrigel's book *Zen in the Art of Archery* was the need for an empathy with the target, even becoming the target in some way, in order to achieve the required state of mind.

In the centre of a Bronzino painting in the National Gallery, Venus kneels, naked, alluring, almost squirming. Cupid tweaks one of her nipples and is thus fleetingly distracted, which allows her to steal, unnoticed, one of his arrows. She is clearly up to no good. The bodies are twizzled round into impossible positions. An art historian might say that this is Mannerist in style and that the glowering green character on the left might represent syphilis, and there might follow a discussion that tries to make sense of the figures in a tussle at the top of the painting. This picture was deeply and utterly shocking to me as a 10-year-old on a Putney High Junior School trip. Six years later, as a practised Galactician, I stood before the painting again, this time allowing myself to be invited in, with no knowledge of the painter or of 16th-century Italy or of classical mythology. Intellect was not part of my relationship with the painting. I was at one with the image, tasted the honeycomb, was drawn into the bluest of blues. Any scholarship followed afterwards, lagging behind as a poor second.

This intense relationship with individual paintings was experienced by other Galaxy members. My sister Annabel remembers the strength of feeling she experienced at coming across a colour plate in a book about Vermeer:

> The woman is standing in front of a window reading a letter and she is wearing a long blue jacket. I was utterly inspired by the beauty of that image. Whether subconsciously or in open emulation, I turned some blue blanket material into a similar shaped jacket. Her jacket was padded satin and mine was wool. Both of our jackets were warm. The shape of my jacket corresponded to the shape of hers. Both of us were pregnant.

Annabel says that this intimate experience was by no means confined to famous paintings by old masters. She describes a similar experience with her discovery of Balinese music: 'I had listened to a recording of gamelan music, which had fascinated me.'

World music in general and gamelan music in particular were pretty much unappreciated outside a small circle of musos at that time. Annabel describes her exploration of gamelan sounds:

> I was taken with the cyclical waves of sound, and using an old bicycle wheel and piece of wooden stick at the Arts Lab, I spun it round to make similar cyclical sounds. This was purely impressionistic, and in no way sophisticated. I was entering into a correspondence with the original work, seeing it or hearing it and then actively relating to it and turning it into something else.

There were three educators within the Exploding Galaxy, each of whom opened a whole new world to me. One of my teachers was Paul Keeler. Before I met him, I had never heard of Kandinsky, Mondrian or Klee. Paul also gave me a broad introduction into conceptual art. Since he had previous church connections, he had interesting friends such as Brother Simon Tugwell of Blackfriars in Oxford, Trevor Huddleston who was bishop of Stepney, and Dom Sylvester Houédard of Prinknash Abbey. It was Paul Keeler who made me aware that there was a world out there way bigger and stranger than my parochial imagination had allowed. Given my liberal background and general nosiness, I might have got there eventually, but this was the fast-track option. Of my educators, Paul was the only one I remember talking about living artists as if they were significant. Fitz and David tended to talk to me more about the ones I recognised as old masters. Paul also taught me the trick of going to a museum to look at just a single painting.

What I learned from Fitz was quite different, in both focus and style of delivery. Another Galaxy mentor, he had a passion for the work of Van Gogh, particularly for the early drawings of potatoes – not in boxes, just the potatoes themselves stretching out to the edges of the page. He thought these were truly revolutionary as artworks, far more than any Jackson Pollocks he had seen, even though those also splashed out to the edges. Fitz says:

> When I was at the Slade and the art historian took us to see some of these paintings and we were looking at *Grass with Butterflies* and she said, 'Isn't it sad, that poor man just staring at the ground like that.' That was what she thought about it and I thought you can walk around in that room in the National Gallery and that particular picture stands out. It's such a superb painting, but there you are, she'd been trained as an art historian.

After one of our Galaxy expeditions to the National Gallery, Jane Ellis bought a postcard of this very painting. Somehow, following a discussion about the need to destroy art, the postcard was torn up and discarded. Fitz subsequently rescued all the pieces from the ground and put them in an envelope. My introduction to this revered Van Gogh image was through these torn fragments, which could be placed on a surface and moved around in any order.

It is almost as if Galaxy members had fallen in love with individual artworks. Edward recalls:

> It was in the Netherlands. We made a special journey to the Kroeller-Mueller Museum in the countryside – where I saw a work by Sophie Taeuber-Arp. She had connections with the Cabaret Voltaire and David was a great fan. The sculpture consisted of flat white blocks. The beauty of it lay in the curves and the way in which she used the space. There were several of these shapes ascending the wall. It was an experience that has stayed with me lifelong.

Our Galaxy mentors had their pet hates, too, and these were also instantly adopted by the younger members of the group. One particular dislike of David's at the time was a Graham Sutherland sculpture, outside the Thorn company in Covent Garden, which we occasionally passed on our long walks through London. The use of concrete in architecture was often derided when noticed, concrete being seen as a material that stifled life. In 1968, the slogan '*Sous les pavés, la plage!*' ('Under the cobblestones, the beach!') became something of a cliché in Paris, but its sentiment summed up perfectly the idea we all had of natural human pleasures being suppressed by flat functional slabs.

Audrey remembers her delight at living in this particular house where museum and gallery visits were almost a daily occurrence. Her favourite was the Pitt Rivers in Oxford:

> It was something like a jumble sale, with everything tumbling over everything else. I remember a beautiful Kathakali sculpture just stuffed under a table. This was in the days when everything displayed was totally accessible. The Pitt Rivers was the most Galactic of the museums because of the way it was stacked with artifacts and we – the Exploding Galaxy – seemed to be particularly interested in making artifacts, things that we could carry about or use.

The third of our teachers was David Medalla. Of the Galaxy mentors, he was the one whose impact was generally mostly profoundly felt. I would describe him as my principal mentor and the person who first gave me the sense that I could be creative in my own right. Audrey remembers him shuffling along, his shoes too big, in sloppy jumpers, always hugging a pile of books and papers:

> David was charismatic. He would just reach up for books constantly. I don't think you could have a long conversation with him without him going to a book or illustrating what he was talking about with a reference. He was engaging and very delightful.

Lizzie remembers herself less as his student and more as a living part of one of his artworks. I saw him as both, my educator – the teacher who made learning cool – and my artistic director, since I saw myself as part artwork and part fledgling artist. This was how he encouraged me to feel.

In those two years I went to more concerts and art collections than at any other time in my life. Money was not an issue since we could walk if we didn't have the money for the 38 bus and since, in those days, art and music came free often enough for there to be no need for a student card. My first experience of the *Matthew Passion* was Galaxy-led, with ten or so bizarrely dressed creatures, scrudges and all, trooping up to the upper gallery of the Wren church, Saint Andrew's, in Holborn.

Andrew remembers how his conversion to classical music came via the Exploding Galaxy:

> Before then I was trashing classical music. Mozart was the stuff my dad liked. As amazing as the Beatles and the Stones and the rest of them were, once I met the Galaxy I suddenly liked listening to Mozart and Bach. Before then I just thought it antiquated and out of fashion. This all came from David. It's amazing, you know, the influence he had on me. Well, I had no education about art, you know, and there was David teaching me everything about the development of art, from the Matisses through to the Lichtensteins. It was almost like a kind of history of art course – like, I suppose, going to art school.

In the years 1967 and 1968, the gradient of my own educational learning curve was near vertical. At the age of 15, when I came across the Exploding Galaxy, I would have described myself as 'not quite a blank sheet'. In addition to school reading, I particularly liked Dostoevsky and Oscar Wilde. Sexual curiosity had led me to read *The L-shaped Room* and *Woman of Rome*. Beyond that, although I had no real interest in *Jackie* and other teen romance magazines, my reading matter had consisted of music rags until *IT* came along. And at the beginning of 1967, my interest in the visual arts was almost non-existent, limited to Botticelli – the ultimate flower child painter.

At the top of the Balls Pond Road house, in the alcove in the front bedroom, floor-to-ceiling bookshelves were bursting with volumes – more than 2,000 at a guess. These were mainly, but not always, on art or Eastern mysticism. Studiously imitating my peers, I took books off the shelves to read at random. One day I pulled down a book called *Baudelaire on Poe*. The reading of this single book connected the names of two 19th century writers I had hardly heard of and led to a kind of exponential curiosity. The fact that, at that point, I had not read either writer and that this was a backwards way of getting into the subject was of little importance. I was riveted by the idea that Poe had been educated a stone's throw away in Stoke Newington. From there came a fascination with gothic writing and later, gothic films. I then started to read the French Romantic poets. No one actually told me to read anything. I was just living in a house where everyone always seemed to have an open book or a newspaper in their hand, and if one mechanism operated particularly efficiently in the counterculture, it was peer pressure.

We went to museums like young people now go to night clubs. We became proper little swats-with-a-difference. Given the fact that the Exploding Galaxy were culture and museum junkies, it is ironic to see headlines about the underground of the time: 'Would you let your daughter go home with these people?'

Apart from my greasy spoon diet, my underground life was almost entirely wholesome. What I was mainlining was, in fact, what lay within the Prints and Drawings Room of the British Museum.

Nevertheless, we were utterly provocative when out and about, especially in a scholarly setting. The general reaction of gallery staff was hostile. Museum attendants in peaked caps, without exception old, white and male, behaved like the prison officer MacKay in the TV series *Porridge*, taking on for themselves the role of drill sergeant to the public.

Michael Chapman was prone to this kind of treatment:

> I was an assiduous visitor to the London museums and would visit the British Museum, National Gallery, Tate and National Portrait Gallery on an almost daily basis. I was, however, often refused entry to the National Gallery on Trafalgar Square, as the guards mistook my long curly hair as being the mark of a drug addict, intent on fixing up heroin in the toilet. Of course, I could not accept this ban and would slip into the building unseen. When the guards discovered me, I would ignore them, and turn to address the other visitors, making a rather loud speech. It became something of a ritual. I entered the museum. The guards summoned the police, the police would read the prevailing laws and order me to leave the establishment. I typically just sat down on the floor and refused to budge. The police then grabbed my arms and feet and carried me outside, to dump me on the pavement... One day I dressed up as a rather tall Arabian princess, using a traditional *burka* over my head that hung down

to my knees, thus hiding my identity. Then I and a very smartly dressed Lizzie drew up in a taxi in front of the steps of the National Gallery. With some daring flair, Lizzie led me up the steps to the entrance and presented me to the guards as one of the members of the harem of a very important sheikh, on an official visit to Britain (or something like that). The guards immediately ushered us in. It was all very funny, especially when I gave my traditional speech.

Some years later, I was invited over to England (I was then living in Amsterdam) by the BBC to participate in the TV programme *24 Hours*. Once in the studio, I suddenly realised that one of the speakers, Bridget Brophy, who was there to defend the rights of artists like the Exploding Galaxy members to claim National Assistance, was also the wife of Sir Michael Vincent Levey, the director of the National Gallery, where I had so often been barred from visiting. I used the occasion to make some very terse comments about the case, and in protest, I began taking off my clothes.

The most prized of all our educational expeditions during that summer of 1967 was our visit to the Saville Theatre in Shaftesbury Avenue to see the Kathakali dancers. This was the troupe's first European tour. The performance showed the whole life of Krishna, taken from the *Mahabharata*. At home in India, this could last all night, but for the European audiences, it was condensed to under three hours.

I was already hooked on stories. If I liked a painting, it was usually because it contained within its frame some kind of emotional narrative. For four years, I had been steeped in the high drama of Scottish border ballads and Irish airs. How could you not be moved by the haunting words of 'She Moved Through the Fair' or the hidden story of rape in the song 'Reynardine'? It took very little for me to be attracted to the high drama of the *Mahabharata* or the miniatures depicting tales from the Moghul courts of India. In the case of the Kathakali dancers, the tale presented on stage was of one family at war with another, a long and bitter battle over rightful lineage. This particular tale of the five Pandava brothers was already ancient by the time of the Wars of the Roses, and was known some 2,000 years before the feud between the Montagues and Capulets was originally acted in the late 16th century.

At the performance, there were enough layers of language to help us recognise the storyline we already knew from David – the facial expressions and, above all, the bulging eyes and *mudra* hands continually at work, swishing around us like a magic force, sucking us up into this virtual other world from our seats in the front row. Even the make-up drew us in: green for the gods, red for the demons and white for the glorious monkey god, Hanuman.

The narrative was packaged in rhythm, fierce stamping and a jingling and chiming of bells, along with a blaze of continually swirling colours carefully lit from the front as was the tradition. This had to be the ultimate psychedelic experience.

Simon Shirley describes the intensity of his first taste of the Kathakali troupe:

> The trippers were blown away by the dancing. The acid had taken away their objectivity. You're like a child – you are in it. As the plot unfolded, loss followed loss. A dice game was lost, the land was lost, then another game lost and then everything was lost – oh, the pain of such loss!

The identification was as intense as if Simon were himself the gambler:

> The pulling down of the curtain was significant, like the pulling down of a veil. Then Krishna entered and the stage was filled with light, which was such an unbelievable relief.

The Exploding Galaxy returned to this same show again and again. On their second tour the following year, the Kathakali dancers were a sell-out at Sadlers Wells, but in the summer of 1967, at the Saville Theatre, there were only a sprinkling of takers, mostly tripping hippies. By the end of the run, Galaxy fans were allowed in free, sitting like groupies right down at the very front for maximum effect.

Ghita Metha has described the two-way flirtation between East and West in the late sixties as a double con:

> The seduction lay in the chaos. They thought they were simple. We thought they were neon. They thought we were profound. We knew we were provincial. Everybody else was ridiculously exotic and everybody got it wrong.[1]

It is true that the simplicity of the unmechanised was wildly appealing to us baby boomers, and also that most flower children were just dabbling, attracted by the exoticism. Josephine recalls:

> I am afraid most of us didn't understand Indian culture and had absolutely no idea what oriental religion meant at all. It was a total mystery. People bought joss sticks, bells and beads. They just seemed pretty and charming, that's all. We could buy highly coloured prints of Indian deities but we didn't understand what it was really all about, the prettiness and bright colours being chosen more as paraphernalia to aid good LSD experiences. Most didn't understand and experienced just a series of charming hallucinatory images. Only a few people actually bothered to read about Hindusim or Tibetan Buddhism.

However, there was nothing sham about David Medalla's interest in Eastern mysticism. He had actually read the texts and studied the *mudras*. His scholarly interest was infectious, and some Galaxy members started to learn earnestly about Indian legends and musical discipline. Since we did not have electricity in the house, storytelling by candlelight became central to our evenings, and David, with his lilting intonation and his infectious enthusiasm, was the greatest storyteller of them all.

Several of the Galaxy entourage took steps to make a serious study of classical Indian performing arts. Annabel studied Indian singing, and I studied Bharatanatyam dance with the Sri Lankan dancer Bala Sundari from the Kalakshetra School. Others like Nick Sawyer and Judith Pertz studied sitar.

The conceptual art world looked askance at this aspect of David the artist, but he was unconcerned, and tales of Krishna and the Buddha remained bread and butter to Galaxy performances. The notion of entertainment taken straight from the Indian cultural tradition gave to the Galaxy a sense of 'the timeless unbowed performance' that was extremely influential in producing the *Bird Ballet*. Above all, the lack of boundaries fitted in perfectly with our desire to pull apart rigid divisions between art and life.

NOTES

1. Gita Mehta, *Karma Cola: Marketing the Mystic East* (New York: Simon and Schuster, 1979).

15

No Two Elephants are the Same

And being with the
Exploding Galaxy street theatre troupe,
When they boarded a train
With a bed frame strung with piano wire
And a crate of ping pong balls.

Unknown to my trusting mother
I spent the weekends with them
Re-enacting scenes from the life of Buddha
With co-opted passers by,
Dressed in a Chinese silk dressing gown
And playing an ocarina.

CHRIS CLARKE [1]

IN THE LATE sixties, most university student unions had healthy budgets which allowed them to hire big names for entertainment. It was autumn 1967 and the start of Warwick University's academic year, and we were on the bill with Graham Bond.

It was cold and we had hired a van – the kind that had very little in the way of bodywork between the front seat and the vehicle ahead. It turned out, though, that we had no driver, except for Simon, who had not expected to be roadie and so had downed an acid tab. This lack of forward planning was typical of the Galaxy and, as usual, we just had to go along with the cock-up. Simon hopped into the driver's seat and I perched close to him in the front, squashed between him and two others. The rest of the Galactic performers had piled into the back, several of them in various states of trip.

If you were going to be stuck in an acid situation, Simon's were generally regarded as the safest pair of hands. It was he who had taught Rakis how to act cool on those first trips in June and July, by showing him how to resist the temptation to stare too much and jump into puddles. This was of particular importance given the venue of many of those early trips – a flat directly opposite a central London police station. Since there were no curtains in either building, members of the force could stare directly into the flat when they got bored with matching their notebooks.

Now Simon was tasting the delights of the astral planes while at the same time successfully negotiating a Ford Bedford along the A425 somewhere near the Warwick campus. 'The road is turning into a sausage,' Simon announced in a matter of fact sort of way. I flinched at his side. 'If you act uptight, I'll freak out,' he said. This was not a threat, just a statement of fact, so for the rest of the drive I sat there pretending to be cool with his state of mind.

Although I had not yet taken LSD myself, I frequently took on the role of guide to other people through their drug experiences, and sometimes found myself talking people down when they went through rogue moments. On this occasion I felt responsible for everyone, since for this gig, few of us were straight ('straight' was the term used by the flower children to mean 'not on an acid trip').

The building itself was not acid-friendly. A typically sixties concrete-and-glass construction, it had only been open for two years, the university having been conceived as a post-war attempt to make higher education available to all. It was getting dark when we arrived, and Audrey was hovering by the large free-standing floodlights that lined the path up to the main complex. As she negotiated each one in turn, she momentarily stood, afraid and trapped by the brightness. Other Galaxy members were dispersing and exploring the grounds. I felt like a sheepdog trying to direct these wayward creatures towards a pen.

Our dressing room was near the student bar, and wherever there was beer, it seemed, there was always the potential for a punch-up, especially when the Exploding Galaxy arrived. We were just too weird and we talked another language when we tried to activate people. Our attempts at re-educating the world were frequently taken the wrong way and seen in the same light as insulting someone's mother. At UFO and Middle Earth, where we were fairly full-on, some people kept a wary but fascinated distance, but we always felt accepted on our own terms on our own turf, the weirdness being sanctioned as a natural result of awakened minds. Outside the London LSD circuit, however, we navigated a path between being circus freaks and objects of ridicule or being inciters who deserved a good spanking.

David Medalla and Gerald Fitzgerald were both present at the Warwick gig. David became deeply absorbed in cutting his toenails, while Fitz entered into a discussion about the limitations of beer and property ownership with a belligerent-looking fresher. David and Fitz were dramatically different as personalities, and each appeared to believe himself the better artist of the two. There was bound to be, at some point, a build-up to a jousting and an ousting. Yet this was not obvious to me then; instead, there appeared to be a strong sense of cooperation for performances such as this one, cooperation of the kind you might find in two hostile nations up against a more menacing third party.

It is not so surprising that a workable and creative truce could have existed between the two. Both were established and confident and saw the group experience of the Exploding Galaxy as central to their own development as artists. Both liked the idea of an entourage of willing people to work with. The group, in turn, benefited from the lack of cultural absolutism provided by the two extremes, along with the eclecticism that allowed Hindu and Buddhist tales to live side by side with Fitz's *Kinetapocalypsoidal Bumping Bodies Ballet* and *Goldifingers and The Bear One*.

Before they met, David and Fitz had each had a grudging respect for the other. Once Fitz moved into the house at Balls Pond Road, there was a liquefying and a melding of two basically different approaches, from which emerged a discourse that was sufficiently unified for common features to emerge. These points in common were key to the unrolling of the Exploding Galaxy as a living artwork. The two key features were the notions of metaphor and transformation that were central to both David's and Fitz's thinking and therefore to everything the Exploding Galaxy did.

David's exploration of these themes can be seen in his discovery of 'the peelable sculpture'. This was anything you could peel and turn into an artwork. Paint on a door that bubbled up in the sun could be transformed into a peelable, as could moss lifted off a rock surface.

In the middle of June 1967, David described his first two peelable sculptures. One measured half an inch and consisted of a piece of his hair and a shred of his skin 'tinted' by a scab; the second, larger peelable was made from various materials – cloth, plastic, wood, rubber and glue pearls – which he described floating down the Thames. He related these peelables to the paintings of Giorgione and, in particular, an adoration in the National Gallery, which he also described as a peelable

The ideas that spewed out of David's head did not need to be confined by the restrictions of reality or by what was physically possible. He saw peelables as the first propositions for his 'Mohole Flower'. He described this flower as growing in the centre of the earth in a non-photosynthetic way, in the darkness.

The notion of the peelable spread in the house, and Galaxy members incorporated the idea into their daily lives, searching streets, bins and market stalls for the perfect peelable sculpture. Favourites came from advertising hoardings which, after layer upon layer of gluing came away, revealed successive strata of unconnected graphics and blurb.

We were all equally absorbed by our encounters with metaphor. An illustration of how far this was enmeshed in our thinking could be seen on one of the many trips we made via the North London Railway line. This overground route formed a semi-circle around London, taking in Kew, Parliament Hill and Dalston Junction. As a number of us were gathered on the platform at Canonbury, Edward examined a sign – a leftover piece of Victorian street furniture in enamel, its corners and screw holes long rusted, depicting a hand in a pointing position showing the way to Platform No. 2. The index finger was scrunched downwards and not at the normal right angle, giving the hand the appearance of a creature with a long trunk. This led to the group having a long interpretative discussion, ending at the proposition put forward by Annabel and Fitz that 'No two elephants are the same'. This concept was thoroughly explored and frequently returned to, almost like a catchphrase. The love of elephants was later extended by Fitz and Umiak, after they formed Transmedia Exploration, into to a fascination with mammoths.

'No two elephants are the same' later reappeared in *Orange and Blue Kinetegram*, at the point at which Orange and Blue, standing there in their respective coloured pools of light, realise they can be any colour.

Once art leaves the gallery walls, it seems to move ever closer to the boundaries of what is possible. More usually – and predictably – the pushing of boundaries leads to the physically explicit, with performance artists using tampons, vomit, slashings and so forth, and audiences walking out and pundits arguing about where to place limits in creative expression. The logical conclusion of pushing these particular boundaries would be the depiction of a real death, and at around this time, a young art student did shoot himself dead onto a canvas.

The Exploding Galaxy had been known, loved and hated for its displays of nudity at some UFO and Middle Earth events, but we actually found the repeated depiction of sexual imagery or acts to be quite centroclinal and a definite sign of straightness because of its reliance on the obvious and the predictable. We would have seen this as hackneyed and as addictive behaviour. We would never have put our own bodies at risk with the self-mutilatory slashings or piercings that some performance artists were relying on. The Exploding Galaxy crossed quite a different boundary.

Our boundary had to do with the nature of reality. If you stopped seeing the world and the objects around you in a conventional way, then anything could be anything. In this way, we were playing with our own sense of reality. The idea propounded by both David and Fitz at that time was that nothing was to be taken for granted. As a follower of this idea, I could describe myself as entering into a chosen kind of madness.

The direction that kinetic art was moving in was all about exploration and seeing what happened, about observing closely and turning the experience of being an audience into a participatory and meditative state. Although not everyone in the Galaxy dropped acid, LSD served this purpose perfectly since things you had always labelled as mundane suddenly became fascinating – the problem with the Galaxy was that, having understood a truth, we felt driven in the way religious converts are, to tell others what they *should* believe. In the midst of a bunch of drunken and rowdy undergraduates on a night out at Warwick, this was never going to go down well. Activating the centroclinal world could look so very smug, and LSD wasn't helping to contain the dynamic. Edward remembers:

> We went to the canteen to get the free meal we were owed as part of our performers' fee, but David had already boarded one of the empty tea trolleys and had decided he was one of the gondoliers in Venice. He was on a gondola and the canteen staff were getting alarmed. Whoever was keeping on top of things, I admire them greatly.

The person attempting to keep on of top of things was, in fact, me. There was more to come. Our kinetic drama had not even officially begun. Although not teetotalers, the Galaxy were fairly disdainful of alcohol consumption. The performance area was now packed and our audience were downing pints. Edward had become concerned:

> I could see the beer going through all the people as though it was actually travelling out from the bar and flowing through their bodies. I actually saw the beer as a thing that was circulating and I saw the electricity connected to the amplified music from the other end of the room, and that was flowing too. I saw the two flowing towards each other and the beer

and the electricity were meeting and making quite a potent and disorienting kind of mix.

Fitz had by now requisitioned an overhead projector and Edward, acting as his assistant, displayed the word 'scrudge' across the back wall. Fitz had found a microphone and was talking to the whole gathering, giving a kinetic interactive lecture, making a visionary proclamation.

Umiak describes that particular moment as feeling that the two of them had pulled off something mad and inspirational. Of the audience she says:

> They seemed to be all in tweed jackets drinking beer. They were very straight, but they had wanted us to come... I think the audience imagined this sort of commune life – this other life. It was another world. The world of the hippies was another world. There was a vision that straight people could have about the alternative life, which caused them to be in either wonder and emulation or sheer hatred.
>
> I was certainly swept up into the magic and high of the whole thing and I think the people of Warwick were too. It was an unforgettable experience like a lot of those hippie happenings were. You couldn't say exactly what performance it was. It was a happening and an experience, and in the sixties, we had things like that.

Edward then retreated to the dressing room and I was dispatched to try to persuade him to come out. This became a pattern for Edward in future scheduled performances, since he was often to be found onstage as an invisible participant – present by his absence.

Things did calm down to some degree, but only temporarily. There was some Medalla-esque dance drama with the *Krishna Lila Ballet*, inspired by our recent experience of the Kathakali dancers from Kerala. Whether this finished or broke up is not clear.

The evening had somehow descended into a boxing-ring battle between two chemically altered states. In the red corner was 'Booze' – bleary and with a bloodied nose, punching the air in anticipation, ready for a ruck. In the other corner, with cerebal cortex unlocked, the sky-blue tripper 'Lysergic Acid' watched, incredulous at the absurdity, uncontained and crowing.

Since the beer continued to flow, punches were eventually thrown and the Exploding Galaxy made a quick exit. We spent the end of the evening outside in the quadrangle, turning ourselves into chess pieces, moving from square to square on the chequer-board paving slabs of the Warwick grounds.

Before we left, a limo pulled up and its chauffeur knocked politely on the door of the van. 'Are you going to be seeing Graham Bond again? He left this book in my car. Could you return it to him?' He handed Edward a copy of an *Introduction to Qabalistic Symbolism,* vol. 2, by Gareth Knight. The reading of this book was to form the basis of Edward's performance in the *Bird Ballet*. Hippie ineptness meant that the book was never returned to Graham Bond.

A sympathetic lecturer offered to put us up on his floor for the night. We all climbed into the Bedford van, except for Fitz, who, still tripping, climbed on to the roof and lay on his back to watch the stars in the night sky, in touch with the cosmos as we drove to our crash pad.

NOTES

1. From 'To Robin Re Revolution', by Chris Clarke.

16

The Bird Ballet

The creation of the world happens continuously. There is neither beginning nor end, everything dies into a new birth, forms of culture grow like grass; life and its meaning does not repeat itself. Everything is born into a death. A good picture paints itself. And man creates his world himself.

SUSANNE WENGER

FOLLOWING THE KATHAKALI dance troupe's debut at the Saville Theatre in London, it seemed natural to David Medalla to produce our own dance drama along the same lines, and the only fitting place to show such an ambitious kinetic ballet was in the beautiful people's favourite venue for a happening: the Roundhouse. This was to take place in the second half of October 1967.

Through September, David sat ensconced at the top of 99 Balls Pond Road, working out the various episodes and convolutions of the epic fable that was to be. Audrey, who was able to observe this creative stage, remembers that it took him no longer than two days working flat out to come up with the whole saga. The storyline, which consisted of 24 'circumsequences', confined itself to the realms of 'plot' plot rather that 'psychological' plot, with the characters exemplifying what we did best: a highly stylised package of good versus evil. Mitja Hinderks describes the plot:

> It is the story of a scarecrow and his disintegration – how his various parts are carried off and then adapted by the birds and then somehow returned and re-assembled to create the scarecrow anew.

Into the storyline were fitted virtually every entry in the *Observer's Book of Birds* plus some fictitious creatures besides, such as those in the 'Denizens of the Bird Underworld' scene: the 'pusher-bird', the 'junkie-bird' and the 'supersonic slogan-bird'. The programme made it clear that the hypodermic needle dance in this scene would not be performed on 29 October 1967, which was the children's matinee. Good characters (the hummingbird, the good flowers, the phoenix and any bird with a pretty-sounding name, such as golden palm weaver or scarlet ibis) were fairly easy to pick out from the baddies (the evil flower, the mad farmer, the razorbill, a disease, the property developer, any carrion bird). The settings switched between a Persian garden, the Galapagos Islands, the underworld, the sea and the whole world's orbit.

Meanwhile, the twists and turns of the plot moved from the mad farmer's death, to the scarecrow's destruction, and his subsequent trial for cruelty to birds, then redemption and finally his destiny as a permanently flying comet that 'zoom-zens' around the world. The thread that wove this disjointed story together was the golden wagtail – the role chosen by David for himself – who propelled the story forward, chased away evil, generally saved the situation and bestowed the gift of permanent fire. Since we admired David greatly, we found this fitting.

The programme described the two circumsequences with amplified music and light shows:

> Circumsequences 7 (storm freak out) and 13 (the underworld) will feature pop groups and kinetic dramas. The pop groups and kinetic dramas will change in every performance.

Among those participating were The Crazy World of Arthur Brown, Graham Bond, The Soft Machine, Dreamland Express and The Sign of Shiva. Acoustic music was provided by flute, alto sax, clarinet, tabla, vina and guitar. In addition, there were homemade instruments, with John Schofield and Paul Keeler playing 'found percussion'. Paul's – a cardboard tube six inches in diameter and the height of a person – later accompanied him on tour to France and the Netherlands.

The Bird Ballet comprised 30 or so dancers in the guises of 62 birds. If there had been 60 performers, 124 different birds could have easily been portrayed, and if 120, there could possibly have been 248 bird explorations. The performance went on as long as it went on, which could be three hours or so.

All the bird roles were allocated by David, but beyond this, we were left entirely to our own devices to create our own performance and costumes. Jane Ellis describes his choosing of her bird roles:

> He chose most of the bird roles for the individual players. You could see the personalities so clearly. And he chose two bird roles for me. I couldn't have explained to myself why they were such true roles for me – 'the goose who warned of danger' and the bird of paradise – but they have continued to be true roles that have somehow remained active in my life.

Edward played the albatross. His dance was inspired by the magician on a tarot card, and for each performance, he wore a skirt made out of that particular day's newspaper (it had to be the paper from that day and no other). He held a metal tarot card figure-of-eight above his head as he read out his bird poem. Years later, when I asked him why he had never explained his albatross–magician choices to other members of the Galaxy, he said simply, 'Because everyone was making their own personal costume decisions at the time.'

The fact was that, if art was truly to enter into every strand in the fabric of life, there was no need for it to be visible to others – there was no need for an 'art' audience. This was for me the most revolutionary aspect of Galaxy philosophy because it made a nonsense of the artist as *auteur*, which remains an unresolved dilemma for young artists trying to break new ground, as well as for those ex-Galaxy members who, long after the group had disbanded, did an about-turn and sought public recognition for themselves as individual artists.

Fitz was totally sculptural in his approach to everyday clothing, so his costumes for *The Bird Ballet* were, although extraordinary, not surprising, and were just an extension of his daily attire. As a parrot, he constructed his beak and plumage from fruit market paraphernalia.

In his other role as priest, overseeing the funeral of the mad farmer, he and Umiak sang out the wording on a Sky Ray ice lolly wrapper in plain chant, enunciating carefully each syllable of the E numbers:

> Firmamentum. Sky Ray. Ingrediaenta: sugar carboxi-methyl cellulose, citric acid, sodium acid phosphate, flavouring, sodium citrate, calcium carbonate, colouring, saccharine.

There then followed the muffled grunting whisper of a congregation uttering the set response: 'Mini-mum contentum: one point nine fluid ounces, fifty-four cc. see Swiss watches – super bar-gain. Free card inside.'

Paul, with all the gravitas of a BBC broadcaster, then read out what was written on the free *Doctor Who* Adventure card:

> As Doctor Who approaches the giant armoured astrabeatle, the monster's eyes flicker towards him, shattering rocks as they travel. Any moment now you will see real Swiss watches.

In this way, a discarded lolly wrapper was turned into a document, and its text of mish-mashed information and marketing was recycled as kinetic drama.

Michael Chapman spent much of the performance attached to a chair by a length of rag, and the chair clattered around after him as he moved around. As the owl, he recited his especially written poem of the same name.

Paul Keeler managed to get a booking for four nights at the Roundhouse. Although not consecutive, they included two Saturdays. This was to be the first ever run of performances by the same theatrical group at the Roundhouse, which was still in its early days as a theatre venue.

When UFO had moved there from the West End a couple of months previously, Joe Boyd and Co. had found the Chalk Farm neighbourhood menacing and had struggled to contend with the local inebriated thugs.

At some point, mods had split into different sub-groups down traditional class lines, with the middle-class mods turning soft and becoming hippies and the white working class morphing into hard mods and then skinheads. The latter were there at 'The 14-hour Technicolor Dream' in their Fred Perry polo shirts and Sta-Prest slacks mouthing off, and they made occasional forays into UFO while at its venue in Tottenham Court Road, usually leaving in disgust on finding that no alcohol was on sale, but occasionally trying to start a ruck.

When Joe Boyd replanted UFO in Camden, he was taking the beautiful people into hooligan territory. The Galaxy were old hands at hostile surroundings. We had already done the same thing in Dalston. Gentrification had not remotely taken hold of the Angel yet, so east of Islington Green was a dangerous place for provocatively dressed hippies. Dalston was a place where the local youth culture was just dying to vent its hatred on the love and peace brigade, and we had regularly run the gauntlet after closing time. However, *The Bird Ballet* was unlikely ever to attract UFO numbers, so at the Roundhouse we avoided the difficulties faced by Joe Boyd and managed to stay below the urban neanderthal radar for the whole of the show's run.

Rehearsals, or 'explorations' as we called them, took place in All Saints Hall in Notting Hill Gate (a favourite haunt of the counterculture originals) and at Middle Earth and the Arts Lab. Then, towards opening night, we rehearsed at the Roundhouse itself which, before it was refurbished to become one of London's top theatre venues, was cold and draughty even at the height of summer.

The playwright Arnold Wesker, as artistic director of Centre 42, was now managing the place, and he would appear from time to time at our rehearsals. He clearly didn't think much of us. Rakis recalled him remarking: 'Funny how you lot always turn up like a bunch of bad pennies.' One time, he came visiting with Lord Goodman – Paul had applied for a grant for the Exploding Galaxy from the Arts Council, and Lord Goodman was its chairman. The two arts moguls left laughing, hardly able to contain their mirth at the thought that we had actually applied for a grant.

The issue of our lack of polish in performance did emerge and eventually divided members of the cast. Jocelyn, in particular, found the haphazard nature of the production difficult to accept. Aside from being remarkably beautiful, she was also a trained and proficient Martha Graham dancer, with the muscular calves and balletic mastery to prove it. She patiently waited her turn to come on as the phoenix, and then with perfect control allowed her limbs to quiver their last against the dying of the light while the rest of us generally bumbled about.

Two schools of thought were emerging at the various Exploding Galaxy gatherings. The straighter ones among us (and that included me) felt that this was a production for a paying public and that, as such, we should give a vaguely professional performance. Those of truly artistic temperament had understood that these were not rehearsals so much as explorations and that, as such, the issue of polish and slickness was a complete red herring. Herzmark was of the former persuasion:

> We had to give people value for money if they were paying. I never had the attitude of 'let everything hang out, it's fine'. I was never that kind of person – not just something that might be spontaneous and happen on the night.

Jane, on the other hand, had felt the rehearsals to be spiritual explorations:

> When we started working on *The Bird Ballet*, we would be pulling things out that were unique and we were enacting something profound and ritually true and it didn't matter what it was. All of this lost its power once the directing came in... Once it became more of a performance I couldn't be bothered so much because we were trying to make it look good at that point. We were doing things to try and tidy up and it had just become bad theatre. Before that point, it had been like Tibetan ritual – with nothing apparently happening except a Tibetan monk chanting in Tibetan. I couldn't dance in the way that dancers dance. I had limited movements because I'd had polio, and in those early *Bird Ballet*

> rehearsals, I had been freed from this and was dancing as expression and not dancing for an audience. I had been transformed from someone with a limp into someone who danced with beauty. For the first time in my life, I was unselfconscious as I moved in front of others.

At a certain point, once the public performances came closer, Paul took over to some degree in the rehearsals. He had not long before been studying at the Central School of Speech and Drama, along with Julie Christie, Christopher Timothy and Lynn Redgrave. His awareness as an actor took over from his explorer self, with the looming vision of an audience paid-up and seated and waiting to be entertained. However, the argument was, in the end, won by a margin by the explorers over the rehearsers. There was some conflict about how things were to proceed, and a discussion took place during which Simon complained that we might end up performing the same show every night 'like *The Mousetrap*'. This produced a sympathetic guffaw from the rest of the troupe. It was finally resolved that Paul should be 'the eyes and the ears' of the ballet. Quite what this meant, no one really knew, but somehow people seemed happy with that.

The Bird Ballet production was therefore a compromise between the explorers and the traditionalists. Like the Living Theatre, we had thrown out the rule book, but unlike them we didn't force the audience from their role as passive observers. In his book *Play Power*, Richard Neville describes the press reaction to the Living Theatre's production of *Paradise Now*:

> They can't act, they can't dance, they can't sing, snorted Fleet Street, tying blinkers to its motor car and galloping forth to measure the hurricane with a slide rule. The night I saw *Paradise Now*, Judith Malina didn't kick her legs as high as Ginger Rogers in *Mame*, angry black Rufus didn't deliver blank verse with the taut aplomb of Sir John Gielgud, but within ten minutes, most of the audience were roaming the auditorium, tense, confused, excited and wholly involved.

He puts the four main underground theatre groups in the same bracket – the Exploding Galaxy, the Human Family, La Mama Troupe and the Living Theatre – and describes them as breaking new ground in new ways, as 'embodying the international, equisexual, tribal, nomadic lifestyle implicit in the movement'.

We didn't have the political punch of the Living Theatre, nor their confrontational ethos, but we shared with them a complete abandonment of theatrical convention.

When Exploders themselves have been asked how good or bad they thought *The Bird Ballet* was, a common response has been: 'No idea. I just know what it felt like to be in it.' It can be assumed, though, that since the audience was required to watch for most of the performance and not necessarily participate, and since the plot unfolded in its own time and in its own way – usually taking around three hours – there would have been plenty of scope for boredom along the way.

Annabel Rutter deeply regretted having dragged her whole family all the way up from Surrey to see the show. She found the experience agonisingly embarrassing, since she felt she was participating in something that was amateurish in the extreme. *The Bird Ballet* was the last Galaxy production she ever participated in.

Indica Gallery's director John Dunbar, having been invited by David to see the show, found the performance boring, but overall enjoyed the evening because he had bumped into an old friend and they had spent the time chatting and catching up.

The Telegraph's Saturday issue described *The Bird Ballet* as:

> The theatre of total influences, with echoes of all times and all environments... unfolding in a leisurely manner, occasionally making its effects but on the whole proving a negative theatrical experience.

It went on to describe the alternating dance, dialogue, music and sound effects:

> The mimetic dances of primitive peoples, shadow plays, the masked dramas of the Far East and even music-hall backchat all merge to create something curiously reminiscent of childhood theatricals on wet afternoons.

The reviewer noticed the new and challenging feature of the production as being its lingo, citing the term 'shimmering density garment' as new jargon for the word 'coat'. This was the first ever reference in the press to the Exploding Galaxy having its own private language.

George Melly, the writer and jazz singer, although filled with rage at what he called the 'bad-tempered law' in its harsh treatment of young people, described his irritation at the hippies' mindless self-regard. He had little time for the Exploding Galaxy, condemning us in the *Sunday Times* as 'a pretty kind of rubbish'. He applauded Charles Marowitz, who had sat through two hours of *Bird Ballet*, and Charles' condemnation on the BBC2 programme *Late Night Line-Up*. George Melly wrote:

> David Medalla, leader of a dance-drama group, sat there in his pretty clothes talking the most wet rubbish (his companion remained sunk in amiable beatific silence), while an unlikely liaison between Al Alvarez and Charles Marowitz tried to pin him down to one concrete statement from which some kind of constructive dialogue could emerge. No such luck.

Further condemnation came from a review that described the ballet participants as clearly enjoying themselves immensely and totally absorbed in a production which he found to be by far and away the most boring piece of theatre he had ever witnessed.

The issue of professionalism in experimental theatre did not go away. Some years later, several ex-members of the Exploding Galaxy formed a new theatre troupe with the Incredible String Band and created a pantomime. By the time backers had been found, the String Band, whose early music was the essence of psychedelia, were heavily into Scientology. Although the storyline was supposed to be created 'democratically' the dancers' function in the end was to ornament the songs written by the String Band for their ponderous, meandering tale inspired by the Scientology concept of the U curve of human emotions. In this role, the 'technically challenged' troupe, working as

Stone Monkey, proved notably inept in the eyes of the press on both sides of the Atlantic and the show's New York producer.

The Americans, in a country where every chorus line without fail contains polished all-rounders who can act as well as they can sing as well as they can dance, had no time for an endearing absence of slickness. In the case of *U*, Joe Boyd always had misgivings. He booked the Fillmore East, where the show died a dramatic and ignominious death, with the pantomime players paid 50 dollars to catch the next flight home.

The Bird Ballet never had to face the scrutiny of a New York audience. In London, we had a largely sympathetic one, not only used to hippie incompetence, but also ideologically in favour of anything produced by UFO progeny. If they could put up with 14 hours of Ally Pally muddle, they could take three hours of *Bird Ballet*. And if not, they could skin-up, breathe in and enjoy the extraordinary assemblage of moving bird sculptures that wandered about the stage.

It didn't occur to me at the time that *The Bird Ballet* was less a theatrical show than it was a kinetic sculpture – a sculpture that, once set in motion, took an evening for its processes to run their own course. Like his mud machine, David had produced a visual construction that had its own momentum and unfolded in its own way. Perhaps this explains why it was that the photographers were the most enthusiastic fans of *The Bird Ballet*. They were the ones who came back night after night and connected most closely with the visual impact of the changing figures before them. Mitja was enchanted:

> When I saw it, everything was perfect: the sound, the props and lighting. The dancing and movement were so original and moving, enhancing and making real the story. The music was superb, exquisite and beautifully played. All of this unfolded organically, the simultaneous creative effort of all the participants. In 50 years of attending performances, this was the one that used by far the least resources. It was also the most original, creative and memorable one.

For me the show was like one of those giant knitted patchworks we bought at Hackney jumbles – not the prissy symmetrical ones in pastel colours you might find at a village needlework display, but the ragged ones produced out of poverty: clashing, lopsided and roughly stitched, but somehow constructed into a meaningful whole. From the wings at each performance, I watched attentively until it came time for me to go on. I was enchanted by the act of watching and participating. To me *The Bird Ballet* was a gift, an experience through which I learned to recognise and value my own creativity. I could see its magic permeating the greyness of straight theatre. The fact that the outside world found the show utterly forgettable was no surprise. We were, after all, trying to convert a world of centroclines.

17

The Tree of Abundance

> *... they had in common [with the Living Theatre] not only the free, swirling quality of their artistic expression, but also their communal lifestyle, which was more like that of some simple, primitive-communist sect than anything previously recognizable as appropriate to the creative and performing arts, even in their more eccentric forms of expression.*
>
> BERNARD LEVIN [1]

THE VENUE WAS Portland Place. The month was November. The Royal Institute of British Architects' winter dinner dance was based on the theme 'The Summer of Love', and this was an unusual gig for the Galaxy. A secretary called Irene had been assigned the job of looking after those performing, who included Mick Farren and his Social Deviants and Yoko Ono, but the film cameras dwelt exclusively on the writhing bodies of the Exploders who, one by one, woke up and joined in the chant: 'Food, money, sex, money, love. Food, money, sex, money, love. Food, money, sex, money, love.'

The cameras were there for a *Man Alive* documentary shoot entitled 'The World Owes Me a Living'. The programme focused on five men from different backgrounds who were living on National Assistance (Universal Credit as it is called now), who attempted to justify themselves on camera. There were two students, an actor, an ex-lavatory attendant and the poet Michael Chapman. Mike was featured because there was particular public indignation about 'work-shy people' claiming the dole and describing themselves as artists and poets. For this reason, the crew were busy shooting the Galaxy, described by the presenters as 'an artistic band of brothers and sisters'.

With the customary confidence common to all members of the Exploding Galaxy, Mike explained his role as re-educator:

> I consider that I am activating people in society instead of the old ideas – the way they are conditioned. I need the state to subsidise me for this, and for equipment as well because I need quite a bit of equipment... I have to live. If they pay other workers money, then they should pay me money.

The interviewer asked him, deadpan, why he didn't take a job and just treat the poetry as a hobby:

> My answer is that I am doing a job at the moment, which is poetry and I couldn't work and do poetry at the same time. I need to be able to go to certain places and meet different people and go through certain experiences to be able to write poetry.

Mike continued by saying that he was aware that some people would see him as lazy – a beatnik even. 'But,' he countered:

> They don't seem to realise that, in fact, their employers are just living off them. I am not living off society. I am helping society by pointing out certain things which they didn't realise before.

Of all the BBC documentary series, *Man Alive* was the most surreptitiously tabloid in its approach. Apparently sympathetic journalists hoodwinked the gullible, egging them on into making remarks that would scandalise the viewing public. After the filming was over, a couple of us sat in the car of a young journalist called Desmond Wilcox, who was conspicuously 'on our side'. Yet in the weeks to come, the outrage created by this particular documentary, along with contributions from *The People* and *News of the World*, created an atmosphere in which gangs of locals felt they had permission to attack our house, and the police felt entitled to plant drugs.

The film crew had been looking for inflammatory comments, and what Edward Pope gave them next was pure gold dust. He was seated in a pose, with a trident of woven twigs in his right hand and a wisp of gauze clipped to the top of his head. Simon sat next to him, listening attentively and nodding, naked from the waist up, except for a scrudge remnants neckpiece.

Edward said:

> The point is that in all societies where it is necessary to do this, there are always elements of mystification… if we could spend all our creative energies making food for ourselves – if we had, say, a little land in Scotland or something – we could do this very easily and make our own buildings. But we involve ourselves in the life of the city, and therefore we have to go to the National Assistance because it is like a tree. We are in the city so we have to pluck from the tree…We are trying to help the other people, trying to change the life of the other people in the city from the decadent situation that they are in.

It's ironic that Edward should say this since he had never claimed benefit in his life and had, in fact, himself been a financial benefactor to other Galaxy members.

The Exploders were not concerned about being accused of living off the state because they felt entitled to government support, but at that time, hardly any members of the Galaxy were actually receiving benefit. Months earlier, in the late spring and summer of 1967, when the house had been one of drop-out London's crash pads, with a transient population averaging a score or so at any one time, this had not been the case and the local Social Security office had refused to process applications from 99 Balls Pond Road. Those were the days, it seems, when an authority could reinvent policy on the spot in answer to a particular problem, with no need for public justification and no obligation to make it apply across the board. So a cap was placed on the numbers who could claim from one particular house – ours.

From the end of the summer of 1967 onwards, there were no more than ten or so live-ins at the house. Eve, Christian, Judith, David and John Dugger would not have qualified for benefits anyway, as they were visitors to the country. I recall that there were no more than three or so receiving the dole. These were Audrey and John Schofield, who signed on locally, and Mike Chapman, who had claimed at Palmer's Green Labour Exchange since early in 1967. Audrey, not knowing what to enter under 'Occupation' on her application form, chose to put 'Shepherdess', because in her last job she had been involved in lambing. This was considered by all to be the perfect application, because not only was it true, but it also provided a dramatic, poetic, idealised bucolic image pitched starkly against the traffic-congested setting we operated in. In addition, she was guaranteed to receive benefit since there were no jobs going for shepherdesses in the region of Dalston Junction.

Michael Chapman, who had featured in the *Man Alive* programme, turned his National Assistance experiences into kinetic dramas in which he activated both the benefit officers and those waiting, who, by the nature of the seating, were a ready-made audience for his poetry readings. These visits were turned into theatrical events by the ensuing reaction to his transformation of the dole office from its recognised purpose.

The *Man Alive* documentary did concede the fact that not everyone living at Balls Pond Road was on National Assistance, but they didn't dwell on this, nor did they give the actual numbers, which would have undermined the thrust of the programme and might have reduced the ferocity of the attacks (both physical and tabloid) that were to follow.

In fact, benefit was only one of the sources of the Galaxy's income. Far more money came through the sharing of hard-earned savings (in the case of Jane, Judith and John Dugger) and the sharing of inheritances (Edward and Rakis).

Despite these benevolent injections of cash, in the two years following my first visit to Balls Pond Road, I witnessed and participated regularly in a state of 'chosen destitution'. I say 'chosen' because, in nearly every case, Galaxy members had affluent homes waiting in the wings, chock full of food, hot water and affection. In my case, Balls Pond Road was akin to a weekend retreat, as I had to return home ready for school on Monday, but for most of the others, this was how they lived month after month. Combined expenditure was extremely low, with the only extravagance being nicotine (alcohol and dope did not figure). More often, cigarettes were obtained by picking up dog ends from the street and reconstructing the contents into roll-ups. This reduced the expense to just the cigarette papers. Our must-buy staples were whittled down to candles, paraffin, rice, tinned fish, milk, tea, bread and jam.

The Sams brothers, originally from the US, started the macrobiotic revolution here. Today they would not be considered anything but successful by establishment standards.[2] However, in 1966 the macrobiotic bookshop in New York run by Irma Paule had been raided by the FBI, urged on by the American Medical Association. Books were taken away and burned and newspaper articles called it the 'hippie death diet'. Greg and Craig Sams were perceived as having infiltrated this country as a nutritional fifth column, intent on brainwashing the British public.

Their Paddington restaurant Seed was *the* hip meeting place in the late sixties, and one of the reasons we often went there was because you could eat free if you did not have enough money to pay. Some of us brought back short-grain brown rice as a staple to Balls Pond Road and some did toy with the newly emerging awareness of alternatives in diet. However, I never saw a truly dedicated interest in this until I came across the Brazilian singer Gilberto Gil in his Chelsea home, who had adopted a fully macrobiotic diet, including chewing every mouthful 50 times.

As in many other aspects of drop-out thinking, there was considerable muddle in the house over diet and nutrition. A book that was passed reverently from one Galaxy member to another stated that tomatoes and potatoes were related to deadly nightshade. I am not sure what conclusion was drawn from this, but an interest in the notion that 'you are what you eat', although vehemently discussed, never truly found its way into practice, since when there was money about, the lure of monosodium glutamate and saturated fat beckoned in the form of Chinese takeaways and West End curry houses. The belief in wholemeal, wholesome and vegetarian lived happily alongside our basic diet, which largely amounted to greasy-spoon fry-ups with lashings of tea bought on tick from the caff a few doors up. We did eat fruit and vegetables, but this was because they could be easily scavenged, not because we were nutritionally conscious.

What saved our health was the presence of a street market in Kingsland Road. Stall-holders were obliged to leave what they dropped. Much of what landed in the gutters was damaged or part-rotted, but there was more than enough to give us the vitamins and roughage we needed. Our 'shopping' bags were string vegetable sacks marked with importers' labels. We cut the bruised bits off the vegetables and cooked the remainder with stock cubes to make soup or with fiery spices to make a more filling stew. Pilchards were a cheap source of protein, and so pilchard curry, cooked by David, was a regular at the house.

Christian, deeply frustrated by the English notion of cuisine, would occasionally swoop in with a leg of lamb and herbs, which he would share, and we would enjoy something akin to a Sunday roast. However, there was not a single occasion in the two years I was around that I witnessed anything raw such as grated carrot or lettuce being put on a plate.

Audrey, being a farmer's daughter, planted wheat in the garden with a view to producing her own bread. This was overly optimistic, given the size of the garden, but it fitted with the concept of transformation and, no doubt, had it ever come to the point of harvest, the straw would have been evolved into scrudges.

The nearby Turkish baker produced giant round loaves, and whenever one of these delightful warm and yeasty mounds was brought into the kitchen, people would appear from nowhere like starving orphans and it would be gone in a trice. The live-in bread buyers accepted the cadging amicably and remained generous the whole time they lived in that house. My pocket money had to cover bus fares from Putney to Dalston as well as anything I consumed at the weekend, and after being stung a couple of times for large orders of spring rolls, I wised up. I noticed that, while the cadgers thought it all very fair, they failed to buy loaves or a round of egg and chips themselves even when they had their own sources of money.

This produced a particular dilemma for the beautiful people. The idea itself was sensible enough: those who were the 'haves' should give some of what they had to the 'have-nots'. This should have worked perfectly well, but some of the 'have-nots' turned out to be 'haves' after all. The problem was that even once you realised this, you were not supposed to mind.

Any selfishness you might perceive in others had to be cushioned by your own lack of materialism. Some people could do this easily and saw no exploitation. I was not one of them. When food was scarce, people became even more territorial about their space in the house, and one person even took to squirrelling away his food supply in a box by his bed. This was reminiscent of the Georgians who lived in shared houses and used boxes like safes. Since this was a Georgian house that was shared, it seems fitting that our way of life was more Regency than post-Second World War.

The only furious row I ever remember in the house was over food – in fact, a jar of marmalade – that had been secretly stashed and subsequently found and tucked into. The accused insisted that they were falsely accused, but there was a dilemma here regardless of the issue of accusation or guilt. Since there was no set of behavioural policies for any of the communes I knew of, everyone carried around their own individual values that, they were convinced, had been adopted or should be adopted by everyone else. So, in the argument over whether it was fair to hide food, both sides were equally right.

Having said this, the sense that we were living the right way far outweighed any trivial injustices.

Those of us who had homes to go to could top up on calories, and as a weekend Galaxy member, I never went hungry. I must sometimes have looked destitute, though: an American tourist, on coming across me in the Portobello Road in bare feet and a Rajasthani skirt, insisted on paying for a slap-up meal before depositing me back on the pavement. I did not let on that I was, in all probability, richer than him and that my ragged look was a fashion choice rather than evidence of the survival of Dickensian London.

For those whose homes were not in London, times were tough. Jane Ellis describes how sumptuous her own bed felt when she at last went back to Sunderland:

> After all that time sleeping on floors and under coats, it was a luxury to slip into my own bed at home on a soft mattress with clean sheets under a warm cover.

Looking back, Andrew puzzles long and hard about how he managed to survive on zero. He remembers scrounging cigarettes on the tube and regularly visiting Kingsland Road market to pick up discarded vegetables, but beyond this he was unable to remember how he supported himself without the help of Social Security. In 1967/68, he became dangerously thin, and on a trip to his home in Colchester, his emaciated state caused great anxiety. His father, who was an army doctor, took one look at the skin and bones arriving through the front door and diagnosed severe malnutrition. Andrew's weight had gone down to eight stone, and it was at this point that he re-evaluated whether he really wanted to continue at the house.

Had everyone struggled as Andrew did while at Balls Pond Road, the dire poverty at the house would have been more apparent and life as a commune could not have continued. The fact was that many Galaxy members felt able to tap into outside sources, including affluent parents or visits to significant others who were working, and this masked the unsustainability and unreality of living at 99 Balls Pond Road. In principle, Exploding Galaxy members liked the idea of being supported by National Assistance because they believed that art should be state-funded and because they felt convinced they were providing an essential service to society, but the trickle of benefit that came in was rather less than it would have been for other groups of young adults at the time. The Galaxy would be more accurately described as self-funded (for example, later on, Judith gave private flute lessons to bring in money) or funded by private benefactors and sympathisers. Had everyone been on benefit as the tabloids stated, there would have been enough money to replace the bucket in the kitchen with a new sink or to pay off the bills and get the longed-for hot water running again.

Following *Man Alive*, the public's opinion of the Exploding Galaxy as spongers caused untold hostility. There followed a copycat article in *The People* with the headline: 'FREE clothes, FREE love – but YOU pay.' The article quoted Gerald Fitzgerald as saying, 'None of us believe in any kind of straight work,' and it said that those who refused to work should be served with what they described as the 'parasite law', and should be sent to labour camps and forced to work as in Russia.

The evening dinner dance at the Royal Institute of British Architects turned out to be a disaster for its organisers. John Schofield describes the scene:

> They were a bunch of rugby-playing architects and there was a lot of alcohol. The whole purpose of the evening had been a gigantic piss-up and here they were having to face all this hippy nonsense, which must have been how they saw it. While Simon was trying to read his lovely poems, they just poured beer over him.

At the end of the evening, two items were found to be missing from the premises. One was a Gladstone bag owned by the evening's organiser and the other was a diner's fur coat, which turned out to be mink and was last seen dancing down the road around the shoulders of a certain David Medalla. The secretary called Irene was sent to 99 Balls Pond Road the next day to retrieve the missing items. She was invited in for a cup of tea and never went home. As things turned out, she had run away to join our circus.

NOTES

1. Bernard Levin in *The Pendulum Years: Britain and the Sixties* (Pan, 1970).
2. They opened the first natural foods store and manufactured organic foods under the Whole Earth brand. Greg invented the original VegeBurger and Craig co-founded Green & Black's chocolate.

18

Flight to Lowlands Paradise

Every one of us became a walking justification of his own life, and honesty became a necessity for those who wished to inspire others with the creative way of life. You might see one of us on a bus, wearing clothes that could be called neither respectable nor bohemian, but you might call them bizarre were it not for the sense in them, or you might call them jokes were they not also full of inventive imagination. By changing their purpose, like wearing a cushion for a hat, or turning an umbrella into a newspaper, or a bus into a church, one penetrates the pretence that life is humdrum, and comes to see one's own life transformed into a part of the life of the imagination.

EDWARD POPE [1]

I REMEMBER FILMS from the forties and fifties that featured an austere-looking secretary in horn-rimmed spectacles, her hair scraped back into a severe little bun and fastened with a hair pin. In saunters Philip Marlowe, or the man from *77 Sunset Strip*, who knows what's what, and slowly and deliberately he takes off her specs and releases the hairpin. Down all her tresses swish and the transformation astonishes. This is a very rough approximation of the complete transformation that took place when straight little miss secretary Irene from the Royal Institute of British Architects joined the Exploding Galaxy. Perhaps it would be closer to compare her with Eliza Doolittle, having to learn a whole new language in a hurry. In this case, Professor Higgins was Gerald Fitzgerald.

Soon after her arrival at Balls Pond Road, Fitz saw her sitting on some density grass (the fake grass used to cover market stalls) and gave her a new name – Uisce Bó, Irish Gaelic for 'water cow'. It was at around this point that Fitz started working on his *Orange and Blue*

Kinetegram, describing the transformation of a centroclinal woman into a fully quaquaversal being. It is unclear which came first, the arrival of Uisce Bó or the seeds of the script, but no one could fail to notice the similarities between this work and Uice Bó's metamorphosis into a fully activated Galaxy member.

Two hip names hit my consciousness in the autumn of 1967. One was the painter Bunk Bessel, who had introduced himself to the Galaxy at a performance of *The Bird Ballet*. I had known about the Dutch Provos from a big feature about them in the *Sunday Times*. They were the young trouble-makers who created the 'White Bicycle' scheme and dreamt up imaginative non-violent 'white' stings and false leads to wrong-foot the authorities. They had already tricked the border police into believing that a large consignment of dog food was cannabis and had started a rumour that the Amsterdam water supply was about to be spiked with LSD. To the London freaks, they were wildly cool, and one of their number was Bessel, who was now inviting us to a massive happening in Utrecht in November.

The other name I came across was Jean-Jacques Lebel, artist, maker of happenings and translator of the Beat poets into French. In the summer of 1967 he had worked with The Soft Machine (who came to be known in France as Le Soft) and had produced Picasso's obscure and plotless play, *Le Désir attrappé par la queue*. He now had plans for the first large-scale all-nighter happening in France.

A meeting was called to resolve the issue of who was going to join the tour – first to Paris and then to Utrecht. Meetings were of extreme importance in Galaxy life and were taken seriously no matter how wacky the people present and no matter how bizarre the propositions put forward. It was at times like this that Paul Keeler's presence was needed. He had the kind of authority that was acceptable to everyone, no matter how far they had flung the rule book. He was the only person for whom there was universal respect and about whom there was little behind-backs bitching.

The problem was this: it was all very well to say that everyone could be and was in the Exploding Galaxy. This had been declared on several occasions. 'Everyone' could mean everyone present in a park or at a gig or indeed everyone in the world. Since Exploding Galaxy members got into gigs free, it was true to say that there were large numbers of self-declared Galaxy practitioners who had never set foot in 99 Balls Pond Road. But as far as the tour was concerned, there was a finite fee to be divided and limited tickets for travel. Certain people ruled themselves out, such as the Fuzzy-Gigglies, because they no longer involved themselves in the explorations. Of the acid casualties, Brian was nowhere to be found and Leighana had announced that she was going back to Texas to kill her mother. Galaxy regulars Gwendolyn, Herzmark and Rag Doll had left to join The Human Family, and Melinda was fast sliding towards the merciless world of smack – she had long since lost interest in Galaxy productions and had left the house with no desire for even a short sojourn away from her source of supply. Uisce Bó, as the newcomer, was not invited along and I opted not to go as I had to sit for my mock O levels just before the end of term. Always the square, I was the one who had not ever tried acid and who, when it came to the most exciting gigs in Europe, watched with my nose pressed against the window pane because I had chosen not to come out to play. I was the biggest centrocline of them all, and I put myself through the further agonising experience of accompanying Eve to a seedy little office in Denmark Street, while she got measured up by some man for costumes. It never occurred to us at the time that only the Galaxy women were being called in to be measured and that there would be no costumes anyway, since we wore our own paraphernalia called scrudges.

And so it was that in that November of 1967, in sandals, bedroom slippers or bare feet, their luggage no more than a collection of cardboard boxes, carpet tubes and fabric remnants rescued from the bins of London's light industries, the Exploding Galaxy set off on a Sally Line ferry for their first foreign tour.

The Paris window gig, 'La Fenêtre rose', was held at the newly built Palais des Sports, similar in style and capacity to the Festival Hall. There were two problems with the gig. First, the auditorium had fixed seating. Happenings could successfully take place in a traditional theatre layout – the Theatre Royal Stratford East and the Jeannetta Cochrane Theatre were examples – but it severely curtailed possibilities. Underground venues were, typically, warehouses or other industrial buildings. The second problem was with the French freaks, who sat, row after row, swigging from flagons of red wine. They had long hair all right, but they dressed without imagination and they did not seem to have a handle on the peace and love thing.

IT described the French response to the imminent psychedelic event:

> The French reaction to this is, so far, somewhat bewildered. The idea of thousands of people coming together to have what amounts to a large pop party with dozens of top performers and an audience as much performers as the performers themselves, is new to France.[2]

These same 'bewildered' Parisians would be making another kind of happening in and around the Sorbonne in a few months' time. Love-ins seemed to sit more comfortably in London and California. By the time the fluffy flowery stuff was eventually exported across the Channel, the whole love and peace thing had been trashed by commerce.

It was the night of 17 November 1967 and it was time for the Galaxy to go onstage, but the management had cocked up. By the time the call came through, the Exploders had been due on 'minutes ago'. The dressing room was a very long walk from the stage so they had to sprint into position.

Then it happened. With the spotlight fixed on him and dressed as an archbishop in a mitre, Fitz walked down the central aisle of the auditorium, chanting e-numbers. A procession moved down through the rows of chairs with the cardboard 'coffin' found in a Soho rubbish pile. The anti-Church message, beamed out loud and clear, was not wasted on the largely Catholic audience. They were ecstatic. On the stage, David Medalla was prancing his *mudras*, and our performance of the ballet *Krishna Lila* had begun. Rakis and Malcolm did their powerful chariot hops across the stage. These were a direct copy of what they had seen in *Khatakali* theatre: both dancers hopping together, but one representing the rider and one the horse-drawn chariot. Meanwhile, Christian walked among the audience. He had found a 'Le Figaro' apron. This was what the vendors of that right-wing rag wore when they were selling on street corners. Christian had also found a piece of broken mirror in the street and was holding it up to random individuals, showing them their own reflections, as if to say 'look at yourself'.

There was something much slicker and more confident about the performance this time. The fact that no one was on an acid trip helped tremendously. John Schofield remembers:

> By the time I went to the Palais des Sports, we had kind of developed a rhythm section. Paul Keeler had found this great big cardboard tube that had been used as a middle of a carpet roll, from a flooring warehouse. It was about six inches in diameter and about six feet long. He made that into a drum. I had a few African drums – not particularly good ones. I don't remember where I got them from. I just acquired a couple of drums. Paul was bass drummer and I was the tenor drum. Judith was the flute player. So we were the music section on the tour.

Andrew had lost his timidity. When newly recruited, this ex-Savoy trainee chef had been asked during *The Bird Ballet* to understudy everybody in the cast. He did this without ever having been to a single rehearsal or knowing anything about the plot line. Worse, he had never even so much as graced the back row of a school play in his life. It was no wonder, therefore, that he had been terrified when Malcolm needed cover one evening. He had been asked to stand in not only as the toucan and the peregrine falcon but also as a disease and snow. Now, Andrew became experimental. To find his costume he went scrudging in the streets of Paris. He found some discarded canisters of 35mm film and quantities of autumn leaves:

> This girl seduced me, and she gave me some cotton and sewing things to put it together. I made a necklace from the strips of film which cascaded down to the ground. The autumn leaves were sewn into it too. I had this massive cloak of leaves and 35mm film, and when the spotlights hit, I was shimmering in front of the crowd and I felt enormous pride at the organic leaves reflecting the autumn and the flashing, sparkling film reflecting the light.

For the river in the ballet *Krishna Lila*, we always used long stretches of sari cloth held at each end by squatting Galaxy members, and the sari was made to ripple and twist as if in flow. (We also nicked this idea from the Kathakali dance troupe.) Andrew was the ripple in the river, exquisitely good-looking with his golden locks, as he danced about stark naked beside the swishing sari under his sparkling strips of celluloid.

This was the Exploding Galaxy at its best. As near to polished as it would ever be, utterly emblematic of the London freak movement in its defiance of any *-ism* except eclecticism.

The weekend of 'La Fenêtre rose' – the night of 17/18 November 1967 – coincided almost exactly with Harold Wilson's announcement that the pound was to be devalued. That week the British nation looked on with dismay at the headlines. Since the Exploding Galaxy was always unerringly at odds with national sentiment, it seems fitting that this was the precise time when they had never felt richer. Paul, who was trusted not only as the eyes and ears of the Galaxy but also as the group's banker, handed each performer a crisp 50-franc note, roughly equivalent to £20. This was good money in the 1960s – if your weekly wage was £20 in 1967, you weren't badly off by our standards. Galactic life was a life of destitution, albeit chosen destitution. This was the group's first ever serious fee for a performance, and Galaxy members were now flush with money, invited to chic parties and fêted by smart Paris, and offered any number of crash pads and seductions.

The Paris experience was not without its downside. There was a meal out that led to a Galaxy-wide food poisoning episode – a kinetic drama of non-stop vomiting lasting several days. Then there was the moment when Rakis was deprived of his hard-earned fee:

> Paul had handled all the money and had given us each one of these big notes – 50 francs. The Palais des Sports was in the Port de Versailles, in a down-at-heel area, with all these heavy sports bars around. We were really hungry so Malcolm and I went to this rough-looking place in all our finery. I paid with the 50 note, but got change for a note of 10. I noticed and made a squawk, but the bar tender just gave me a beefy shrug and his big friends just stood there. He didn't give us the money back. I forget if it was old francs or new francs, but to us then, it was a fortune.

Cannabis played virtually no part in Galaxy life at that time, and there was a strict rule about bringing drugs into the house, but we looked differently on acid when it was used when we were out and about. There had been occasions like the Warwick University gig when performance and acid trip coincided, and so it did not seem odd that John Schofield should spend some of his birthday money on a bulk purchase of acid tabs for the Galaxy tour.

> For my 21st birthday the previous month, I got a cheque for £21 from my mum. By that time the trip to the Palais des Sports and the 'Flight to Lowlands Paradise' had been organised and I had been invited to go along, so I spent £14 of my £21 birthday money on buying 40 acid tabs. I just told people if you want a trip I've got a little tin box, and by the time we set off for Utrecht, there were 35 acid trips left.

They went through Belgium, and at the Belgian–Dutch border, two customs guys got on the train and said, 'Right, everyone, we want you all off the train here.' It was just a little border station. They said, 'Could all the women please go in this room, and all the men in that one? We'll come back and see you soon.' Schofield got worried:

> I thought, Oh God, we're going to get searched. So I started getting worried with this tin burning a hole in my pocket, so I said, 'Look, I've got 35 acid tabs here and I think we should get rid of them. So if anyone wants to take one – you might have to take two or three each.'

Fitz refused, as did David and Paul. Quite a few other people turned down the offer. Schofield understood that this was a big favour he was asking, but the low take-up meant that others would have to consume the extra. In the end, there were about five or six of the Galaxy men and a couple of hangers-on who agreed to 'get rid' of the 35 tabs. Rakis took his share, as did Simon. Malcolm was cautious after the Ruy episode, so only took two. Andrew Forrest took three (this was his first-ever acid trip). Schofield took the remaining seven or eight. He recalls:

> We swallowed the whole lot, silver foil and all to get rid of all the evidence. I breathed a huge sigh of relief when the final one had gone. Then the customs guys came into the room with a big clipboard and said, 'Right, we need to know how much money you have because we can't let you into the country if you can't support yourselves.' And, of course, Paul had got loads of cash from the Palais des Sports, so he just kind of produced this money and the customs guys said, 'Oh well, that's fine. There'll be a train along in ten minutes.' So, after all that, there was no search.

It took about another hour to get to Utrecht, and those who had taken the acid started getting more and more 'swirly colours' after about 30 minutes. The sun was setting over the Dutch marshes – a beautiful sight – and they stood at the window watching that. The men were flying by this time. When they got to Utrecht, it was almost like a civic reception. There were lots of press people there, and as the Exploders got off the train, they were greeted like rock stars. People were taking photos and asking for press conferences. The newly arrived troupe were totally off their faces, so just stood there smiling.

The Exploding Galaxy's arrival appeared to be a highly rehearsed, well-prepared performance. The waiting posse of Dutch press were impressed by the choreography: the Galaxy women walked forward purposefully in a coherent line towards the welcoming party, while the Galaxy men dawdled their way or stopped as if distracted. Some even retraced their steps or turned to walk in the opposite direction towards the far end of the platform. Among them, Andrew – on his first acid trip multiplied by three – was high up on stilts, in his wax-spattered civil defence coat, striding about in any and every direction.

The 'Flight to Lowlands Paradise' is now an annual festival with ten stages and 200 acts. It pulls in top international bands and crowds of 60,000 or more – the Dutch version of Glastonbury. It is held at the right time of year – August – and at the right location: a vast campsite near Amsterdam. The two original 'Flights' were held at the butt end of the year and were dogged by organisational problems. The second 'Flight', in 1968, was beset with difficulties, due to a change of date in a bid to book Jimi Hendrix. The first 'Flight', by contrast, had fewer known names, although Arthur Brown and the Social Deviants played, as well as the band known as the Dutch Pink Floyd, The Zipps. Apart from these, the 18 hours were padded out with body painting, poetry, massage and experimental theatre – several people remarked at the incongruity of having traditional Dutch clog dancers on the same bill as the extremely experimental approach of a guitarist called Sha. It cost 10 guilders to get in, and if the very unlikely estimate of a crowd of 10,000 is true, someone made a lot of money that evening.

If the 'Fenêtre rose' venue had been unsuitable because it was too obviously a theatre, this venue was doubly wrong but in an entirely different way. The vast aircraft hangar of a building, now known for its international winter fair, was a cross between Earls Court, Olympia and Fairfield Halls in Croydon. This was far too large a space for the likely numbers prepared to part with 10 guilders per head to see dubious fringe acts with no massive-draw pop names. If Paris had been the high point, Utrecht was to be the low one. Rakis remembers:

> We'd been on the road a long time and had been sick with diarrhoea in Paris and then we'd all dropped this huge amount of acid. Malcolm and I could see that it was becoming more Fitz's troupe and we didn't like the way he explored ideas.

> The whole Dutch experience of the 'Flight to Lowlands Paradise' was not a pleasant one. Arthur Brown was there, but even the music didn't sound good. Maybe it was the hall. It was a stark huge space with no warmth at all.
>
> At that time, people had a very romantic view of the provos – the white bicycles and all that. Malc and I had been billeted with this leading provo. He had this stupid girlfriend who was really suburban, who wore proper dresses and stockings and shoes with straps. Nobody did that in those days. I remember the sterile little flat and this sterile little girlfriend. Amsterdam was a great disappointment. Everything was kind of phony and hollow. After that, everyone just went their own way. Everyone just said: 'See you in London, man.'

To top it all, the promised fee did not materialise. Paul did his best, trying to evoke a sense of fair play. At one point, the hippie Paul even said to the wad-carrying anarchist impresario, 'This isn't cricket.' Needless to say, we went away empty-handed.

By Utrecht, serious cracks had begun to appear between the group's two leaders. Judith describes the difference in style between David Medalla and Gerald Fitzgerald:

> David had a knack of recognising the strong and creative qualities in the people around him and letting them express that and allowing that to be a part of what he was creating. It was very interesting how he was able to work with people... This was almost exactly the opposite of Fitz. Fitz was more conceptual and directive so Fitz would have the characteristic of correcting what he didn't think should be there and David would have the characteristic of using what was there to fit into what he was doing, so the contrast between the two is interesting.

It was by now impossible to gloss over this extreme difference in approach, and it was becoming clear that neither of the artists had much time for the other. There was no open warfare between the two men, but it was fairly obvious that there was a growing coolness. From then on, what took place in any performance tended to be two completely different styles of kinetic drama, lumped together under the label 'Exploding Galaxy performance'.

It was while on tour in the Netherlands that key members of the Galaxy drifted away. Simon decided to go walkabout and set off to travel to Afghanistan and beyond. He left unannounced, and the shock of his loss was felt instantly. Malcolm and Rakis left at this time, too.

A week into the stay in the Netherlands, the Exploding Galaxy were back to their status quo: in other words, a state of perpetual hunger. The setting was a different, harsher one, lacking the cohesive cosy comfort of a shared home and the ready food source provided by vegetables dropped at the nearby market.

As November moved into December, the anticlimax was palpable. Sleeping on floors under coats had been fine in the warmer months but was difficult to cope with when temperatures dipped down below zero. The 'Summer of Love' had really ended and the penniless troupe were bracing themselves for the harshness to come. Nothing could have prepared us, though, for just how coldly unjust events would turn out to be for the Exploders in the year following that *annus psychedelicus* of 1967.

NOTES

1. *Planted*, a report compiled by Paul Keeler, 1968.
2. *International Times*, issue 21, 17 November, 1967.

19

Liverpool Eight

We were all on this ship in the sixties, our generation, a ship going to discover the New World. And the Beatles were in the crow's nest of that ship.

JOHN LENNON

BY DECEMBER 1967, London's two key hippie arts venues had come into their own. The Roundhouse had enjoyed its first theatrical run. Unfortunately for Arnold Wesker, the production was by his least favourite troupe – the Exploding Galaxy – but the old brick building was becoming recognisably more of a theatre space and less of a freezing and hazardous railway shed, although it was still largely booked for one-offs.

Jim Haynes' Arts Lab had been up and running for some months. Its particular success can be put down to the new formula of mixing social space and performance space within an arts centre, and also the fact that, as a shell and not a formal theatre or gallery, it could be transformed at virtually no financial cost. In addition, the *IT* listings column released the management from having to pay for costly press adverts. Free listings were to be the single most important factor in developing experimentation in the performing arts at that time because they produced audiences without any outlay. The Arts Lab was to be the first of many arts centres that provided viable opportunities to produce near budget-free works that were truly experimental. Jim Haynes describes one of his favourite productions as *Tea with Miss Gentry*:

> I knew someone who lived down the street called Miss Gentry; I didn't know how old she was but she was up in her years and she had been a hat

designer for theatrical productions. She lived in a little room about four or five flights up and just loved to talk.

So we'd chalk this sign up saying '*Tea with Miss Gentry*' and sell about ten tickets, then put up a sold-out sign. Then ten people would be led down Drury Lane and up these rickety stairs to Miss Gentry's flat. I would knock on the door and say, 'Miss Gentry, your guests are here,' and I would lead in these ten surprised individuals, who had no idea what they were going to see or do, and place them in her sitting-room where she would serve them tea and talk about her life. It was a very big success – one of our longest running productions – because she loved it.[1]

A feature of Jim's personality was that, if you said to him, 'Do you choose yes or no?', he would most likely choose yes. Combined with this was the fact that there were several talents working with him at the Arts Lab able to turn it into one of the world's most exciting and experimental arts venues. Jack Henry Moore had created a theatre space that could be transformed in minutes, and it was to become the home venue of his troupe, The Human Family. Dave Curtis ran a basement cinema-with-no-seats, and Biddy Peppin ran the art gallery programme with Pamela Zoline. It seemed that anyone could suggest an idea and it would be given a chance.

Biddy had been artistically active from early on and had been a great fan of Fitz's work since her Slade days. She chose his work as the Arts Lab's launch exhibition: 'The Evolving Documents Show'.[2] This turned into a Galaxy free-for-all with Exploders graffiti-ing the walls.

Not long after the Arts Lab opened, Yoko Ono approached Biddy. John Lennon had produced an artwork and she wanted to know whether it could be displayed in the gallery. No one in their right mind would say no to John and Yoko. John had been to art college, and most people knew his drawings from *John Lennon in His Own Write*, so he was already respected as an artist, but this piece was different – it was an *objet trouvé*: a drawer with the back part missing.

Biddy liked challenges and, of course, would love to display a Beatle sculpture – this would be a first. However, there were certain problems. One was the strict instruction that under no circumstances could it be made known that John Lennon was the creator of this work. The second was the fact that the Arts Lab contained no plinths or display cases. Over the course of a week, large amounts of debris would accumulate, and so it was likely that an old drawer with its back missing would be mistaken for rubbish. Biddy's solution was to give the piece its own space, but to have someone guard it at all times – a hippie guarding a broken drawer. The exhibit remained there for several weeks, and eventually it got out that this was John Lennon's artwork, so of course, it was regarded with suitable reverence.

Mike Chapman regularly gave readings there and suggested a mud event to Jim Haynes, who this time regretted saying yes. Mike remembers:

> I once organised a mud-in at the Arts Lab in Drury Lane and commissioned Graham Stevens to make me a large inflatable mud bath, into which I deposited one ton of prime earth. The one-metre-high pool was placed in the foyer and was slowly filled from a hosepipe to produce a thick muddy paste. The event was accompanied by a recording of the *Hippopotamus Song* by Flanders and Swann. Anyone around was invited to take off their clothes and jump into the mixture to enjoy the experience.

The event ended with mud splattered in generous quantities all over the floor, walls and ceiling of the reception area. Jim Haynes was furious and announced to Mike that he was now 'top of his shit list'.

The Exploding Galaxy was booked for the Architectural Association's Christmas Ball at the Roundhouse. With key members of the troupe still abroad, especially David Medalla, we were a leaner group, but were enough of a crowd to make an impact. The two explorations for the evening were led by Fitz and Malcolm, who were polar opposites in both temperament and artistic approach. Malcolm had dreamed up a caveman-discovering-fire ballet. Fitz, in contrast, read out his 'Players Number Six' poem. This consisted of descriptions from the cigarette vouchers catalogue.

It was on this occasion at the Roundhouse that three of us, among the younger ones in the group, decided to take our first trip. The acid was definitely good Sandoz Pharmaceuticals quality – the real

McCoy, not your average street acid. But we were impatient, and having waited twice the allotted time for it to take effect and finally believing we had been given duds, we downed the three remaining tabs. Then, almost immediately, *whoosh!*

Architects could be relied on to produce a good theme park setting for a ball. Eight-foot models of playing-card royals towered over us – the King of Clubs, the Jack of Hearts and so forth. A stage was set up to one side of the circular cobbled turntable, with a gantry above and a gang plank for the psychedelic lighting. Onstage were some cowgirl strippers dancing topless. The underground bosses always did that, hauling in professional girls for some glamour and titillation. They did that at UFO, too, paying go-go girls in lurex to waggle their bottoms at the audience between bands. It always seemed so straight to me, so unhip.

Rainbow-eyed, I approached Joe Boyd, who was standing with the cool crowd watching the striptease. In his hand was a tangerine, which he had been peeling. I snatched the fruit and plunged the segments into my mouth. The intensity of their taste was more gorgeous than any tangerine I had ever known. Barefoot on the freezing December cobbles, I felt no cold. At some point, I came adrift from my friends and floated up the wooden steps to the balcony and looked down on the party. Then the terrors started. Two concerned young men with faux afros approached, the drug turning their faces into demon masks. I tried to climb the balustrade on to the gantry gangplank above the writhing pit below, screaming for my friends. The lottery that decided whether you live or are taken out as an acid statistic went my way that night, and I found myself back with my Galaxy, waiting to make my entrance as 'rain'. My costume was what I had been wearing all evening: a thirties Jean Harlow-style off-the-shoulder jumble gown. It was translucent and cut on the cross so it clung tightly to my body as far as the knee, where it suddenly flared and kicked out in swirls at each step.

Jocelyn was worrying about professionalism again, thinking that the acid would affect our performance. She had no need to worry.

Cavewoman, also tripping, was grunting brilliantly, and as Rain, I swished and writhed my way across the floor – a 16-year-old virgin on acid in a see-through frock, extinguishing the fire that Caveman had just discovered. The Exploding Galaxy went down a storm that night.

Post-first-acid-trip, my treating life as a total artistic exploration intensified. The two strongest sensory memories I have are of the Beatles' *Magical Mystery Tour*, which was a permanent audio backdrop that month, and the posters of the experimental artist Peter Max, who used a split fountain technique, which allowed him to blend inks at the moment they went through the rollers. He described this as playing the printing press like an electric organ. The resulting effect – vintage photographs splashed with extravagances of colour – delighted my newly heightened state of awareness.

My LSD experience had strengthened my ability to see the extraordinary in the ordinary. Now, my clothes were getting wilder. I had graduated from mini-skirts to a semi-circle of grey army blanket attached at the front with a kilt pin. I now added a new scrudge – a wheel taken from a pre-war dolly's pram and suspended by knotted quarter-inch knicker elastic so that it bounced at my hip. A few months later, on a visit to see the Brazilian artist Sérgio de Camargo at his flat in Paris, he and his wife Aspasia asked me what its significance was. I was unable to say, apart from that I liked the way it moved as I walked along. As a 16-year-old, I was a good listener to evaluations of the aesthetics of objects taken out of their everyday context, but when it came to proposing ideas that could be taken seriously as 'artworks', I had neither the life experience nor the reading under my belt to justify my choices. Nor was I an artist – but then everyone was an artist, weren't they? I just generally got into the spirit of the thing, making absolutely no attempt to make myself look sexy. My new style ideas pushed this to the limit. I took to wearing a Mary Whitehouse-type hat because its artificial petals blew about randomly in the wind.[3] These hats were typical of middle-aged women, hugging the head firmly to set off their methylene-blue-rinse perms. The Queen

Mother wore these head-hugging bubble hats with above-the-knee outfits on official visits, as I remember. They were hideous.

The Exploding Galaxy as a group sneered derisively at any contemporary performers other than themselves, and this included the London Beats and the Liverpool Scene. One Galaxy observer has even gone as far as saying that we were only prepared to commend dead artists, composers and poets. Whatever the truth of this, there was no mistaking our overt contempt for other performers as we sat waiting our turn. We could be jaw-droppingly arrogant. I can remember times when it was really shame-making to be present at gigs where the Exploding Galaxy, either as performers or as audience, disapproved of the set-up or medium. If we disapproved of an event, which was frequently (since we were the only ones who understood the true aesthetic nature of performance), we would mutter to each other about linear thinking. I remember feeling uncomfortable at these moments, especially when the Liverpool poets were on. I had bought *Underdog* magazine and *The Mersey Sound* anthology and really liked the scouser humour. There was a pop-directnesss in their poems that I connected with. Trapped as I was in my middle-class bubble, I could not then have formulated the thought that they were a genuine challenge to the privileged elite's stranglehold on the arts.

Mike Chapman was happy to read his poems anywhere. However, he was nearly always overlooked by organisers and poets on the regular Beat circuit. He therefore felt completely entitled to usurp the programme at the gigs he attended. He recalls:

> I would get angry at not being invited to any official readings and would sometimes interrupt scheduled poetry events, such as the Liverpool poets, Adrian Henri, Brian Patten, Roger McGough. I would just get up on the stage and demand my democratic right to address the audience, much to the dismay of the other poets, especially after the roars of approval from the public.

Mike was not alone in believing in his own artistic superiority. He has pinned it down as 'a sense of self-importance (missionary – save the world type of thing), which eventually seemed to become on occasions, self-righteousness'. In the Exploding Galaxy, we really did all believe that we were the only valid form of artistic expression out there, and so we had no qualms about our lack of respect and diplomacy towards other acts.

My friend Kath had been in a six-month relationship with one of the Liverpool creatives. His name was Brian and he performed regularly on the poetry circuit and had gained an international reputation for the childlike innocence of his verses. The relationship had deteriorated, because according to Kath he had only remained interested while she was aloof and ethereal. She rang me on Boxing Day. There was nothing aloof or ethereal about her desperation to join him in Liverpool for a few days. A couple of us hitched up with her as moral support, arranging to stay at Adrian Henri's place in Canning Street, while Kath stayed with her poet in a bedsit around the corner.

'Why do you have to go today, so soon after Christmas?' My dad sounded disappointed and uncomprehending, resigned to the loss of one of his daughters during the Christmas break. As I left the house, I could hear Stravinski's *Les Noces* blaring from the upstairs bedroom.

We looked extraordinary: three leggy young women, dressed like mad but beautiful hippie bag ladies, standing on the slip road to the M1 with our thumbs up, showing a card displaying the word 'Liverpool'.

They say, 'Start as you mean to go on,' and our start in Liverpool 8, after we had been plonked on to a street corner near the Anglican cathedral, was a six-year-old 'mucky kid' approaching us, sticking his face up towards us threateningly and shouting, 'Smash yer face in!' We were going to be in for a lot of scouse pie for the next few days. It is hard to describe just how rundown and shabby Liverpool 8 was in the late sixties, having been through all that bombing. One of my sister's schoolfriends, who went on to do her degree at Liverpool University, described the city as a bomb site ruled by scary children. During her time there, this same schoolfriend had the extraordinary experience of being knocked to the ground by two girls, both under 10.

Our billet was cold indoors as out. Adrian Henri's place was a giant three or four story early Victorian terrace in Canning Street, with open fires but no central heating. On the wall as you walked up the stairs was a large canvas with a real dead pigeon painted into the surface.

One of the big differences between the Galaxy and this new crowd, was the frequenting of pubs. The Exploders had no money for drink and generally looked down on the consumption of alcohol. We stuck to soft drinks, Turkish coffee Dalston-style or black tea – buckets of the stuff. There were two fashionable pubs in Liverpool: the Philharmonic and O'Connor's. I noticed that the men would not walk with us, even though we were staying at their place. It was like some parts of Asia, where men and women walk in separate groups. This particular section of Liverpool's hip crowd seemed somewhat segregated, gender-wise, but once in the 'Phili', they would talk to us. They asked me why I wore what I wore and why I chose to put on old ladies' granny lace-up heels that looked like orthopaedic shoes. They clearly preferred minis worn with thigh-high boots.

When a young child draws a picture of a tree, the trunk is long and significant, topped by tiny near-invisible leaves almost off the page. To my patronising mind, this was how some of the scouser intellectuals saw us women – long and significant legs dominating, with a prominent slit nestling at the junction, topped by giant breasts and the tiniest of near-invisible heads and faces almost off the page. Encounters between the genders seemed much like those famous Christmas Day football matches at the front during the First World War – a bit of a romp between the trenches/sheets at an agreed time, with everyone scurrying back to defensive positions as soon as the final whistle blew.

Kath's first faux pas was to wear her bloke's Afghan jacket to go down to the shops. It was made from uncured sheepskins and it had a distinctive embroidered pattern (they were all slightly different). Everyone knew it as his property, and as Kath walked down to the corner shop, it became a flag advertising to the whole local area that she was his girl. This was an uncool thing to have done. Brian was irritated and it didn't happen again.

My final memory of Liverpool was going to Paddy's Market and being pelted with tangerines by 7-year-olds. In my brazen Galaxy gear, I looked like a Martian to the folk of Liverpool. However, despite these occasional abrasive moments, going to the city had been like a pilgrimage to a holy site. It is hard to convey the impact of Merseyside's writing and musical talent on the nation in the early to mid-sixties. None of the arts was left untouched by the tremendous creative energy coming out of that city. Never again could the Home County-ites sit there smugly, certain of the supremacy of their culture.

Kath's relationship with Brian ended soon after that trip. She made one more attempt to speak to him after a poetry reading somewhere in London. He was talking to a girl when she approached. 'You fucking fuck,' he said to Kath. 'You just lost me a fuck.' Those were the words that ended her relationship with one of the great bards Liverpool.

NOTES

1. Jim Haynes, *Thanks for Coming* (Faber, 1984).
2. This show has been called the 'Invasion of Ideas'. Edward remembers, however that 'The Evolving Documents Show' was the opening exhibition at the Arts Lab and that 'The Invasion of Ideas' took place at a space in Notting Hill.
3. Mary Whitehouse was a social campaigner against the permissive society and opposed the way this manifested itself in the British media.

20

The Forces of Centrocline

Frederick Greenwood, editor of the Pall Mall Gazette between 1865 and 1880, met in his club Lord Riddell, and in the course of their conversation Riddell said to him, 'You know, I own a paper.'

'Oh do you?' said Greenwood. 'What is it?'

'It's called the News of the World – I'll send you a copy,' replied Riddell, and in due course he did so. Next time they met, Riddell said, 'Well, Greenwood, what do you think of my paper?'

'I looked at it,' replied Greenwood, 'and then I put it in the waste paper basket.
And then I thought, "If I leave it there the cook may read it" – so I burned it.'

J W ROBERTSON SCOTT [1]

THE EXPLODING GALAXY had spent the previous two months in freezing mainland Europe at two giant hippie festivals, one in Paris and the other in Utrecht. In ones and twos, they trickled back through late December and early January. Not everyone had been overcome by the deprivations of the tour. John was kept away by a new romance, and Mike, delighted by both Utrecht and Amsterdam, stayed on. He was with Eve, in a student flat on the Wibaustraat near the flea market: 'Each night, a lamplighter would pass along the streets with a long stick and taper to turn on the gas and light the lamp-posts. It was very romantic.'

Another exception to the steady flow back to London was David Medalla, who had been wrong-footed by the authorities and was prevented from returning. His visa had expired on 7 December, and despite previous assurances, the Home Office was now refusing to renew it. Over time, it seemed to us that the police, the Home Office and the gutter press were 'all in it together'. David described his reasons for staying abroad longer:

> I wanted to prolong my stay in Holland, as by then I had started an essay on oriental sculpture, and I wanted to study the collections of oriental art attached to the Rijksmuseum in Amsterdam, the Tropenmuseum (also in Amsterdam) and the Ethnology Museum in Leiden... I was given to understand by the Foreign Office in London that all I had to do was go to any British consulate abroad and my visa would be automatically extended.[2]

On 16 January, having still not received his visa, he left the Netherlands for Paris. Almost a month, and many phone calls later, he was still waiting. The Home Office was now asking for further information, which included questions about his finances and also about his 'group'.

Fitz had travel document problems, too. He needed to renew his passport, and on the form, he had entered his eye colour as 'Lapis lazuli'. He argued with the civil servant at the Passport Office in London's Petty France that this was a more precise description, but she had insisted that he put down 'Blue'. He did manage, however, to get the following past her:

Occupation: Transmedia activator
Hair colour: Raw umber
Special peculiarities: Unspecifically striking

All of this was written out carefully in regulation turquoise ink. In Fitz's passport photograph, half the shot was taken up with one of his quaqua-manuscripts proudly displayed under his chin. Border security was different in those days.

Arriving back at the house in mid-December, Fitz was horrified to find that a visiting well-wisher had bought a number of cut-price single bedsteads, helpfully taking the trouble to bolt them together and arrange them two or three to a room through most of the house. In a commerce-out-of-the-temple-style confrontation, Fitz insisted that they be immediately taken apart and removed. This was the first sign of Fitz's serious commitment to 'activated space'. Two years later, this concept was taken to a whole new level by Fitz's new troupe, Transmedia Exploration.

The beginning of 1968 marked a change in the artistic balance at 99 Balls Pond Road. Previously there had been a tense equilibrium between two very different artists, who underneath it all did not seem to like each other much. What kept these forces in play was the enthusiasm of the young Exploders. It was us, the juvenile worker bees, who busied ourselves, picking one idea from Fitz and then another from David. We were the pollen mixers who had allowed the two very different approaches to flourish and become something quite new – something that belonged to neither of the two artists themselves. Now this democratic creative mix became lopsided, and Fitz came to the fore, at least until David was back with *The Buddha Ballet* in the late spring.

And so it was that several Galaxy members started work on the *Orange and Blue Kinetegram*. Fitz's kinetegrams were not like *The Bird Ballet* explorations because we were rehearsing something that was Fitz's own creation. In a Medalla production, we were encouraged to explore our own consciousnesses in our own way and use what came out. With this new work, there was not much room for interpretation.

It was now just over a year since the opening of UFO, and the picture was disappointing to say the least. The belief in a utopia, and our belief that the flower children could change the world by being kind to each other and preaching peace, had been replaced by one gradually dawning truth: that human nature was exactly as it always was – generous, good, bad, worse and utterly evil.

It was the beginning of February 1968 and the Vietnam War continued unhindered. It was now three years since the start of the continuous bombing raids known as 'Operation Rolling Thunder'. In January alone, there had been 1,202 combat deaths, with 336 young Americans recorded as missing in action. That was just the toll on the American side.

Nothing was the same, not even the LSD, which was no longer the pure chemical, straight from the Sandoz factory in Switzerland, but now came, more often than not, cut with speed. In London, countless people cried out that they had been busted and/or fitted up. What had once been the idealism of an elite and cosy community of intellectuals, who immersed themselves in Beat poetry, CND and lysergic acid diethylamide, had been steadily and almost invisibly worn away by the straight world. The forces out to destroy us were powerful.

The most obvious force of repression was police persecution and, in particular, the activities of the drugs and vice squads. One by one, representatives of youth culture had been raided: the *International Times*, John Hopkins, the Rolling Stones and many more. Where there was no incriminating evidence, it appeared to us that this could be taken care of with a little 'Dropsy'.

The police seemed to have a specific interest in hippie meeting places. In addition to the targeting of prominent individuals, they attempted to take the venues out, one by one. In the case of UFO, this had been easy enough: they just had to lean on the manager, Mr Gannon. Joe Boyd writes of UFO's expulsion from the Blarney Club, its Tottenham Court Road home at the end of July 1967:

> When the *News of the World* spiced the nation's Sunday breakfast at the end of the month with shocking tales from the hippie vice den, Mr Gannon got a call from a local policeman: if UFO opened that weekend, a warrant would be sought for a raid and his licence could be lost.[3]

The club did not survive its move to the Roundhouse for long, and it closed down at the end of September 1967. As for Middle Earth, it took two raids and a little help from some market yobs to dislodge it from its home in Covent Garden. In his book, Nick Butt of Middle Earth gives a blow-by-blow account of the police raids, the invasion by Covent Garden market traders and the subsequent failure of the police to arrive while the club was being smashed to pieces.[4]

Jim Haynes, anxious about a raid, approached the police to reassure them about activities at the Arts Lab. Despite this, there was a subsequent but thwarted attempt at planting drugs. A staff member became suspicious about somebody loitering and then found and removed the illegal substances from the premises. This was shortly before the arrival of the police.

In terms of police interest, the Exploding Galaxy ticked all the boxes: a well-frequented haunt (99 Balls Pond Road), people in the public eye (the Galaxy members), and being unnervingly anti-establishment, if in an indefinable sort of way.

It seemed to us that we had got to a stage where the fuzz felt they could act with impunity. At their side and helping them all the way was the second centroclinal force: the Fleet Street hacks. In fact, there was no attempt at disguising the collaboration between the police and the press. Rag Doll remembers vividly that when the Covent Garden Hotel squat was raided in March 1969, they arrived together.

It appeared that certain elements of the gutter press were working closely with members of the Metropolitan Police. From celebrity tip-offs, it was possible to feed information to the squad who in turn, post raid, would feed the baying hacks with titbits. The more unscrupulous of the latter allowed their sordid imaginations free rein, safe in the knowledge that their carefully ambiguous wording was defamation-proof. What was not actually printed was disseminated as gossip, which spread like wildfire. Thus, for over half a century, one of the lovely emblems of that era remains permanently fixed in the public imagination with a Mars bar inserted between her legs.

It is interesting to compare public opinion now with what it was in the late sixties. Post-2010, the degree to which the Met and the press had been in cahoots came as a horrendous shock to the whole nation. Some of those in the media have tried to suggest that 'it never used to be like this'. Those of us who had been the targets of this sort of sleazy coverage were in no doubt that the red-tops and the boys in blue had been locked in a permanent and very sordid act of coitus lasting at least five decades.

The worst culprits were the *News of the World* and *The People*, who took it in turns to terrify parents and ridicule their offspring. Richard Neville described *The People* in the following way:

> ...a vile organ, akin to the *News of the World*, racist, mean, jingoistic and deceitful, with a horror of the unconventional. But their circulation was bigger than the population of Australia. [5]

It is of curious note that at this time, the general public were far more afraid of the hippies than they were of the link between the police and the press and the serious danger this posed to democracy.

It was as though the police and press were willing soldiers in a cultural war. It was a war between the generations rather than a war against crime. At the time, it was perfectly acceptable to discriminate because, as yet, there was no consensus that cultural difference and minority belief systems were something to be valued. Three years before, the first Race Relations Act had outlawed discrimination relating to access to public places. Nevertheless, this was still a time when you could put a notice in your boarding-house window saying: 'No children, no blacks, no Irish, no dogs.' Equal opportunity and anti-discrimination were in their infancy.

I remember a friend of mine making an appointment as a new patient at a doctor's surgery in Putney. He was freshly bathed, but had long hair and stubble. He wore sandals and a poncho, and if he had not been wearing glasses, you would have said that he looked like Jesus Christ. The GP took one look at him and, without exchanging a single word, ejected him from the building. Intolerance towards otherness permeated every aspect of life, from skin colour and the choice of clothes – to absolutely everything. One of the difficulties in putting together this book has been to try to convey just how utterly shocking counterculture appearance and behaviour was to the straight world.

In January 1968, there was a new arrival at the house. John Dugger was a veteran of a collective in San Francisco's Haight-Ashbury. Through a chance meeting with Andrew Forrest, he and his friend wound up unrolling their sleeping bags on our floor. Young Americans were wealthier and healthier than us and seemed fond of the outdoor life, having frequented summer camps as youngsters and spent their vacations hiking and fishing. Of young Londoners, it was said that the best exercise they got was coughing up the previous night's phlegm. In the United States, every house had two TVs and a giant fridge, and it sometimes even had two cars parked outside in the drive, or at least that was my impression at the time. On his first night at the house, Dugger and his friend joked about toothpaste dispensers shaped like Roman face masks – I had no idea what a toothpaste dispenser was. These visitors seemed to come from another planet.

When Dugger arrived in London, bomb damage was still evident wherever he walked. The cityscape was still full of gaping holes filled with water and debris and torn and ragged brickwork, and the greyness of the winter landscape furthered his belief in our deprivation. But he stayed on. As an ex-art student, he was curious about the house and our life there. He found a painting by David and was bowled over by it and very soon started making his own sketches and artworks.

Dugger was a breath of fresh air at 99 Balls Pond Road, like a Second World War GI bringing treats, only instead of nylon stockings, he brought us muesli. Lizzie remembers the start of a new daily ritual, thanks to his purchasing power. At the breakfast gathering, there would now be cereal and fruit and even the luxury of milk (tea had been drunk black for as long as she could remember). But as an American who had been called up for the draft, Dugger was significantly more politically aware than most of his Exploding Galaxy counterparts.

At the time, there was a journalist in Fleet Street by the name of Kay Windsor who specialised in righteous indignation features. (Audrey still says she would dearly like to slap her, and I still say that she never actually existed and was just some hack fabrication.) She had just done a hatchet job on a youth leader – later sacked because of the article – who was employed by the YWCA to make their gatherings more appealing to young people. Given the public's concern about Harold Wilson's devaluation of sterling in November and given the national anxiety about young layabouts, her next article, on the scroungers called the Exploding Galaxy, was minimum-effort eye-catching copy that was bound to hit the spot.

It was February 1968, and Dugger had not been in the house longer than three weeks or so, when there was a knock at the front door. The people at the door wanted an interview, saying they were freelance journalists. Dugger called Fitz. I am still, after all these years, at a loss to understand why they were allowed across the threshold. Fitz knew they were gutter press and that they would want to describe a cult of flower children, complete with photographs to alarm parents. We had seen it all before in the underground – the rigged photo of the junkie shooting up, casually thrown in with the caption: 'This is what our cameraman spotted.' Despite this, Fitz was always prepared to talk to reporters about our work, as if he would be able to win them over. But, in his own words, 'They usually ended up telling quite another story':

> I was surprised by their complete lack of politeness. They said they wanted photographs (which they had already begun to take) and were writing an article about Diggers. I told them we were not Diggers and suggested other places where they might find some. I made them tea and tried to reduce the curious hostile atmosphere they brought with them. I said I would be happy to answer their questions about the Exploding Galaxy and its art, which I did, but their lack of manners knew no bounds. I had to tell them a number of times to listen and make notes of my replies to their questions (they had a habit of inventing replies for me). I was disappointed to find that most of their questions were about money ...[6]

Clever in its libel-evading tactics, the article conveyed the impression of women as public property and said we were all on benefit. Neither comment was correct, but we were advised that we could not sue. Its purpose was to generate hate and disgust in the minds of the readers. Fitz already looked fairly eccentric in his cloak and quaquacrown, but to make him seem crazy they distorted the image by cutting around the contours. The article described how the whole group sallied forth, dressed in shredded paper, shopping bags, eiderdowns or bits of tinsel:

> So help me, here's another bunch of scruffy, long-haired, unwashed wash-outs who believe they have solved all life's problems.
> With callous conceit they reject all the rules which ordinary people live by and are busy setting up groups where everything will be common property. And I do mean everything...
> In Britain today there should be little sympathy – and even less help – for these scruffy lay-abouts who have their heads in the clouds – and their hands in our pockets.[7]

During the *People* interview, various members of the Galaxy were seen leaving the house. Fitz explained to the journalists about our rehearsal at the school around the corner. Within two hours of the journalists leaving, there was a police raid on the school premises.

NOTES

1. J W Robertson Scott, *The Story of the Pall Mall Gazette*, Oxford University Press, 1950.
2. *Planted*, a report by Paul Keeler, London, 1968.
3. Joe Boyd, *White Bicycles: Making Music in the 1960s* (London: Serpents's Tail, 2006).
4. Nick Butt and Richard Marris, *ElectricNick: No Direction Home*, (e-book, 2013).
5. Richard Neville, *Hippie Hippie Shake* (London: Duckworth Overlook, 2009).
6. *Planted*, 1968.
7. *The People*, 25 February, 1968.

21

Plant a Flower Child

'A good police force is one that catches more criminals than it employs.'

SIR ROBERT MARK, COMMISSIONER OF THE METROPOLITAN POLICE [1]

MIKE CHAPMAN COULD be a liability, like when he thought up the mud incident at the Arts Lab. Mike was, in fact, a talented performer. His delivery of poems was extremely funny, so I often joined his readings at the Arts Lab. I even once adoringly followed him in a Galactic convoy to the BBC when he did a recording for John Peel. The ranting and the anti-religious writing were, to me, the most exciting aspect of his output. It was an outpouring, a spewing rage delivered in an utterly deadpan manner, and this delighted me.

My only doubt about his contributions was that he seemed to have a need to be the most prominent person in the space – and by 'space' I mean auditorium, government building, museum, London square, TV chat show, other person's gig or any other public arena. This could be entertaining, as it was on the evening several of us went to see The Living Theatre at the Roundhouse.

The Living Theatre had a hard-hitting overt political message. That night they talked about Che Guevara in the foothills of Bolivia and they chanted, 'We can't take our clothes off in public.' This was repeated again and again: 'We can't take our clothes off in public' on and on, until Mike Chapman stood up from the audience and chanted, 'Oh, yes, we can. We *can* take our clothes off in public.' There was a stand-off period of several minutes. Then Mike took his clothes off and turned round to the audience. 'You see,' he said, 'we *can* take our clothes off in public.'

I watched with derision as The Living Theatre continued their original chant – they couldn't deliver an improvised response.

But Mike's attention-seeking could also be irritating, like in *The Bird Ballet*, when his entrances were sometimes noisier than everyone else's. I also found it centroclinal that, to achieve maximum attention, his poems were filled with references to sperm, copulation, ejaculation, pee and farts. He seemed to want to press the prurience buttons in the same way as the tabloid press. But then, I was incredibly strait-laced.

Mike, with his tendency to stir things up, was just about to cause major havoc for the rest of the Exploding Galaxy.

We had been working on the *Orange and Blue Kinetegram* in the annexe of Whitmore School in Grange Street, Islington, and had the agreement of the director to use the premises for explorations. The Inner London Education Authority liaison officer had also been informed.

The annexe, called Group Theatre, was separate from the main school building, although within the school boundary, and was primarily used for adult education classes. These included voice production, Shakespearean interpretation and mask-making. We had the space for two weeks, and this would culminate with a performance on 18 February 1968 in the same building in its role as a theatre.

This was the start of a really promising arrangement, since the space was not only tailor-made for Galaxy explorations but also within close walking distance of the house.

No matter where we went, the Exploding Galaxy always attracted attention, and never more so than from kids in fairly rough areas. My most vivid experience of this was when we rehearsed at the Lisson Gallery, where the kids constantly called through the letter box. At the Whitmore, a number of local children abandoned their after-school club and hung around Group Theatre to watch our explorations. They took to Eve, Audrey and Andrew, in particular, and were invited to bounce balls as part of the *Orange and Blue* exploration. The bouncing balls were, in fact, full stops at the ends of sentences, so this was a particularly educational piece of transmedia, possibly a first thorough introduction to punctuation for these children.

With his customary turning of a blind eye to outrage, Mike dug out a copy of the soft porn *Parade* magazine when visiting the Group Theatre. Publications like *Escort* and *Parade* were hardly titillating by today's standards. There was little that was explicit – just topless women in big bloomers throwing beach balls. However, in an act that was to have major repercussions, Mike asked the kids whether they wanted some naughty pictures. He recalled the event in Planted:

> Hearing this, a lot of them broke out into shrieks of eager longing at which I tore the *Parade* into sections and distributed them. Then a little old lady crackled up and herded the reluctantalised kiddies out on to the pavement outside the gate.

The fallout from this was an outraged head teacher, who contacted both the Inner London Education Authority and the police. For this reason, our agreement with Group Theatre was terminated. Not surprising, really.

This incident occurred on 15 February, but it was agreed via the Group Theatre manager that we could continue working there for a few more days until our performance on the 18th. It was in this context that we received the uninvited visit from *People* journalists at Balls Pond Road the next day, on Friday 16 February, followed by an unwelcome visit from the police at our rehearsal later the same afternoon.

The Group Theatre bust was disastrous as far as the police were concerned. There were a number of officers involved in the raid and among their number there was someone present who was prepared to act illegally. It is not possible to plant evidence effectively if your search area is used by a number of people not associated with the target individuals. It turned out that the studio was shared by lots of others, so if you put cannabis in an unidentified bag, you could not be sure whether you were fitting-up a Galaxy member or a random adult education student. In fact, whoever it was who placed the drugs there had mistakenly planted drugs on one of the teachers at the school – unless, of course, it was the teacher who owned the drugs. Then there was the layout of the building. To execute the swift placing of incriminating evidence, you needed the privacy of blind spots and corners. In this case, the whole studio had been swept that very afternoon by the council liaison officer. The only two suitable dropping areas were a kitchen counter and a curtained-off changing space. By an extraordinary coincidence, that is exactly where the drugs were found.

Then there was the behaviour of the plantees. They were clearly not in any kind of drugged state. They were watching absolutely everything that was happening and did not miss a trick.

'Watch that man,' Paul had said to John Dugger. In their matching statements the police said there was no obscuring curtain or kitchen counter, and no cry of 'Plant! I saw him plant it!'

Dugger had a lot to lose – if deported, he would be thrown directly into the arms of the FBI as a 'draft dodger' – yet he was spectacularly unintimidated. (The arresting officer described him as 'haughty'.) Dugger recalls:

> They found a knife – a paring knife – and handed it to one of the junior members of the squad. He held it by the blade. I pointed out to him that it was bad action to hold the knife by the blade because he would leave his finger prints on it. An older officer approached him and suggested that he should not hold the knife by the blade.

No substances were found on any of the Galaxy members during the strip-search, nor among any of the Galaxy's possessions. Interestingly enough, no fingerprint checks were later made on any of the six exhibits used to support the police claims. Three pieces of hashish had been found in three different places within three minutes. A carrier bag containing Exhibit 2 – '6 grains of cannabis resin' – was subsequently explained as 'lost'. This was the bag that belonged to the teacher. In Paul's words, the whole procedure had just been 'the old magician's trick of hiding the cards in the hands'.

Paul Keeler described his treatment at the hands of the police as extraordinary. He stated that at the theatre one officer had asked him to strip, but in omitting this from all police accounts, it appeared that Paul had stripped for no reason at all, giving him the appearance of being in an abandoned state. At the police station Paul asserted that he was made to strip again, this time in front of the desk sergeant and six or seven other officers, and that in the interrogation room he was thrown to the ground and kicked. He maintained that a passing officer showing disapproval made them moderate their actions to hitting him over the head with a rolled-up copy of the *Police Gazette* and then threatening him with its theft.

The officers did not have free rein. Once at City Road police station, it was clear that some officers there either did not know about or did not care for what was happening – the problem for coppers who pushed the limits was that not all coppers pushed the limits. Several Galaxy members were remanded in custody overnight, but by the morning just four were charged and taken to Old Street Magistrates' Court: Paul Keeler, John Dugger, Eve Ridoux and Uisce Bó.

It was at this point that my sister Annabel was drawn in to the Exploding Galaxy and through the court case eventually came to marry Paul Keeler. Up until this point she had been no more than vaguely curious about our activities. Following the first arrests, she received a call from her close friend Umiak, and Annabel and I immediately turned to our father, Denny Drower, for help. Although not trained as a lawyer, Dad had worked for both prosecution and defence in courts martial during the war. He once wryly commented that, during all that time, he had never come across a single soul who was aquitted. This had given him a nose for injustice and now he smelt a rat.

On one issue there was no disagreement – we all believed that the authorities were set on eradicating the Exploding Galaxy. This fitted with the Home Office's behaviour towards David and his visa and the persistent police interest. To us, it appeared to unfold as a coordinated assault by the Home Office, the police and the gutter press.

For this reason, it was obvious that another raid was imminent and that this time it would take place at 99 Balls Pond Road. We knew that the police would get us 'bang to rights' this time and we felt utterly helpless, believing that magistrates would be unwilling to reprimand officers publicly, even if the officers' honesty was in question.

On the morning of the first magistrates' court hearing, my father had said that the Galaxy needed protection from further persecution by the police. Annabel remembers:

> He made out an affidavit, which my mother typed out, stating the Galaxy's fears and said that, if such a document were signed, dated and kept in the bank, it might be useful evidence should there be another plant. When we got to court, my father was involved in the business about bail. I brought out the affidavit for the Galaxy to see. Some signed; others wouldn't sign immediately because they weren't sure of the wording and wanted to discuss it further. In the excitement and confusion, some people did not see it. The matter was postponed, but wasn't taken up again in time.

Umiak's father, Roy Price, was a solicitor high up in the Treasury. She went to see him on the Tuesday following the Group Theatre raid, saying that she and her friends were in 'grave danger' from the police. Roy said he thought it not at all improbable that the police planted evidence 'but was sure they had their reasons'. Umiak said that the whole country was in danger if the police could get away with such crimes. Her father suggested that, if they wanted to protect themselves, they should 'invite some responsible person to the house who could be a witness in the event of further raids'.

Umiak immediately thought of her friend, poor unsuspecting Caroline from Putney High School, who was granddaughter of the painter Augustus John and, more to the point, daughter of Sir Caspar John, First Sea Lord until 1963, Admiral of the Fleet, retired, and chairman of the 'I'm Backing Britain' campaign. Caroline was just off to Italy as part of her gap year. Had she known what lay ahead, she might have done well to stay away. As it was, she took the No. 73 bus over from Barnes, accompanied by her border collie, Flossie.

From the house, Caroline made an excursion to Kingsland Road Market, paying for the ingredients for a big meal, which she proposed to cook for the whole Galaxy household.

There was just one unexpected guest that evening, someone looking for Fitz, who was out. He was allowed in and, once more, the Exploding Galaxy laid themselves open to potential danger. According to Umiak:

> The man sat down with us to await Gerry Fitzgerald's return. He tried to get information about ourselves from us for an alleged book that was being written by a hippie-girl from San Francisco. He was very vague about the nature of the book, but provided vital statistics of the author. He also tried to take photographs of me but I stopped him, because he could not be precise about what he wanted them for. Later Fitz spent quite a long time talking to the man about his art. I got bored and left. But there was something insidious about the man none of us liked. He wore jeans, but they were very new. His casualness seemed studied. Moreover, he seemed always to want to steer the conversation towards vaguely suggestive jokes. To our relief, he left.

In their report on drug offenders and the law,[2] Caroline Coon and Rufus Harris describe the use of fit-up tactics 'to enter houses on pretexts other than to search for drugs so that the plant could then be arranged'. In fact, as Fitz was being bundled into the van the next day, an officer said to him that one of their lads had been round to visit the previous evening.

It is hard to understand the degree to which the Galaxy were prepared to overlook obviously bogus explanations by people wishing to enter the house. This was our major weakness, our Achilles heel. My opinion now is that it was less naivety than our messianic conviction that we could persuade anybody of the validity of our way of life. For this reason, the group had defied caution and let this man cross the threshold. It may well be that the man who came into the house the night before the raid was just doing a reconnoitre, but whatever his role, one thing is certain: that at least one officer out of the 16 who entered the house on 21 and 22 February planted drugs.

At 8.40am the following morning, 22 February 1968, there was a sharp bang on the front door, but unlike the previous year when it had been broken down, the police waited for Galaxy guest Caroline to open up. The lead officer announced that he had a warrant to search the premises for drugs. He entered the house accompanied by other officers. At the same time, more entered at the back, having gained access through a neighbouring house and climbed over the garden wall. Amongst their number was a dog handler with one of London's only two drugs sniffer dogs, named named after two cartoon bears, Yogi and Boo Boo. Altogether, there were a total of 16 officers, with ten Galaxy members and two dogs present in the house. It seemed that the police were searching for particular named members of the group. What also later emerged was that, although none of the officers in the second raid had attended the first, one of them had been present at the previous magistrates' court hearing the morning after the previous raid. My guess is that they had already been gearing up for the second raid and needed someone to identify the owner of the house – namely, Paul Keeler – but it just so happened that, on the morning of the second raid, Paul was in the West Country, rallying support.

Once they were in the building, the police fanned out in different directions. Yogi was not doing very well as he was distracted by Flossie, the Border Collie. One officer went straight down to the basement, and straight to a particular overcoat, which was hanging in the hall. This was John Dugger's coat. He 'pulled out' a whopping 63 grains of cannabis from the pocket without the aid of a torch, an essential aid since the space was dark even in daylight and permanently without electricity. Caroline actually witnessed the downstairs 'discovery':

> I remember being down in the basement, and observing through a hatch police searching or questioning people. And at one point… there was the appearance of a piece of cannabis resin which was golden in colour like a little rock. I remember seeing it and thinking it looked like a dog biscuit, and saying that.

Until the actual trial, the police took no interest in Caroline. They realised she was a visitor to the house and didn't even bother to make a note of her name.

Next came the defiant voice of Uisce Bó from upstairs saying, 'I strongly protest my innocence!' In fact, the first time Uisce Bó had ever seen cannabis was at the Group Theatre six days before, when the police had shown it to her. This was the second time, and the quantity was 23 grains. Four people had been sleeping in the middle room, but the officers ignored Val and Eve, instead making a beeline for Fitz, almost as if there had been a prior plan to nobble him. Fitz's space was separated off by market crates, turning it into a partitioned sleeping area called his 'quaqua-tent'. Since he shared this space with Uisce Bó, she got nobbled, too.

Other officers moved straight upstairs to the top floor. Christian had witnessed what had happened to Fitz on the middle floor and was irate. There followed a miraculously quick discovery of drugs in this room too, a typical hallmark of cases where the police were accused of planting. Out of the mountains of books and papers in Christian's room and again without the aid of a torch, the officer swiftly pulled one postcard-sized British Museum paper bag and without hesitation put his hand straight in and, hey presto, pulled out a little lump of something. He held it up. Christian lunged and snatched it from the officer and made as if to throw it out into the street. Despite being pinned by the shoulders, Christian flicked it not out of the window but over the officer's shoulder on to the carpet. Audrey, who had been standing nearby watching, calmly walked over and stood on the exhibit. With the lump held between her toes, she walked slowly downstairs and politely asked one of the officers if she could use the bathroom. In this way, the planted evidence was flushed down the toilet. Christian was instead charged with obstructing a police officer.

Later that day, he enacted the following real-time kinetic drama at Dalston Police Station:

POLICE OFFICER: What's your name?
CHRISTIAN: Christian Ledoux.
POLICE OFFICER: What do you do?
CHRISTIAN: I live.
POLICE OFFICER: [*reading out what he wrote*] Liver.

Uisce Bó and the 19-year-old Dugger, as the only two also charged at the Group Theatre, were remanded in custody at Holloway and Ashford, respectively. Pete Brown, the musician and poet, stood bail for Fitz. Christian was granted bail of £150, but on condition that he report every afternoon and surrender his passport.

There were a large number of officers involved in both raids. John Dugger, who was victim to planting both times, has himself said that he does not believe all present were rotten apples. But it only takes one or maybe two to carry out the deed. The outcome was that members of the Exploding Galaxy were charged with possessing drugs on two separate occasions.

From HM Prison Holloway in Parkhurst Road, on regulation prison stationery, Prisoner 860 Uisce Bó described her surroundings as 'dense, ugly and mocking'. She spoke of the urgent need to get sympathetic reports from the press to counter what was in *The People* and described how she thought the police had filled her father's mind with corruption – 'I must try to undo this.' She finished with: 'Love, love, love, love Always, your Uisce Bó.'

The officers had a problem with Uisce Bó. She was a combination of the virtuous and the forthright, and since it was obvious to all that she was telling the truth, she was a major obstacle to the prosecution's case. Get her in the witness box and the whole case against the group would fall apart. Charges against her were dropped.

At the Committal to the Crown Court, sureties were needed. At court it turned out that Guy Brett's offer to stand bail was not sufficient, despite his establishment-sounding job (art critic of *The Times*). The police said that they did not have to give a reason for not accepting him as a surety. On hearing about the plant, my father, Denys Drower, had immediately agreed to stand bail, so he stepped in. He remembered the Committal Hearing:

> A police officer approached me outside the court and asked me if I was the man prepared to stand bail for the accused. I said I was. He asked me for my name and address. I gave it.
> He then asked how much I was prepared to put up. I said £500. He said, 'Each?' I said, 'Are you crazy?[3]
> He then said, 'One is an American and one is French. They might easily skip the country.' I said, 'That's ridiculous, they don't have any money' or words to that effect... I went and sat down on a bench next to my wife and daughter. The officers then came over to me and asked me if I realised what would happen if the accused did not surrender their bail. I said, 'Yes, of course – if they don't turn up, I lose the money.' One of them said, 'You know, you could even go to prison?' I smiled and said, 'I'll take that risk...'
>
> The magistrate, questioning me on the subject of bail, asked me why, since I hardly knew the accused at all, I was prepared to stand as surety. I replied that, although I myself did not know them, I knew of them and that my daughters knew them well. I was satisfied from what they had told me that the accused were not guilty of the charge. I felt that the evidence as far as I knew was most unsatisfactory and I feared an injustice was being done.[4]

Bail was finally set at £150, which was no small sum by the standards of the day.

Uisce Bó's father had come down from Sunderland to stay the night with our family. Denys described him as being completely out of his depth. The hippie thing had really only happened in London, and what did he know or care about what we stood for? He emptied gas meters for a living, and he read the tabloids on Sundays. He was horrified by the weird crowd his daughter had befriended, and sympathised with the police. (Uisce Bó's letter said of her parents: 'They really believe I am insane.')

When he met his daughter on her release on 2 March, he strode across the hall and slapped her smartly across the face in front of the police officers. This incident more than any other brought home to me the issue of class, which was so deeply engrained in relations between the hippies and the straight world in 1967 and 1968. Events as they unfolded over the next few months did nothing to alter this opinion.

NOTES

1. Sir Robert Mark was Commissioner of the Metropolitan Police between 1972 and 1977. This famous comment was made during his inaugural address.
2. Caroline Coon and Rufus Harris, *Release Report on Drug Offenders and the Law* (London: Sphere Books, 1969).
3. Today's equivalent would be approximately £7,500.
4. *Planted*, a report compiled by Paul Keeler, 1968.

22

Parliament Hill

I sat with him in silence there
below a circle of some twenty cedar trees
which standing heavy with their age
now stooped like just so many grandfathers

And there we chewed on honeycombs
and supped a sherbet made from
secret saps and herbs

ROLY DROWER [1]

IF YOU LOOK from Parliament Hill, at the exact spot where the engraved landmark indicator stands, and you face south, what you see is quite different from what would have met your gaze in the spring of 1968. The then essentially low-rise cityscape is now pushed through with thick verticals, the London Eye, an outsize Ferris wheel, being the most surprising of the new additions. But there, too, are the old faithfuls – Crystal Palace mast, just discernable through the haze down towards Croydon, St Paul's (now a protected view from this spot) and the Hilton Hotel, open for business in April 1963. Nestling down towards the right is our beloved Roundhouse, its conical hat smartened up in what at first appears to be the green of copper. Gazing like this is like watching a film called *Learn to Paint in Watercolours*, with the view being built up layer upon layer over the decades through a series of jump cuts.

The name Parliament Hill is austere, with its Civil War connotations and the hint that it was parliamentary troops who held this piece of high ground in the 17th century. I prefer its other name, Kite Hill, which carries with it the playfulness evident there on any windy weekend and is a more evocative description of the place as a favourite haunt of the flower children. It was here that the beautiful people celebrated weddings and birthdays and it is here that pagans like to welcome in the spring equinox.

There is some old footage of our favourite underground DJ, Jeff Dexter, who in the spring and summer of 1967 would take revellers up to Parliament Hill in the early hours from Tiles discotheque to dance in the dawn. This film, shot in the daytime during that year, sums it all up so well – a giant ring o' roses at the summit with a long chain of 40 or so smiling, long-haired grown-ups holding hands, rolling down the slopes and generally being children to the sound of strumming, flutes and improvised percussion. Even the children are seen joining in, pretending to be children. We believed that our innocence could counter all the ghastliness of the world and could show it up for what it was.

It was in the summer of 1967, that Edward Pope had the idea of a Galaxy visit to Parliament Hill at dawn, which he called the 'Snail Exploration'. This was one of the events that several of the Exploders particularly remember from that time. Edward recalls:

> The idea came from the spiral of a shell. The point was to erect a kind of a structure that had an outward spiralling effect. It was a happening that involved no real audience apart from the Galaxy itself, because there wouldn't be an audience on Parliament Hill at dawn – except the park keeper, who tried to throw us out. He was our audience.

Edward's initial idea was minimal, with the expectation that a creative outcome could be evolved. The notion of exploration, as opposed to a rehearsal or performance, had really begun to take hold among the Exploding Galaxy. Edward describes what Fitz wore for this one:

> It was a classic of the incongruous – a costume with a straw hat which had not originally been made as a hat, but as some sort of packaging. It looked rather like the Tin Woodman except made of straw, so it had Oz resonances and out of the top came this film reel – a loose piece of film, which again could be a reference to *The Wizard of Oz*.

Edward describes this early exploration as an indulgence on the part of David, Fitz, Mike and Christian and as a kindness, in that we felt that we should do something that would be Edward's. He remembers that 'they appreciated my creative input but it was generally considered that my things worked best on an intimate scale'.

Almost a year after the 'Snail Exploration', in June 1968, the *Hampstead Express and News* chose a mocking, 'Some mothers do 'ave 'em' style appraisal of Galaxy explorations on Parliament Hill, with the headline: 'It's either them or us that's barmy – and I know which it is. we are getting used to THEM up here.' In the article, the park keeper who had been the only audience of the 'Snail Exploration at dawn' the previous year, gave a damning account of the various performances he had witnessed:

> We were very interested in watching them at their antics. They seem to be quite harmless and we would usually leave them alone. We have had them here before attaching strings to the ground from little sticks and telling us they are having telephone conversations with worms.

The position in the late spring of 1968 was as follows: we had been targeted and zapped by an out-of-control and corrupt police force, which had more in common with the Greek and Brazilian military juntas of the era than with the bobbies benignly watching the right to free speech being demonstrated at Speakers' Corner every Sunday. We were traumatised by what had happened and afraid of what lay ahead.

However, by comparison with the three accused following the drug raid on No. 99, my experience of spring 1968 was both untroubled and entertaining. It is true that I was fully immersed in the aftermath of the busts – my sister and I had found bail for two of the accused by asking our father. I also visited Uisce Bó in Holloway with a parcel of home-cooked food and rallied round in whatever way I could. However, it was different for me. I was not the one who had been falsely accused, and I did not have to stay every night in a house that was regularly jeered at and bombarded with bricks. Nor had my passport been confiscated.

I had been having French coaching with Madame Deuchar, and because of this, I managed to wangle my parents' agreement to a trip to Paris on the pretext that this would help my French, ready for my O level in June. I stayed with Eve Ridoux at her parents' house in Rue Vergnaud, in the 13th arrondissement. My diary for April and May of that year is devoid of entries, but I do know that I was walking down a Paris street on 5 April when Eve stopped at a billboard: 'Oh, 'ow sad, 'ow terrible. Look – Martin Luther King, 'ee 'ees dead!'

Galactic life in the French capital was remarkably similar to that in London, except that the Parisians were truly shocked by my pre-grunge ragged clothing. They scowled at me as though I were 'a dirty hobo'. As in London, we perpetually hung out at museums, looking at oriental antiquities, our preferred venue being the Musée Guimet. The Gustave Moreau Museum was for me a particular treasure trove. Josephine, by now studying alongside Freddie Mercury at Ealing School of Art,[2] had persuaded me to read Huysmans' *À rebours*, which mentions Moreau paintings and was a favourite of those art school hippies interested in the romantic symbolists. Although I did not really get the hedonist stance, I loved Moreau's paintings.

David was briefly back in Paris showing his bubble machines. Mike also made an appearance and was given the task of finding washing-up liquid to pour into the artwork's tank. This was meant to produce the magical swathes of foam, but he came back with a soap that didn't froth, so there we all were at the opening, standing around a tall, humming, bubble-less cube.

Although it was not yet May, the streets on the Left Bank were hotting up. Eve led me there and we stood with the young crowd who were shouting abuse at a very frightening wall of police shields. Had she marched forward towards Odéon, towards the shields, I would have followed willingly. With no understanding of the importance of the events that were about to unfold before my eyes and a belief that I was invulnerable, was I innocent or just incredibly stupid? Luckily, Eve led me away and into a side street. It was only a matter of weeks before it all erupted.

Eve's parents were communists but, by Paris student standards, were extremely straight, so dinnertime at the Ridoux household could be very noisy. While I was there, some of her friends, who were always welcome, came to dinner and embarked on a political argument. Voices were raised and there was an abrupt walk-out during the third course of the five-course meal. My impression of young French people at that time was that they did a lot of walking out in disgust.

Miraculously, and by sheer fluke, I came back from Paris speaking better French and managed to pass my O level.

The person with most cause for anxiety following the police busts was John Dugger. If convicted, we believed that he would almost certainly be sent back to the US where, he believed, an FBI welcoming party would be waiting to greet him. It was remarkably unlucky for Dugger that, within weeks of arriving in the UK, he had found himself twice charged with possessing drugs and doing ten days in Ashford Remand Centre as an underaged alien.

For Dugger, the only way to cope with the fear of conviction was to put all his energies into creativity. He joined forces with David, now back in the country, to devise the longest running of all our performances, *The Buddha Ballet*. From May 1968 until the end of that summer, just before the Crown Court hearing, we could be found almost every week at the summit of Parliament Hill, enacting tales taken from both Hindu and Buddhist texts.

Throughout that spring and summer, I joined the throngs that grew in number there. In this way, I became familiar with stories enacted from the *Mahabharata* and with the Buddhist Wheel of Transmigration.

Not all the press coverage of Galaxy events on Parliament Hill was negative. In one sympathetic article, Asians from Southall described how they had travelled across London weekly to see the tales taken from the *Mahabharata* and dramatised on Parliament Hill. In the summer of 1968, David wrote:

> The first two explorations of *The Buddha Ballet* were held indoors, towards the end of April, at Shoreditch and Covent Garden. After the second exploration, John Dugger and I agreed that we should evolve *The Buddha Ballet* on Parliament Hill, Hampstead. Since May until now friends have been evolving *The Buddha Ballet* on Parliament Hill... Some of the explorations of *The Buddha Ballet* have been very beautiful. The latest one involved people going into the forest of Kenwood, climbing trees, moving through ferns and calling each other throughout the wood with animal and bird sounds.

The 'people' mentioned were members of the public, there on the Hill by coincidence or design, who willingly joined in and took on roles as instructed by David Medalla. In this sense, it was truly exciting as a piece of audience participation.

David describes the development of *The Buddha Ballet* and how this piece was explored by the Exploding Galaxy:

> After telling the story to the people gathered on Parliament Hill, we invited people from the 'audience'. Five young men took the parts of the five Pandava brothers... while various boys and girls played different animals living in the forest surrounding the lake. People standing about became the trees, while eight girls played the poisoned water of the lake, with the help of a sheet of green polythene which they rippled at suitable intervals during the unfoldment of the dramatic action. To establish the symbolism behind their roles, the five Pandava brothers went separately into the crowd and acted out their respective senses. Thus the youth playing Arjuna looked into the eyes of the people in the audience, Bhima listened to the audience's conversations, occasionally 'throwing sounds' into the air which he would 'catch' while moving amongst the audience. The youth playing Yudhisthira touched the bodies of the people in the audience, while the two youngest Pandavas, who are twins in the story, alternately 'taste' and 'smell' the audience... Only when the audience were sufficiently articulated and actively involved in the sensory exploration of one another did the drama proper begin. The people in this exploration were mostly strangers to one another, but by the time our exploration was ended, new channels of communication opened up amongst us.[3]

These stories were carefully chosen and adapted so that a maximum number of the gathered 'watchers' would feel inclined to participate. At the Arts Lab, the story would be typed onto stencils and duplicated on the banda duplicator in sufficient quantities for most people to have sight of it. Guy Brett describes *The Buddha Ballet* encounters in the following way:

> ...these latter events were really gigantic games into which Medalla and... John Dugger would endeavour to attract the passing public. Once a human body was formed out of the linked bodies of dozens of people, and strode off like a ragged giant over the hill, Medalla rather romantically incorporating every anarchic or disruptive element, such as rowdy kids who were treated as fleas and expelled from the giant's hair with a massive comb.[4]

For me, the most exciting of these stories was entitled 'The Questions of King Milinda'. When I first heard it, on a dark candlelit evening when we were sitting round the fire at 99 Balls Pond Road, the story enchanted me. Guy Brett describes these extracts from the Pali canon as 'a wonderful document of how two enlightened cultures (the ancient Greek and the early Buddhist), with their two different but completely complementary systems of thought, encountered and transformed one another'.

Among the regular attenders at Parliament Hill on Sundays were Hermine Demoriane and Hugo Williams, who brought their young daughter Murphy. One time, Hermine, who had been training as a tightrope walker, set up her rope between two trees near the summit.

Graham Stevens often brought his 'transmobile', an inflatable structure which was a totally new experience for many. With team cooperation, it could be taken up and down Parliament Hill for no reason other than that it was tremendous fun. It was a totally simple structure, but utterly intriguing for adults and children alike.

The writer Sheila Robotham lived near the Galaxy house. She knew Graham Stevens and joined us at Parliament Hill on one of those final Sundays in 1968. She writes:

> As we danced on the grass, I did feel an extraordinary sense of open delight being generated within the little group, which appeared to spread outwards to embrace passers-by. I did, however, retain sufficient scepticism to suspect that part of the popularity came from the startling beauty of Graham's partner, Merdelle. One aspect of the hippie underground was the loving playfulness, which it is easy to be cynical about. Looking back, I think they had an insight which I would value now more than I did then.[5]

For John Dugger, all this came as a welcome distraction from what lay ahead. The fact that he was so deeply involved in this project kept him sane during those anxious months and cemented his creative partnership with David Medalla, a parallel working relationship which lasted into their 'Artists' Liberation Front' and 'Artists for Democracy' phases. At the time, David described *The Buddha Ballet* as still being in its first stage of evolution. He said, 'John Dugger and I believe that, in time, *The Buddha Ballet* will grow and flower into a great social art, created by everyone for no one.'

NOTES

1. Roly Drower, *Bramblespit and other Poems and Stories* (Scrudge Books).
2. There was a strong connection between music, the underground and art colleges. Freddie Mercury, Ronnie Wood and Pete Townshend were all students at Ealing College of Art.
3. *Planted*, a report compiled by Paul Keeler, London 1968.
4. Guy Brett, *Exploding Galaxies* (London: Kala Press, 1995).
5. Sheila Rowbotham, *Promise of a Dream: Remembering the Sixties* (Allen Lane, 2000)

23

We Can't be Everywhere

We must understand straight away that the Exploding Galaxy are 'us', that their rights are the same as ours and in no way affected by the way they look and live

MARY HOLLAND, *THE OBSERVER*, 1968

BACK FROM PARIS, I went to Balls Pond Road, but less often. The anxiety there was palpable. It was partly the fear of another bust. We did not think that the police had finished with us yet. Eve, who had been arrested in the first raid at the theatre, knew that if this happened again, it was likely that she would be remanded in custody like John Dugger and Uisce Bó. She approached her solicitor after the second plant to ask how she could protect herself against the police:

> My solicitor said that it will be better to leave for a while the house because the police will be able to plant us a third time. He said that has happened already to other people... I decide to leave for two weeks to stay in a friend's house on the advice of my solicitor.

In addition to fuzz persecution, we were now afraid of the locals, who had lapped up the 'bunch of spongers' copy from *The People* and now knew about the police case against us, and, as a result, were becoming bolder in their harassment.

In the late 1960s, the people of Britain were unified by two parts of our communications infrastructure. The first was television. In 1968 there were just three TV channels, so that everyone who watched telly would be tuned in to the same programmes, from *Steptoe and Son* to *Panorama*. Everyone, from the Queen to the laird in his castle to my old man the dustman, watched the *Morecambe and Wise Show*. Despite the gradual mellowing changes brought about by migration, this shared viewing gave a strong sense of shared mono-identity, even to those who disapproved of sixties sitcoms or *The Man from U.N.C.L.E.* Even for those who hardly spoke English or held strong anti-TV views, the box was still somehow revered and fascinating. The whole nation, apart from a few Jehovah's Witnesses and the newly arrived, strode lock-stepped into the same information stream.

The other unifying force was the red telephone box, designed by Sir Giles Gilbert Scott of Battersea Power Station fame. By the end of the sixties, there were heading for 70,000 of these kiosks countrywide. Of all items in daily life, the public call box was the fiercest leveller in our class-ridden society. Even if Lord Romtitom of Upton Hall sent his butler out to the corner shop and never had cause to talk to a labourer or a char lady, he would still find, when out and about, that he had to wait in a queue with the Turkish café manager or the Jamaican nurse to make a call.

There had been a telephone at Balls Pond Road, but when things got tight, a drop coin box had been installed in the hall. In a desperate moment, the box got raided, so that phone was cut off. When Galaxy members now wanted to make a call, they had to stand in line in the street with other locals.

It was in 1967 that demand for the phone box outside 99 Balls Pond Road increased dramatically. Galaxy members suddenly started popping out at the slightest excuse to call their parents or people abroad. This was all due to Katy. There must have been a telephone insider friend-of-a-friend who knew the code used by engineers to make free calls. What you did was to dial 'K-A-T-Y' and then wait for a click, and then dial the whole number, including the international code, and you got through free. The news spread like wildfire through the Galaxy and beyond. People were ringing long-lost friends in far-flung places to chat about nothing very much at the drop of a hat. Katy was irresistible because everyday phone calls were expensive enough as it was, but calls abroad were utterly prohibitive, even for people who were earning. Eventually somebody at the Post Office twigged and

Katy stopped working for us, but there were several delicious months of thumbing our noses at the system.

The idea of being attacked by an angry mob in the place where you are meant to feel safe is terrifying, but this was now a distinct possibility given local feeling, and it was doubly frightening because we had no phone of our own to call the emergency services if someone was breaking down our front door. And this is exactly what happened.

In Christian Ledoux's statement about the events of 30 March 1968, he wrote:

> I had walked back from a concert of *St John's Passion*. Most of the people in the house were asleep and I shared a meal with two or three Exploders who had not gone to bed yet. At about half past one, we heard some very harsh and unpleasant shouting outside. Four men and three women were pointing at and making for the house. They looked about 40 years old, which from our experience was very unusual. They came into the front yard, taking a dustbin lid and my bicycle. The three married women were enticing the men to get in and rape a girl, Mal, who was watching them out of an open window. They said she was naked, which she was not, and called her a prostitute. Mal, who is herself married and has a 3-year-old daughter living in the house, panicked. By now everyone was awake. The shouting outside was heavier and heavier. We got frightened and tried to use a neighbour's telephone. Nobody would wake up. We tried another house through the garden. Same thing. There was no way to call the police, which was the only thing we wanted to do, as we would not fight these men who came here probably to spend their alcoholic energy in threatening us with their coarse voices, and breaking a few things (like works of art, noses and knuckles).[1]

The four men started banging on the door shouting: 'We want peace!' They managed to burst the door open, punching Christian on the nose and leaving him unconscious, while Edward was able to step past Christian to push the door closed and then barricade it.

A fortnight later, at about 3am, a large lump of concrete came through a window in the upper ground floor, into the room where David Medalla was sleeping. When John Schofield went to inspect the damage, he found splinters of glass and wood covering the bed and floor. The bottom half of the window had been completely shattered. The concrete had come through with such force that it had broken the lower wooden strut of the window and had landed eight feet into the room.

Particularly worrying for the women in the Galaxy was the degree to which they were now in danger out on the street. When walking back from Hugo and Hermine's house in Islington one night in March, Audrey was set upon by a group of youths. It was after 11pm and she wasn't sure whether to take the bus back or to walk. At that moment, a boy of about 17 tried to grab her arm from a doorway. He called to his friends and soon Audrey, who was pregnant, found her way blocked by about a dozen young men. One of them said, 'I know where she lives. She's from Balls Pond Road. She's one of them. Let's get her.' Another got close and whispered, 'I'm going to get some tits from you tonight.' It was at this point that Audrey was saved by the arrival of a No. 38 bus. As she jumped on board, the boys beat on its side and yelled.

The harassment continued into the summer, and on 26 August 1968 there was a further attack. This time a group of between four and six youths threw two half-bricks though the basement and ground-floor windows. John Dugger and David Medalla made chase, but there was little they could do with the police so half-hearted about catching and charging.

The police had been contacted after each attack on the house, and they showed a curious lack of interest in what was normally regarded as a serious crime – attacking someone in their own home. One of the hardest things to do in the late sixties was to convince the general public that the Metropolitan Police was a corrupt force – people still saw it as *Dixon of Dock Green*. No convictions resulted from any of the offences against 99 Balls Pond Road. It seems that the police were always on an especially slow 'go-slow' when it came to protecting hippies.

At around this time, the Government issued some publicity designed to reassure the population that the police were doing their very best to protect them and solve crimes under difficult circumstances. The poster depicted a friendly bobby's face with the caption 'we can't be everywhere'.

Fitz, like John Dugger, had to cope with an impending court case. His pre-trial project took place at the Arts Lab. He had had a good working relationship with Jim Haynes and had been at the Slade with Biddy Peppin, one of the people running the Arts Lab gallery. He approached Jim and asked him if he could paint the whole lobby dark blue – the blue of a policeman's uniform. Jim said his usual yes. The musician and poet Pete Brown, who believed an injustice had been done, not only stood Fitz's bail but also paid for the vast quantity of emulsion needed to turn his idea into an exhibition. Fitz then made hundreds of copies of the police poster – the helmeted police officer benignly looking straight to the camera. If you went to the Arts Lab during the display, whichever way you turned, what you saw was that nice bobby telling you 'we can't be everywhere'.

Paul Keeler is always at his best when rallying on behalf of a project. He had been arrested at the theatre raid and kept through the night of 16 February at Hackney police station. As sole owner of the house, if he had been present at the raid on the house, he would be charged for allowing his property to be used for the taking of a Class A drug, even if he had no knowledge of any illegal substances on the premises. Paul knew the law and was adamant that there should never be illegal drugs in the house. By convicting Paul in this way, the authorities could effectively close the whole show down.

Their years as directors of Signals Art Gallery had given David and Paul a very large circle of sympathetic supporters from all walks of life, from Brother Simon Tugwell of Blackfriars Monastery in Oxford to the French critic Jean Clay to Caresse Crosby, wealthy American publisher, peace activist and patron of the arts. These people, all well respected in their fields, rallied around and offered help. Among them were a number of MPs.

Paul started by approaching members of the press he thought would be sympathetic. Mary Holland of *The Observer* was superb. In her feature in early May entitled 'Is it the police versus the young?' she described how Paul had been made to strip naked in the hallway of the police station (defence solicitors at that time said that this was not uncommon); how during his interview he had been threatened with being charged with attempting to steal the *Police Gazette*; how legal aid had been refused because the magistrate thought that public money should not be spent on 'cases of this kind'; and how, when the case had been thrown out, costs were not awarded to any Galaxy members. In addition to this blow-by-blow account, she wrote about our way of life and went on to attack discrimination based on appearance. Her article was an early plea for the toleration of difference, something that would later be enshrined in law.

Paul now had plans for something altogether more ambitious – a report. He approached several people, among them Benn Levy, playwright, veteran of two world wars and Labour MP. In the face of the obvious threat to the rule of law and civil liberties, Benn, among others, willingly offered to fund Paul's idea for a report about the circumstances of the Galaxy court case. The document would be a report highlighting the inconsistencies in the prosecution statements, and would explain the Exploding Galaxy's philosophy and creations. It would also lay the story out clearly for the defence team, to make their job as easy as possible. But the ultimate aim was to provoke a public enquiry into police corruption. Paul called the book *Planted* and the print run was 500 – enough copies to distribute to all the people who were sympathetic and concerned about the case.

There was one drawback. Nothing could be mentioned in the book about the second raid, the one that took place in the house on 22 February, since that was still *sub judice*. The report therefore confined itself to details of the first raid at Group Theatre on the 16th.

Through all of August, my semi-detached home in Campion Road, Putney, became the Exploding Galaxy's campaign centre. For a time, it seemed as though everyone was working in harmony again, as a team. In addition to fulfilling its civil liberties role, *Planted* was an opportunity for artistic exploration and display.

Planted was divided into sections. The aim of the first was to show that the two raids were not isolated incidents, but part of a pattern of police activity. The purpose of the second part was to introduce the ideas and aspirations of different members of the Galaxy to show the diversity of their interests. Thus, *Planted* included an introduction by Fitz called 'The Quaquaversal F', poems by various Galaxy members, the programme notes from *The Bird Ballet*, all of the kinetic drama, *Orange and Blue*, a speech given by Edward Pope at the 'Festival of Poetry' in Struga, Macedonia, extracts from Michael Chapman's plans for a film, a proposition for a kinetic structure by John Dugger, and notes made by David about *The Buddha Ballet*.

Statements were examined microscopically, counter-statements were written, plans were drawn up and inconsistencies itemised. From our own experience, which until then had been a fragmented impression that we were being harassed, emerged a cohesive picture of how the police, the gutter press and the Home Office had worked systematically to end the Exploding Galaxy as a group. Of particular interest was the chronological account of the difficulties faced by David in getting his visa renewed. Through this report, our story was at last being told. Countless parallel stories from the underground movement were still submerged and would remain so for ever.

Preparation of the report gave our house in Campion Road the urgency and dedication you might find in a deadline scene from the film *Citizen Kane*. Typists came and went, Josephine was brought in to draw up plans and Mum even prepared the headings. Pots of tea were on the go the whole time. We were also providing refuge for frightened Galaxy members, some of whom would bed down at night in our sitting room. Mum was delighted to be involved and found her chores whisked away by eager helpers. Dad, although sympathetic to the cause, was just plain confused.

Once it was off the presses, Benn read through *Planted*. He was aghast: 'You can't show this publicly! People will not understand!' He was particularly concerned about the articles at the back from the gutter press, reproduced in all their nakedness, with such a scandalised slant. As a key figure in the fight against censorship, he was aware of how people in high places would react, but we believed in including all the accusations so that they could be revealed as fabrications. Benn also seemed confused about our artistic theories, saying to Paul, 'You know, I've read it through very carefully and I can't for the life of me understand a word. I have no idea what you stand for.' Nevertheless, he continued to support us through the trial and wrote and delivered a statement in our defence. He remained a steadfast supporter of our unfathomable ideas and even hosted an evening for all of us in the wonderful home he shared with the actress Constance Cummings in Old Church Street, Chelsea. Here is part of his statement for the defence:

> There are no articles of association, no recruitment. Newcomers gravitate towards the group, find it congenial and stay or uncongenial and leave. They are unacquisitive, as oblivious of elementary comfort as a classical religious order, unselfconsciously ascetic. Their boardinghouse is furnished with mattresses, sleeping bags, packing cases, bookshelves and little else. There they live in cheerful penury working away like beavers on projects that offer no prospect of serious remuneration, that may at best earn them a week's supply of baked potatoes, raw carrots, bread, jam, cabbage, Mars bars and occasional eggs. They dress and coif themselves egregiously, prompted not by fashion but by individual fancy. Their clothes are not only a proclamation of non-conformity but often an expression of surrealist humour.

It was at around this time that I took my mother to 99 Balls Pond Road for the first time. She was enchanted by the Exploding Galaxy but had never seen the house. The place always looked much worse during the day, needing the flattery of candlelight to look at its best. This was daytime. As Mum stepped into the reception room, she was confronted by a sea of solidified candle wax that had seeped into every fibre of the fitted carpet and hardened. Completely unshocked, she turned to John Dugger and cheerfully gave him some housewifely advice:

> She told me how easy it was to remove hardened candle wax just by using paper and a hot iron. I didn't have the heart to tell her that there was no electricity in the house for an iron.

As the court case loomed, our spirits were in a sorry state. I sensed for the first time that this group, which I thought would take over the art world and revolutionise the nation's aesthetic values, was in danger of collapse. What lay ahead was an epic real-life drama and a legal artwork rolled into one.

NOTES

1. *Planted*, a report compiled by Paul Keeler, London, 1968.

24

Kinetic Drama at the Crown Court

The cry of planting has become a standard, I might almost say, statutory defence in cases of this nature.

MR MCGILLIGOT, OLD STREET MAGISTRATE [1]

THE INNER LONDON Sessions House Crown Court, to give it its full name, is typical of civic architecture completed between the wars. A judicial building since 1794, it is situated on Newington Causeway south of Waterloo.

As I remember, the Galaxy case was 'listed', which means that we had advance warning of the date. I found the printed list pinned up in the court foyer and saw in black and white: '*Regina* v *Dugger, Fitzgerald and Ledoux*'.

It was the first time I had ever watched a court hearing, and until this case, I had not understood the degree to which it was both theatre and game. It was inevitably theatre – both sides had to convince an audience, in the form of the jury. This was done through well-projected voices, artful delivery and, above all, pauses in just the right places to milk the moment. It was a game because strategy was used to win. Whether the protagonists were nice people or were being unfair or underhand was not relevant because the unfolding drama was all about strategy.

Game it may have been, but there was no mistaking the seriousness of the occasion when the clerk called out, 'All rise!'

I remember that both prosecution and defence barristers objected to individual jury members as they took their place. I could not see the reasoning behind any of these objections, why one particular person was challenged while another was not. What I did understand, and it seemed grossly unfair, was that the prosecution could strike out anyone they chose, but the defence were limited to two objections.

If you are going into the dock, it is best to dress for the occasion, in the way that normal people do when they are attending a job interview. You go to the barber, buy a suit, polish your shoes and so on, so you appeared normal. The three Galaxy defendants appearing at the Inner London Crown Sessions that week had all taken great trouble with their appearance. Christian was the most conventionally dressed. Even so, he wore a white suit that gave him a flamboyantly Left Bank presence. His cinematic bone structure and dashing Gallic looks made him seem every inch the film star, and he delivered his evidence with eloquence.

With the principal exhibit flushed out of existence, thanks to Audrey Vipond, and only a few cannabis crumbs remaining in the British Museum bag, the main evidence against Christian revolved around his obstruction of the officer who he said had planted the drugs. Here, his defence ran into difficulties. Two members of the Exploding Galaxy were not going to give evidence: Paul and Audrey. Neither was prepared to say under oath that they had never in their lives smoked cannabis. Certain people believed that saying 'never' was a wise and necessary part of convincing the jury, since the members of the latter were likely to believe that someone who had *once* been guilty would *always* be guilty. Audrey not being called to the witness box was a particular problem for Christian. The prosecution was quick to notice this, and made sure that the jury knew that some potential witnesses were conspicuous by their absence and that conclusions should be drawn. It is easy to look back and see how we could have done things differently, but the reluctance of judges in the sixties to favour the defence when cases were tried in court using evidence tainted by obvious police corruption has been well documented. Had Audrey gone into the witness box and described how she had done a tip-toe job on the offending lump, she would have been charged with obstruction or even perverting the course of justice. The fact that she did not go into the box made the jury suspicious of Christian's honesty. Why would she have anything to hide if he were innocent?

Fitz also appeared in court in his 'Sunday best'. Of all the Galaxy members, he was the most austere and openly disapproving of what he called 'addictions', which could be anything from watching TV and consuming alcohol to doing the same thing in the same way, week in, week out. He was the least likely to fall prey to the vices of cannabis or alcohol. When he first took the stand, he wore his green velvet cape and his 'quaqua crown' – a huge Hieronymus Bosch-like bird's-nest affair of twisted aluminium ribbon, with a span nearing two feet.

John Dugger describes how Fitz came across in court:

> Fitz took the stand with his quaquacrown on. There was some debate and then he was asked to take it off. Having lost his headdress, he was then just a bald guy sitting in the dock talking about crazy ideas, because to those 12 good men and true from Bow, quaqua didn't mean a blind thing. The question was, did he have drugs, and when he finally said, 'No, I don't even drink whisky,' he sounded absolutely crazy. I think he misunderstood who the audience was. The audience was there to judge the Exploding Galaxy, not to read a criticism.
>
> It seemed to me that it was Fitz's idea that somehow he could linguistically convince the court, and he could point out the contradictions of language and show that it was all illogical. But this wasn't going to work. Courts are run on their own precedent and their own linguistic interchanges, and by the way, they are better at it than the rest of us. You might put on a costume or a dress up and act like a Celtic bard, but these men in front of you who are wearing equally ridiculous dress – they've got the law on their side and they know exactly where to turn and exactly what to do, and when you fall foul of that, they've got you.

When he came to sum up, the prosecution barrister turned to the jury and, pointing in the direction of Fitz, said, 'He is asking you to believe that he does not even drink whisky.' He stopped for dramatic effect and then delivered the punch line: 'An Irishman who doesn't drink whisky!' The jury found this hilariously funny.

John Dugger's wardrobe was also carefully planned. He wore white navy-surplus trousers and a white shirt. Each day, after court, he would re-dye these garments so that by the time he was called to the stand, his outfit had changed from white to pale yellow to deepest saffron and positively 'glowed' in the courtroom.

The general wisdom in cases of this nature was to 'deny, deny, deny' and force the prosecution to 'prove, prove, prove'. In many cases, this strategy worked. However, the Crown always had the advantage, by virtue of the 'unimpeachable' nature of police evidence. Although the accused were supposedly innocent until proven guilty, the testimony of the police would usually be given extra weight against defendants.

Dugger was treating the Galaxy trial not as theatre of the absurd but as a life and death struggle. He stated that, yes, he had smoked cannabis in the past and had tried alcohol, but he now lived a different life. Dugger's solicitor was Bernie Symons, who, given the seriousness of the situation, had brought in a highly qualified barrister, a QC called Jeremy Hutchinson[2]. Neither had expected Dugger to admit on the witness stand to having ever smoked cannabis. John Dugger recalls:

> When Jeremy Hutchinson asked me the question 'Have you ever smoked cannabis?', I said that I had. My tack was I just walked into this thing. However, since being there now I have been helping do this theatre piece called *The Buddha Ballet*. Part of the fact was that I had been studying Buddhism myself. As a religious person I was the first to admit – as someone who believes in an ideal – that I had done the wrong thing, but I had not been guilty. When Jeremy Hutchinson asked how I explained the presence of 63 grains of cannabis in my coat pocket, I pointed right at the policeman seated in front of me. Still pointing, I stated, 'That man planted me.' The prosecution objected but it was not struck off, and the damage had been done.

John Dugger came across well. He did not particularly agree with all the Galaxy doctrine. As an artist with his own ideas, which included the validity of conventional drawings, he objected to having to spout a lot of Galaxy jargon in order to convince the world of our legitimacy as an art movement. For him, it was easier than that. He had the misfortune to arrive in England and almost immediately have drugs planted on him, and if he were found guilty, he would be shipped back to the States to face a law enforcement welcoming party US-style.

The chief witness to support Dugger's evidence was Caroline John, our respectable friend from Putney High School, the one invited by Umiak to stay the weekend.

As a witness, she was not allowed into the courtroom before her appearance on the stand, but enthusiastically met up with us during the breaks while she waited to be called. One day, she went off to buy ice lollies, and as she returned to the group, laden with 15 or more of them, they were unceremoniously snatched from her without so much as a thank you. We could be so arrogant. Caroline might not have been a member of the Galaxy in-crowd, but she was nevertheless a great source of generous gestures and an essential witness for the defence.

The prosecution barrister, Jean Southworth, was on her feet. When cross-examining, she had a peculiar mannerism of hooking the pigtail of her wig out from under the stiff white collar around her neck. Rottweiler Jean was about to take on teenager Caroline.

I simply did not understand the game then. As far as I could see, nobody could doubt Caroline's honesty as she talked about Flossie and dog biscuits. But Rottweiler Jean was having none of it: 'You did not do this. You did not see that. I put it to you that you are lying.'

In general, it is not good to blub if you want to show strength; I knew this from my school days. In a court case, this was an act of total submission. In the face of such cold aggression, Caroline broke down, and as a result, her evidence was not thought by most to have been helpful to John's defence. She had tried to do the right thing, but the Galaxy was not big on empathy – there was no tea or sympathy nor any words of gratitude. We did not even notice her leave. On the platform at Elephant and Castle, a kindly defence barrister chatted to her for a while and then ... that was it. Unsurprisingly, she felt pretty sore about it afterwards.

Partway through the trial, an article appeared in the *Hackney Gazette* with the headline 'two spiritualists and a poet on drugs charge'. The paper may not have been a Fleet Street heavyweight, but the article used the same old tactics – a fictitious nude in a shawl answering the door, the long hair, the men in bed with women, all shocking details in the late sixties. Who knew how many of the jury read that piece. It was not going to help our case. The article also brought up the accusations of planting. Quoting Judge Llewellyn's question 'Is there any truth that you planted the cannabis?', the piece rounded off by giving the police the last word: 'There is no truth in that suggestion.'

There are many explanations as to why the rule of three is central to story-telling. It appears to have been universally internalised by all those who sit down to write a speech (Martin Luther King, Winston Churchill), tell a joke (an Englishman, an Irishman and a Scotsman) or recount a fairy tale (Rumpelstiltskin, Billy Goats Gruff). The theory I prefer is that two instances are enough to set up curiosity about a pattern, ready for the third to knock it all sideways, and this is what most satisfies the human hunger for narrative. In the case of fairy tales, there may be three wishes or three characters, three temptations to resist or three attempts to attain a goal. In our fairy tale of the Inner London Crown Court, there are three kinetic princes. Their challenge is to slay the ogre called out-of-control-police, acting as arm of the state. Each prince comes from a different foreign land and each wears armour of his own choosing. The French prince chooses directness and eloquence, the Celtic bard attempts to explain his world and the American shows that he is a devout monk.

It is the custom in fairy tales to hear the outcome of each attempt as the story unfolds, but in our case, we had to wait for the whole case to play out before we knew what befell our three princes.

The jury deliberated for an afternoon and much of the following day, so over a meal at Balls Pond Road in the evening, we speculated anxiously. Most people believed that Christian had done the best job in the witness box. During the trial, I had made a point of examining the jury members from the public gallery, and I thought I knew who were the most sympathetic. I felt confident that there were enough open-minded people on the panel to make convictions impossible, so the result the next day came as a shock.

Fitz was found guilty and fined £40. My mother, who had been at the court throughout, immediately offered to pay this. Umiak remembers:

> Fitz said, 'I'm innocent and therefore I don't want to pay the fine.' He saw it like that. He didn't want the fine paid. He also saw that £40 was a lot of money and he said, 'They wouldn't pay me forty pounds to do a performance, but they'll pay the fine.' He struck attitudes and so the fine was never paid.

In Christian's case, the cannabis part was not proved. The obstruction part was somehow dropped along the way and never picked up again by the police. To me, this shows that the police were to some degree wary in the face of articulate people crying 'Plant!'.

John Dugger was found not guilty. In a case where a judge feels particularly strongly, he or she can go further, and this is exactly what happened in Dugger's case:

> Lord Hutchinson explained to me afterwards that, upon the jury acquitting me, and because of the seriousness of the charges against me and my position in Britain as a young American, the judge had me immediately removed from the dock as 'innocent of the charges'. This would mean that I would not be stigmatised by the trial at a later date in any applications for leave to stay in the UK. By law, being found not guilty is not enough to stay the Home Office's hand in considering deportation – after the fact – and Lord Hutchinson had argued that I alone stood to

be punished doubly for the crime we were charged with, first by Britain and then by the US.

There was a surprising twist at the end of this story for Dugger: he had not, in fact, been drafted to fight in the Vietnam War. It emerged some time later that a letter had arrived at his home in the States, releasing him from the obligation to present himself for military service, but his father had not forwarded the information.

The artist and journalist Caroline Coon remembers our case well. In 1967, she had founded Release, an agency set up to provide legal advice and arrange legal representation for people charged with the possession of drugs. When the arrests took place at No. 99 Balls Pond Road, there had been phone calls to Release. Caroline remembers:

> Everyone was naïve about the level of police corruption... All those officers in the sixties and early seventies, they didn't get the sack. If any of their skullduggery was exposed, they were allowed to retire on the grounds of ill health with a full pension.
> Both the drugs and vice squads were riddled with corruption, but the government believed that the British bobby could do no wrong. In the late sixties, we tried to bring this to the attention of the authorities, but they tried to deny it ... For our generation, the 20-year-olds in the mid-sixties, to come up against this level of corruption was utterly horrendous.

In 1993, Lord Denning decided to make a drastic reduction in the amount of material stored at the Public Record Office. It was decided that just 5 per cent of all criminal cases should be saved and the rest should be put into the incinerator. Thus, some Old Bailey, notorious and celebrity cases like the Rolling Stones' have been kept, but the vast wealth of legal documentation from that time has gone up in smoke, along with any chance to reinvestigate some of the most obvious cases of police corruption.

It was sometime towards the end of the court hearing that Michael Chapman rolled up outside the Inner London Crown Court with a new toy – a super-eight camera. I think I was then aware that this equipment had been paid for by a wealthy benefactress who was supporting young film-makers in Paris. Over the next months, Mike shot reels and reels of footage – blurred images taken from night buses, random leaves and random crowds. Mike also had the good sense to film our gatherings outside the Inner London Crown Court – the toing and froing at the entrance – including shots of high-ranking police officers, our team of lawyers and the Exploding Galaxy in all our finery.

If it had not been for Mike's film and my mother's contemporaneous notes, which she wrote in her immaculate hand throughout the whole trial, you might be forgiven for thinking that the case called *Regina* v *Dugger, Fitzgerald and Ledoux* was nothing more than a fairy tale.

NOTES

1. Mr McGilligot was the Magistrate presiding at the Galaxy Committal Hearing at Old Street Magistrates Court in March, 1968.
2. Jeremy Hutchinson was the criminal barrister who defended Christine Keeler, George Blake and Howard Marks, and played a key role in the Lady Chatterley trial.

25

The Dandies of Zanzibar

Les Filmes Zanzibar sont les filmes sans histoire.

CHRISTIAN LEDOUX, 1968

IT GRADUALLY BECAME clear to many young people that the British authorities, seeing how the French government had almost been toppled and fearing copycat action at home, had started to involve the secret service. Monitoring of the avant-garde continued through the seventies. All sorts of events – from open-air gatherings to scientific meetings at the Royal Institution – were frequently attended by 'a couple of suits' from MI5, there to spy on the activities of anyone whom they thought associated with hippie thinking.

The Exploding Galaxy were seen as subversive, and I think that the only reason why our phone was not tapped by the police was that it had been cut off long ago. However, I do not believe that the targeting of us as a group went to 'the highest levels'. John Dugger does not wish to speculate about who was behind the attacks against us, but he does see the police and press action as 'concerted and orchestrated' and he remembers the climate of 1968:

> I believe that the purpose of the police raid on 99 Ball Pond Road and the trial that followed had been to convict us and thereby break us up as a group. Ours was not an organisation that was resilient enough to withstand such an attack.
>
> The defendants in the court case were an American, a French man and an Irish man. There was no English person charged. It seems to me that the authorities would have loved to have turned us into some kind of international agitators or anarchist commune instead of basically a dance theatre company that had zero politics.

I do not believe that MI5 had latched on to us as the English answer to the Parisian agitators. I think the authorities saw us as idiotic clowns, and they had better things to do on the university campuses and within the unions. If they had fixed on us, it would have taken them next to no time to see how we filled our days. Anyone who monitored us for a single afternoon would see that we were nothing more than a harmless bunch of paupers who spent their days scavenging the dustbins of London for trove with metaphorical value.

The Exploding Galaxy was not typical of the counterculture in general, which was politicised in any number of ways. Our stand was against police corruption and state suppression as it affected us as artists. It was not generalised. Despite our sympathy with countercultural causes, I do not remember a single conversation about Black Power, civil rights or the Vietnam War, although, of course, we agreed with the general underground consensus. Discussion in the house always revolved around aesthetics, 'shimmering density', our costumes or our performances. It is only with hindsight that our rebuttal of consumerism and our carbon neutrality appears radical. According to John Dugger:

> The fact is we didn't have any politics at all. Probably that was the biggest criticism you could have of the Exploding Galaxy. We had so little politics it was embarrassing. Everyone else was standing up and what were we doing? We were dancing about on Parliament Hill. We were fighting a different battle. It was called 'the perfect artist's battle'. We were fighting the great monster for the sake of artistic freedom.

The Parisians had their own approach – the French students had almost brought their government to its knees. Some veteran barricade dandies travelled from Paris after the May 1968 revolt and paid a call on Balls Pond Road as if they were dignitaries visiting a fellow rebel state. But what did they find? Edward took their visit as an opportunity to explain to them his idea called 'Servacow'. He felt a need to contribute to the French action – the soft equivalent of assassinating a dictator – so he had come up with 'SEmi-Violent Riot Anti-COntrol Weapons', which ranged in severity from using soapsuds, custard pies, slippery surfaces and slapstick to fomenting rebellion by employing carefully placed jokes. He had not thought this through, though, because 'there were always a million propositions and only three realisations'. 'Servacow' remained in the zone called 'unrealised ideas'.

It is interesting to realise how, despite this, the French radicals admired us. One of them was Patrick Deval, an old friend of Christian's – they had made a film together in 1966 in which Claude Chabrol played a role. They were part of a loose group of creatives in Paris, among them Philippe Garrel, Jacky Raynal and Sylvina Boissonnas, who were interested in making films.

Patrick still has strong memories of his first impressions of the Exploding Galaxy. He had seen Michael Chapman activating in the streets, and thought, 'He is doing it, while we just talk, talk, talk.' He had been enchanted when Eve had gone up to a fountain and carefully placed cake papers on the water.

French New Wave cinema had been just the beginning. If the Nouvelle Vague version of art house film-making defied convention with its long takes, its jump cuts and its focus on the preoccupations of a younger audience, then what came next took French film-making one stage beyond the pale. It was called Zanzibar, and Zanzibar was anti-*auteur*. The Exploding Galaxy's connection with Zanzibar came through Patrick Deval's film *Achéphale*.

It was in the summer of 1968 that I first heard the name Sylvina Boissonnas. I never got to know her well, so what I heard came second-hand. Sylvina was a Schlumberger. Some decades earlier, the two brothers Conrad and Marcel Schlumberger had invented 'wirelogging', a method of using electricity to locate oil deposits that became vital in oil production. Ever since this discovery, their business had been at the cutting edge of technologies related to oil and gas extraction. As I understood it, every barrel of oil that was pumped from the ground added to their unimaginable wealth. The Schlumberger family was also keen to support the arts, and among Sylvina's parents' generation of the family, there were collectors of everything from Picasso to the Surrealists and Lichtenstein. There was also in the family a history of philanthropy, so it is therefore not really surprising that Sylvina should take it upon herself to fund artistic projects. Having reached the age of 21 and from the seemingly infinite interest accruing to her inheritance, she began to develop her own style of patronage. She had been a student at the École des arts décoratifs but had subsequently turned her attention to film projects and had started to finance them. It was a courageous act, not just to finance experimental cinema without the interference of the state or the demands of the corporate world, but also to finance nobodies to make films. Anyone could present themselves and use the format of their choosing: 35mm, 16mm or Super 8. Jackie Raynal described her open-door approach:

> Anyone could come forward, really anyone, with a project of painting, photography, film, music, publishing, and could receive a cheque from this unbelievably tall woman who was curious and eccentric, and who never asked for an accounting on the use of her money.[1]

Rue de l'Échaudé was where Olivier Mosset lived. An artist who at the time specialised in painting zeros, his place had become the centre where this group of young artists and film-makers could view films and discuss their ideas. When the flat became too small for the numbers interested, Sylvina rented a larger space in Rue Thimonnier near the Place Pigalle. The group came to be known as Zanzibar after Rimbaud's attachment to the place and in honour of the fact that for a short period, prior to April 1964, the island nation had a left-wing government, earning it the nickname, 'the Cuba of Africa'.

Zanzibar films had certain distinctive features. They were characterised by extremely long takes and panoramic shots, were usually filmed in black and white and were sometimes lit by candlelight. They had protagonists – Sally Shafto in her book on the Zanzibar film-makers has described them as 'witnesses' – but little or no plot line. For me this was a challenge, since my liking of folk ballads made me crave plot – psychological plot, 'plot' plot, any plot. The problem I often found with iconoclastic art was that it was great to produce it yourself, but not so much fun to watch. As far as I was concerned, Zanzibar films were ultimately romantic in nature, with the themes of destroying art, zero and nothingness all being a reference to the moment when the revolutionaries officially turned their calendar back on 24 October 1793, setting it to zero for the previous year.

Most controversial of all in Zanzibar's *modus operandi* was Sylvina's decision to pay the unskilled to make films. This was in keeping with idea of breaking with the tradition of the *auteur*. Credits were absent from the group's films and they were often made through consensus, although 'collaborative decision-making' often meant that the strongest personalities got to make the choices. When Sylvina funded Serge Bard's *Détruisez-vous* ('Destroy Yourselves'), she was bank-rolling someone who had never made a film before, and when she backed Jackie Raynal's film *Deux fois* ('Twice upon a Time'), she was allowing a film editor to be a film director. Sylvina later explained this use of the non-specialist:

> There was an idea of conquering freedom for many of us, of leaving behind what Guy Debord had memorably called the 'society of the spectacle' and of participating in several areas at once, without however ever being a professional in any one. We were in synch with the youth movement in the US in the 1960s and 1970s, as well as with the Chinese cultural revolution (or how it was perceived in the West). We also sought to put into practice a collective management, to reject a delegation of authority. We dared to think of making films without being professionals, by using reduced crews, often made up of friends as technicians.[2]

In fact, this deliberate use of the non-skilled was very widespread within the underground, especially in England, where we have always adored amateurs and 'also-rans'. In the Exploding Galaxy, it was part of our currency of expressiveness, with only a smattering of highly proficient performers, such as Judith Pertz, Jocelyn de Warren Waller and John Taylor. The Incredible String Band were also taken with this idea of the everyman artist. Robin Williamson explained how these ideas were used in the planning of their 'surreal parable in song and dance' called U:

> I had been pushing for a while to get a visual element into what we were already doing musically… I liked the notion of everybody having a go, regardless of their particular abilities; using all people at their various levels. This was something that Medalla, Malcolm and the Stone Monkey had already imbibed, in the notion of street happenings, getting people to generally explode. These people were already doing Indian movement ideas, Indian street theatre ideas, Japanese, Burmese and Thai kind of puppet notions. For better or worse, we tried to flush all those things in there.[3]

Patrick Deval did have experience, but he was far younger than was usual for a director . The film *Acéphale* was shot in a single fortnight in the summer of 1968, filmed in a disused railway station and a disused zoo. Christian was due to have a central role, but because of the problems with his passport caused by the Galaxy court case, he could not get back to Paris until part way through the shoot. His place was taken by Laurent Condominas.

The name *Acéphale* was taken from a journal produced by Georges Bataille. The title in French has a transgressive connotation, but *acéphale* translated into English does not sit well – 'headless' makes one think of headless chickens and 'brainless' indicates total stupidity. As the prefix 'a–' is used, meaning 'without', I would prefer to translate the title as 'a-brained' or 'non-headed'. Thinking in underground terms, I would compare *acéphale* to our use of the word *strange*, which is how we liked to call ourselves in the US and in England. What we meant was: in a state that is more present and more sentient and which transgresses normal perceptions. We saw it as an awareness of otherness.

Acéphale was one of a dozen or so films to have come from the 'dandies' of Zanzibar. 'Dandies' is a good word to describe this loose crowd of highly creative artistic investigators. If you look at pictures of them, they are all young and good-looking. A photograph of Philippe Garrel shows him standing, hand on hip, looking for all the world like a swashbuckling Errol Flynn, and Serge Bard, swathed in a headdress, is a fair version of the young Rudolf Valentino. The women of Zanzibar were largely ex-models. From the appearance of these people, you might be forgiven for thinking that they were more closely aligned to the flamboyant, hedonistic corners of Hollywood than they were to the radicalism of 1968.

I saw *Acéphale* three times. The first time, I thought it wonderful in every way – there were the Exploders at work on screen. The second, I saw it as self-important tripe, and the third, I found it extraordinarily beautiful and poignant, and an accurate document depicting our late sixties bubble.

In London, scavenge art continued to blossom. Where the French used copious numbers of words, we used street detritus. London definitely had the edge when it came to dustbin thinking. Artists such as William Green, Gwyther Irwin and Stuart Brisley had stood us in good stead. Mark Boyle and Joan Hills were also working with the discarded. They had put together a film called *Ends*, made from footage scavenged from the bins of film companies in Soho. This they showed at a momentous evening event named 'Suddenly, Last Supper'. During the screening, they did a vanishing trick by loading up and moving house while their guests were being entertained downstairs.

The Exploding Galaxy, too, worshipped at the shrine of transformation: take something out of a skip, and turn it into something else. Our mothers had been trained during the war to draw pretend seams in eyebrow pencil up the backs of their legs. The parentage of our artists' medium was rationing. Wartime newsreels from British Pathé, such as *Seaweed Belt* and *Fishing Net Hat*, show the way in which women were encouraged to use their imagination. I even remember seeing some footage once where milliners were encouraged to save curled woodshavings in order to decorate hats.[4]

Perhaps the most extreme offering to come out of that sixties period of film-making was made by Anthony (Scottie) Scott, who scrudged the whole 48 hours of footage for his film from the bins of Soho. *The Longest, Most Meaningless Movie in the World* is registered with the BFI, yet cannot be found. Zanzibar is also a story of the lost – lost films, lost money, lost equipment. Several films either disappeared or were never distributed. In this way, those makers of the 'lost footage' have turned themselves into true practitioners of the art of the invisible – the ephemeral as it ultimately should be: gone for ever.

NOTES

1. Sally Shafto, *The Zanzibar Films and the Dandies of May*, 1968.
2. Shafto, *The Zanzibar Films.*
3. Shafto, *The Zanzibar Films.*
4. Cinetopicalities In Brief No. 96, Pathe News, 1940 and Fishing Net Hat (Issue Title : Hands Wanted), 1939, Net Result, Pathe News ,1940 Painted Stockings, Pathe News 1940.

26

The Money Mules

There were only two White Panthers and Mick Farren was the leader. I went round to his flat one day and Mick was always telling me about this 'property is theft' stuff. He had some Gene Vincent LPs that I was rather keen to own, so I said, 'I don't feel as strongly about it as you do, but I'll take these Gene Vincent LPs,' but it turned out that property was theft except for Gene Vincent LPs.

JOHN PEEL AND SHEILA RAVENSCROFT [1]

THINGS KEPT DISAPPEARING. One by one, I'd notice items go missing – my Kurt Geiger boots, for example, and a Westaway Fair-Isle knit, an oriental embroidered belt and pieces of treasured jumble junk. I was not the only one. Rag Doll, who earned his living by working as a DJ, had lost his record deck and entire collection of LPs from the house. Audrey's watch also went, as did Judith Pertz's motor scooter, the one she had originally used to get to London from France.

To start with, when the house was overcrowded with perhaps 30 people crashing at any one time, there were two people I can think of with serious drug habits, in bad need of a fix, and this might present an explanation for the thefts. But the 'No drugs' notice had been put up in the house in July 1967 and the druggies had been squeezed out soon after. So it is interesting that items continued to go missing.

Thefts from the unsuspecting over a period of two years or more would have provided a slow but steady stream of income via a pawnbroker. The person concerned had a strong sense of entitlement but was skilful enough to remain undiscovered for the whole time they spent working with the Galaxy. I suppose the rest of us, despite throwing out the rule book, had assumed that respect for other people's property would not be up for renegotiation or at least, if it were, that there would be some discussion about this by the whole group. This was foolish, given the political climate of the time.

Theft was not part of Galaxy philosophy, and the shadow of these disappearances obscured the truth about the house at Balls Pond Road – that, in general, it was a place where whatever each of us had was generously shared.

Of course, for those of us who had the nicest things, it was difficult not to have some belief in personal property. You were not supposed to mind if others took your things because, after all, you were one of the beautiful people and not a materialist. Lizzie always said that it was tough, having to sit there looking tranquil, while someone else walked off with your favourite scarf – or your boyfriend.

Money was in short supply, and what followed next might seem the answer to anyone's prayers - a lottery win of sorts, or more precisely, several lottery wins. Sylvina Boissonnas, the Paris-based benefactrix, now turned her attention in the direction of the Exploding Galaxy.

I am not sure at what point Sylvina broadened the scope of her donations from just film-making. It was either Lizzie or Christian who gave her a copy of Paul's report, *Planted*, and she read it with concerned interest. Across many countries, youth culture was united in rebellion against the system, and here in London an arts revolution was being brutally suppressed. The report ended by seeking donations in support of the Exploding Galaxy. None of us could have imagined the extent of patronage that Sylvina was about to give.

News spread swiftly that those members of Exploding Galaxy wishing to travel to India should make their way to a particular flat in the 9th arrondissement, where they should make their request in person to Sylvina.

Sleeping arrangements at Rue Thimonnier were as they always were when crashing – you found yourself a corner and then put down a cloth to mark it as your area. You used rolled-up clothing for a pillow and you became accustomed to the hard floors. In my case, I found what I thought to be a room, but it turned out to be a vast airing cupboard emitting intense dry heat. At least, though, it was my own space.

The first non-film 'pitch' to Sylvina, or rather the first Galactic pitch, had come from David Medalla, who proposed travelling to Kerala in India with the aim of studying with the Kathakali dancers in their home town on the river Nila – his lifelong dream, perhaps. David had not wanted to travel alone, so Sylvina was asked to pay for 'anyone in the Exploding Galaxy who wished to travel East'. Since Galaxy members had various other projects in mind, this 'journey East' was soon broadened to other kinds of creative proposals.

In Wales, things were tough. Rakis had been sharing with Robin and Licorice of the Incredible String Band, but moved out to a cottage nearby. He was so cold that winter that he and his writer friend Peter O'Connor took it in turns to sleep with Malcolm's Jack Russell, the dog acting as a joint hot water bottle. When news came through from Malcolm that Sylvina was giving away money for projects, Rakis appeared in Paris in the blink of an eye. Paul Keeler had successfully secured a sum to put on a concert in Paris, and this dovetailed with an idea of Rakis' to do the same at the Roundhouse as part of a project to bring the glorious talking drums of Oshogbo from Nigeria to Europe. He was good friends with the artist and Yoruba priestess Susanne Wenger, who believed in the healing power of these drums, and would be able to convince the drummers of the value of this ambitious project. The first stage was to film the drummers *in situ* in Oshogbo. Sylvina agreed, and after cashing her cheque for £2,000, Rakis sat with Malcolm at a café on the Île Saint-Louis, and the two of them worked their way through 14 sorbets.

Malcolm Le Maistre did better than Rakis, coming away with £5,000 for his theatrical project called 'Stone Monkey'. This was to be a dance drama troupe like the Exploding Galaxy, but it was to be leaner, 'more focused' and less amorphous.

Andrew Forrest also approached Sylvina at about this time. He, too, wanted to travel to India – not to study Kathakali dance but to take photographs. Along with the ticket to travel to the sub-continent, he bought a camera and rolls of film. He describes his pitch to Sylvina:

> She invited me to a viewing of her own film at the Cinémathèque. Afterwards she asked my opinion and I was honest. I told her I thought it was a piece of pseudo-Warholian pretentious drivel. It didn't stop her giving me a large sum of money. I later contacted my sister Lesley and she bunked off school to get over to Paris, and, with her Sylvina money, she joined me in India. As Sylvina handed me the cheque, she said in a kind, not unpleasant way, 'Don't ever approach me again,' which I didn't. Some years later, though, when I was living in Paris, I passed her in the street. As she walked towards me, our eyes flickered in recognition. Nothing more.

There was a protocol to asking Sylvina for money. You gathered with other hopefuls at Rue Thimonnier. You might have to wait for several days – later it became weeks. She would then visit, listen to the pitches and send you off with a cheque to a particular bank (one owned by her family, it was rumoured) to cash the money. One evening, I was witness to the ritual pitching. Sylvina came across as businesslike but warm. One by one, she addressed the people seated on the floor, and one by one, they told her about their proposal. She seemed to say 'Yes' to everyone. I was sitting in the corner knitting, which for me felt like a political act there in Paris – perhaps I had seen too many guillotine films. At the end of our audience, she looked directly at me and said, 'What about you, Jill?' I said, 'Thank you, but I don't want anything.' The audience was over in a few minutes and her personal fortune had been diminished by approximately £9,000. This figure needs to be multiplied by 15 to get a rough idea of such a sum in today's money, but it was drop in the ocean at that point.

Of course, it was one thing to receive a donation from Sylvina. It was quite another to carry the money back to London. The French custom controls were strictly enforced: you were not allowed to take more than the equivalent of £50 out of the country. The consequences were serious, so each individual had to dream up their own kinetic smuggle-drama. One person put the trove in her garter, another in his underpants, and another in a baby's Moses basket. The most ingenious of these 'mules' was one of our number who smuggled the money in a hairdo, pinning the tight tube of notes into the centre of a French roll. We are talking here about upward of £1,000 per journey, but in the case of Malcolm and Rakis, they had pooled and divided their money to smuggle it across, and carried £3,500 each, carefully folded into newspapers tucked under the arm.

Mike's first sponsorship from Sylvina paid for his trip to India and a Super 8 camera, with which he planned to make his own film. By the spring of 1969, he was being funded to set up a printing press in London, using the staggering amount of £50,000 from Sylvina, enough to buy a medium-sized property portfolio in central London, had he wished to set himself up for life financially:

> After the Indian journey, I returned to Paris, and together with Sylvina and some associates, we launched an international political satirical magazine called *L'Idiot international*. The magazine was quite slick and the general plan was to release French and English versions simultaneously. The English version tied up with a project of mine to mount a printing factory in London which would be rented to unions and left-wing organisations to enable them to produce their newsletters. Sylvina gave me the whole £50,000 in currency at her bank, which I then stuffed into my haversack and took to London on the boat train. When the British customs officer opened the bag and saw the money, he gave me a very wry smile and let me pass.

Umiak and Fitz had less luck. They had approached Sylvina as a couple, wanting to acquire warehouse space in Covent Garden. When Sylvina asked 'How much will this cost?' they were unable to answer, so were forced to return home to find out how much a warehouse in Covent Garden would sell for. In the meantime, they made do with the usual £1,000. Back in London, in the flurry, they left the lot in a carrier bag in a telephone box at the end of New Oxford Street and had to dash back across London to recover it. In Paris once more, having found out that the price of a warehouse in Covent Garden was £8,000, Umiak was told that she could not have it because Sylvina was no longer able to fund these projects.

What caused the Sylvina bubble to burst so soon was the number of people who were now traipsing across to Paris. Rue Thimonnier was not the only place where money changed hands. In the 1960s La Coupole, a grand Art Deco restaurant in the Boulevard Montparnasse, was a must if you were young and considered yourself an artist.

It was here that Sylvina would dine with her courtiers, and here that she would hand over cheques, rendezvousing down in the toilet lobby for financial dealings. There were often a smattering of Exploding Galaxy members present, particularly Lizzie, Christian Ledoux and Michael Chapman, and there were members of the Zanzibar crowd, including Jackie Raynal, the only woman film director apart from Sylvina herself. Patrick Deval, Michel Fournier, Olivier Mosset and Phillipe Garell were also often in attendance. Serge Bard was frequently seated close to Sylvina. His hands were stained with the traditional henna designs of the Touareg, and he would gesticulate and twist them in a way that no one could fail to notice. If you were at the 'top table', then Sylvina would, of course, pick up the tab. If not, then you had to fork out for your own meal. I can remember, more than once, sitting with French friends at some table on the periphery. They would take their time mulling over the menu, humming and hawing until after long deliberation they would order the *soupe a l'oignon gratinée*, which I believe was the cheapest item on offer to diners. I would go there without money, so would most times sit in the equivalent of the saloon bar to the side of the restaurant, where I would take all evening wincing my way through a single *citron pressé*.

I am bound to say that I did not understand La Coupole at all. The place served meals to any number of the revolutionaries of 1968, including Daniel Cohn-Bendit. Yet here they were in what most students would have considered an outlandishly expensive restaurant.

These young troublemakers were supping oysters along with the lawyers and bankers. Did anyone really want such hypocrisy in charge? Why did they have such impeccable table manners? Why did they not choose to eat in the Coupole des Pauvres – a perfectly good, cheap eatery for working people, near Chatelet? Four years later, that great outsider, Buñuel, put his finger on this peculiar muddle in his film *The Discreet Charm of the Bourgeoisie.*

In his book *Dancing Ledge*, Derek Jarman mentions seeing a Galaxy performance at the Coupole. Nearly all Galaxy members frequented the Coupole at some time or other, and since seating in such a large hall makes a perfect audience for a Galactic exploration, it was not long before Mike climbed on a table and did his extraordinary recitation of the owl with David beguiling the captive audience with his *mudras* and light footwork. After some anxious moments, the waiters relaxed as the dining hall burst into spontaneous applause. Were the Galaxy still activating? Or were they merging with the spectacle we so despised? Were we starting to become a band of performing bears, there to please the over-comfortable?

Certain people could describe themselves as loosely Galaxy. At this point, there were approximately 12 core Galaxy members. 'Outer' Galaxy included occasional participants on Parliament Hill, ex-Galaxy members and people who might have once stayed the night – a category that increased the Galaxy number well into the hundreds. There were also, of course, the imposters. They had always been there, using our name to get into venues free or to increase their own artistic credibility.

Jim Haynes had done us lots of favours, so I suppose he could at a pinch claim to be 'outer' Galaxy. Jim describes his meeting with Sylvina in a café on the Boulevard Saint-Germain where she asked him how much the Arts Lab needed:

> I told her anything from £5 to £5,000! Well, she paused... and wrote out a cheque. We carried on talking for a while and then she had to leave. After she'd gone, I slipped the cheque out from under the saucer and took a peep – it was for £5,000! I was stunned.

Hermine Demoriane – certainly outer Galaxy – asked for money to study avant-garde art in Brazil, which seemed like a worthy choice. Stan Siegel, one of the young poets who hung out at the British Museum café, gave half the money he received from Sylvina to his parents to help them out, and then spent the rest.

Although not core Galaxy, at least Hermine and Stan had participated in our events. But Galaxy 'fringe' turned into Galaxy 'friends of friends' and then into all and sundry. Now people started appearing at the flat in Rue Thimonnier who looked like business executives and, for all we knew, read the *News of the World*. Sylvina had no idea how rash it was to have agreed to fund 'the Exploding Galaxy'.

By this time, the flat in Rue Thimonnier was half doss house and half waiting room, filled with people hoping for a handout. It was like a doctor's surgery, full of anxious faces. When I next went there, I encountered an influx of strangers who had no connection whatsoever with 99 Balls Pond Road, but just as before, all they had to do to gain entry was to say they were in the Exploding Galaxy.

The last person to get an audience before the doors banged shut for good was Andrew's sister, Lesley Forrest. Andrew, terribly excited, had stopped off at Colchester before going to India. Lesley was a school student aged 17:

> Andrew urged me to join him in India and gave me £30 to go to Paris. I said I wasn't promising because it seemed too ridiculous. I wasn't part of the Galaxy, and why would Sylvina give me money? Andrew said, 'You've danced with us,' and because he'd offered to pay for me out of his Sylvina money, somehow I felt morally obliged. I was terrified, so I took along a school friend. Now she definitely wasn't part of the Exploding Galaxy. I told my parents I was staying with a friend in Henley-on-Thames for the weekend.

When we got to Sylvina's hotel, we knew that she was no longer giving money to artists and was only interested in donating to the political press. We were just walking off when she came running up the road, calling after us. She invited us in, offered us tea and apologised for the packing cases, saying, 'You are lucky to catch me because I am just off to make a film in Africa.' She asked after Andrew and said, 'You must be dying to join your brother. How much do you want?'

After that, my friend, who had been quiet as a mouse all this time, piped up that she had always wanted to go to Japan.

It was pouring with rain and we went shrieking down the street. Sylvina had just parted with 40,000 francs. At the border, they asked me how much I was taking out of the country. I said, 'Only what's in my purse,' and smiled. Since the 20,000 francs was in my purse, I was not lying.

My father, when I told him, said that he had worked all his life and never had anything vaguely approaching that sum. The next day he opened a bank account for me at Coutts.

The amount they were given was the equivalent of £16,000 in sterling. This meant that at £8,000 Lesley had walked away with the equivalent of over £120,000 if you were comparing recommended retail prices with what they are today.

And that was the last of the Galaxy's Sylvina money.

NOTES

1. John Peel and Sheila Ravenscroft, *Margrave of the Marshes* (Bantam, 2006).

27

The Ballet of the Hippie Trail

> *Crash! A large sausage fell on to the middle of the table. Loppi angrily remarked that with the arrival of the sausage their first wish had been fulfilled. He told Lappi how stupid she was to waste one of their three wishes, and cried, 'May this sausage find its way on to the end of your nose!' The second wish was now fulfilled. The sausage was dangling from Lappi's nose, and try as she might, it would not come away.*
>
> *Now the poor couple realised at this moment that they must use their final wish to set things back to how they were before. All three wishes were gone, and Loppi and Lappi had to continue living as poor woodcutters. For some time afterwards, they expected the beautiful stranger who had granted their three wishes to return, but this she never did.*
>
> *The moral is: whoever fails to take sensible advantage of unexpected luck will lose it for ever.*[1]

LIZZIE WAS ON a jet plane, headed for Paris. Mike Chapman had saved her life, of that she was sure. She had been in Kuala Lumpur, suffering from bronchial pneumonia and getting weaker by the hour, and he saw to it that she got on a flight home. In Lizzie's words:

> Chapman thought I was going to muller, and he bunged me on a plane from Kuala to Bombay – in one of those planes without stabilisers. I then flew Air India to Paris, and when the pilot announced that we were over the Caucasus, I looked down and thought, 'My God, that's the Iron Curtain!' I had a cup of tea at Prague.

Then the magic was over. Lizzie was in the ladies' lavatories at La Coupole when Sylvina appeared. Far too well mannered to cause a scene or raise her voice, Sylvina said sternly that she regretted the whole Galaxy thing. Lizzie was abashed, mortified. She adored Sylvina and would have protected her to the death, and now, as she looked into those blazing green eyes, all she saw was anger. Sylvina was asking questions. How was it possible that Galaxy members who had asked for money to go to India had not gone to India? How come some of the people approaching her were not even members of the Exploding Galaxy? How could it possibly be that people were sending telegrams asking for top-ups when living in India was so cheap?

One thing was clear. People had not been able to be moderate. Lizzie herself had always shown a taste for the civilised. I remember that once when we were catching a train – I don't know where to or where from – Lizzie nudged me and said, 'Let's go first class.' So the two of us sat there as our train shot across the English landscape, while we scraped marmalade onto toast, sipping English breakfast tea all the while and resting our heads against crisp white antimacassars. Another time, when we were in Paris, we all stayed at the very same George V hotel where Princess Diana would make her final exit over three decades later. This was the equivalent of staying at the Dorchester, and the next day, of course, we did not have so much as a bean with which to take the Metro.

Michael Chapman had said that poor people, when given money, wanted to act like the rich. This was certainly true in the case of that first Galactic expedition. You only had to look at some of their India trip itinerary choices – the Orient Express and a luxury liner, followed by five-star hotels, including, of course, the Raffles Hotel in Singapore. To be fair, the first Middle Eastern leg had been thwarted by the after-effects of the Six Day War the previous summer. Nothing was going through using the usual routes, so David and Co. were forced to take the slow boat – port-out-starboard-home style. Could the Galaxy really explode in this context? Were the Galaxy going to challenge these people's values just by travelling alongside them? On that voyage, there were long hours of boredom, punctuated by scheduled entertainments like a fancy dress competition, which Lizzie and David Medalla entered as the 'Emperor and Empress of Paper'.

This was pre-package-tour India. The motley Exploders were heading for the home base of the Kalamandalam Kathakali dance company in Kerala. They eventually found themselves in a place called Udyogamandal. John remembers:

> It was a massive culture shock. To a Westerner in 1968, it seemed the most godforsaken place you could ever imagine. We were picked up and taken to this compound that was on the road that led down to the local river. It was just as the Shivaratri festival was beginning, which meant that the entire night the main road was filled with people, many of them beggars. We didn't have access to any running water so we looked a mess. David had written these grand letters, and once we arrived at the school, we looked like the bunch of shit-poor artists. The Kathakali troupe was expecting some proper dance company from London. What they got was the Exploding Galaxy.

There were problems with expectations on both sides. As far as the hosts were concerned, it was clear that none of the new arrivals had clocked up 10,000 hours of physical discipline.

Another strand of the Sylvina-financed hippie trail led to North Africa, and here, too, there was disappointment. There were unheard of quantities of drugs being consumed such as had never been known at Balls Pond Road. One member of the Galaxy's North African contingent wrote back, astonished, to London:

> There is a white butterfly skidding about in front of the hills and then he drops down into sea and ah – he is gone... Oh, it's so complicated and sordid the whole money business. I think Sylvina's money is jinxed... The two-and-a-half million she gave was burnt in Marrakech in a fire the night we arrived there! A kindly piece of poetic justice for those who went out to smoke and left the candles burning, so their fric went up in smoke. So I left there quickly for it was alarmingly drugged – the city, the French and the Americans there. No talk of anything except acid and hash. So I arrived in Algiers... ill and with body lice, quite the most irritating parasites.

This impression was remarkably close to what George Harrison had experienced when he visited Haight-Ashbury in San Francisco.

He had imagined romantic figures with craft tools working away at making paintings and carvings. Instead, he saw a bunch of layabouts, who had travelled across the States to get to this 'Mecca of LSD'. As he walked along, people tried to hand him gifts – native american artifacts, books, incense and drugs. He turned and walked fast back to the limo and drove straight back to the airport. He later said of that episode, 'It was like any addiction. So at that point I stopped taking it actually, the dreaded Lysergic. That's when I really went for the meditation.'[2]

The exodus east was still in its early days. It was not until 1970 that the first travel trail guide was published in London. The guide, the brainchild of Hoppy, was a bundle of stapled foolscap sheets with a pink cover bearing the title *BIT Guide* (the name was inspired by *IT*). The idea was that it could be regularly updated by those on the road – a kind of pre-blog blog. Names soon became familiar: The Pudding Shop in Istanbul, Chicken Street in Kabul, and Freak Street – the road to Kathmandu. Already, major drug consumption had become part and parcel of the hippie trail. This was unmistakably a mass travelling event, akin to the Grand Tour of the 18th century, but the exotic stop-off points were not the frescos of Florence or the ancient ruins of Rome but, instead, good smoking destinations such as Chitral, Kashmir and Manali.

Some looked east not to indulge in the exotic but to re-evaluate, and many came back converted to one or other of the religions of that part of the world. The drummer John Alder, known to most as Twink, was at the centre of the London psychedelic music scene. He had played with, among others, the Pretty Things, Tomorrow and the Pink Fairies. He had been drinking heavily, taking drugs and partying hard, and by 1971 was in a bad way. He realised that things had to change, and it was at this point, while in Morocco, that he converted to Islam. Others were drawn to Tibetan Buddhism and still more followed – through gurus – some hybrid form of Hinduism.

Simon was the first Exploding Galaxy member to make the journey east. On the Galaxy tour he had stayed three weeks in Amsterdam, walking the canals in the freezing cold and having absolutely no money. He returned briefly to Balls Pond Road, which also was unbelievably cold. He had effectively moved out anyway:

> I decided to go to Turkey with my girlfriend Mally. At the time there was this sense that anything was possible and we travelled using our own savings. I left without saying goodbye as I was frightened that the Galaxy would beg me to stay. I got to Peshawar via the Khyber Pass, which presented no problems at all. It was 45 degrees and April 1968. Afghanistan was truly a paradise.
>
> The idea of a 'timeless unbowed performance' had been extremely influential in producing *The Bird Ballet* and so I was already initiated. I was acclimatised to the nature of performance in India, and these went on all night as a normal occurrence. We eventually wound up in Kerala and then went to Sri Lanka. This trip gave me the sight of devotion at first hand and I gained a thirst for God.

Most Galaxy members had already become acclimatised to some degree to the world they were entering. They knew many of the tales of Krishna. Some had started to learn Indian musical structure. The complicated rhythms, the quarter tones and the *mudras* were not unfamiliar to Galaxy travellers.

We saw our journey as more of a pilgrimage. Patrick Deval firmly believes that, as a generation, our journey was different: 'We did not go to conquer, but to learn.' However, it was also perfectly possible to travel the hippie trail in a Western bubble and learn precisely nothing.

Richard Neville, editor of *Oz*, had left Australia for London in April 1966, taking the slow route. He therefore had plenty of advice to share with those embarking on the hippie trail three years later:

> Third-class compartments break the Geneva humanitarian codes, but then most hitch-hikers escape payment, so you can't complain. Look the Indian railway guard in the eye and say, 'I am not going to pay.' He will go away. If he persists, ask: 'Didn't I meet you at Oxford?'[3]

His advice for Thailand was:

> If you want to avoid paying fares, (1) pretend not to understand what the conductor requires, at the same time creating an embarrassing exhibition, with wild gesticulations and shouting, and he will leave you in peace, or (2) point to another European and say that he has paid. He can return the gesture. These two ploys are common throughout the East, although in Thailand you won't have to pay anyway. Not due to any discriminatory generosity on the part of the transport minister, but because the Thais are too polite to ask you.[4]

It would be hard to imagine that anyone taking this advice would have learned anything during their 6 or 12 months on the road.

Meanwhile, the saga of the Sylvina hand-outs had turned into a circus. The accidental burning of the all the film finances was not the only piece of hippie incompetence and it was not to be the last.

Rakis' idea, perhaps the most exciting of the lot, was to bring over to the Roundhouse the talking drums of Oshogbo in Nigeria. This was an early attempt to introduce African musicians into Britain – in 1969, world music was not even a category in music shops. Through his friend Nick Hosker, he acquired a cine camera in order to get some advance footage. The day came in Oshogbo when the finest drummers were assembled, and handsomely compensated, and a crowd of hundreds gathered. They were all in position and ready to go, but Rakis went home empty handed. The concert went down a storm, but he was unable to get the camera to work, try as he might. He returned to find out from Nick that he had left the safety catch on.

In Paris, it sounded like things were getting ugly. People had started to squabble. David and John Dugger made allegations against Mike, who was himself now fully absorbed in his plan to start the printing press. A top-of-the-range Heidelberg printer had been purchased and he had leased premises somewhere in Shoreditch.

My understanding is that Sylvina was not the only French heiress giving away big money in 1968 and that this was an unwelcome financial drain at a time of national emergency in France. Lizzie is certain that she read a newspaper article that puzzled over the seeming drain from French coffers. If the extreme left were attempting to de-stabilise the country financially, then one possible way was by getting very large sums out of France through willing money mules. Lizzie, who knew people at the heart of the movement, firmly believes this was part of their strategy. I wonder if this story is really so very far-fetched, given the strict £50 limit that had been placed on taking money out of the country at that time.

By now, Lizzie was dispirited and destitute – she had just given away her last sous. She declared that the Sylvina money was Rheingold. What she meant was that whoever possessed it would live in eternal anxiety and that those who did not, would desire it. If you took a cool look at outcomes, you might be inclined to agree.

In the late 1980s, Lizzie's husband was trawling a second-hand bookshop and found a copy of Richard Neville's book *Playpower: Exploring the International Underground*. At the back was a section on free money, in which Neville explains how to create a false identity and a false address by using a bombed-out property. There is also a paragraph that came to haunt Lizzie when she learned of it. The book was originally published in early April 1969, which coincides with the exact moment that the Rue Thimonnier became a feeding frenzy:

> Sylvina (the woman in Paris) doesn't enter the philanthropy stakes... 'How much will you need? OK.' No strings, no medals, no bread and butter letters. Only a Japanese delicacy... she is spending her capital. Less and less is safely invested in the system. She's decided not to play that game. The people who know how to contact her are the Exploding Galaxy.

Lizzie was mortified. Her lack of caution had meant that she might as well have published the information herself. From then on she believed that she had unwittingly betrayed the person she most wanted to protect.

As for Sylvina, I believe that these days she is an architect. I don't know what has become of her artistic contribution to Zanzibar, *Un film*. I wonder whether people have attempted to approach her since that time, wanting the details of this fascinating scoop or hoping to make a biographical film cut in with footage from the Paris of May 1968. I imagine that where people once wanted her money, they now want her story, and it is an irresistible one – the woman of great wealth who gave up her boots of Spanish leather and left the castle to live with the raggle-taggle gypsies for a while.

NOTES

1. From *The story of Loppi and Lappi*, an Estonian version of the three wishes fable.
2. George Harrison: *Living in the Material World*, A film by Martin Scorcese, 2011.
3. Richard Neville, *Playpower* (London: 1971).
4. Neville, *Playpower*.

28

Tropicália Comes to London

There is no such thing as a neutral education process. Education either functions as an instrument which is used to facilitate the integration of generations into the logic of the present system and bring about conformity to it, or it becomes the 'practice of freedom', the means by which men and women deal critically with reality and discover how to participate in the transformation of their world.

RICHARD SHAULL

THE EDUCATIONALIST PAULO Freire, exiled in the 1960s from Brazil, would have approved of our Galactic approach to learning. We, the Exploding Galaxy juniors, continued our education through exploration, but now turned our gaze to two other established artists. Neither David nor Fitz was around at this time. Fitz was out activating new spaces in Islington, developing his own troupe, which now called themselves Transmedia Exploration. David was still out of the country, on his 18-month walkabout courtesy of Sylvina. So it fell to the youngsters to find other mentors, and the artists Lygia Clark and Hélio Oiticica fitted the bill perfectly. We all had admired the Brazilian artists, long before they swooped in on London.

I had already met Sérgio de Camargo and his wife in Paris. There was something organic about all those clusters of small slanting wooden cylinders he produced. They grew out of the flat surfaces they inhabited, as if animated. In his relationship with Signals, Sérgio had been, according to Guy, a kindly uncle figure, and he remained that for us throughout 1968, firmly attentive to whatever the Exploding Galaxy was getting up to.

Most members of the group had seen, if not the exhibitions of the Signals sculptors themselves, at least some of Clay Perry's photographs of the works in action. Long before Lygia visited London, I had spent time at Guy's place in Southampton Row, turning the hinges of one of her angular metal constructions that were called *bichos*,[1] and Audrey was familiar with what she has described as Lygia's 'pregnancy space suits' with all their pockets and textures. Most people living at 99 Balls Pond Road were fairly literate, kinetically speaking. What we hadn't realised was just how close Lygia's and Hélio's explorations were to our own Galaxy investigations. When they came into our lives in person this hit us like a bombshell. There was an instant rapport and mutual enchantment.

Hélio had started with flat surfaces of colour, which were then suspended. Explorable box-like constructions and containers followed, which led to encounters with capes and whole environments. A look at Hélio's photographic archive shows how much took place outside in the street and on the '*morro*'.[2] Despite the rain and the cold in our part of the Northern Hemisphere, the outside felt the natural place for the Exploding Galaxy to operate, too.

One Galaxy member who consistently took the opportunity while out and about to engage passers-by in discussions on aesthetics was Edward Pope. Edward stayed with Lygia Clark in Paris in autumn 1968. He recalls:

> Lygia had a famous sculpture which was a little plastic bag with water and a stone. I borrowed it to take around Paris and show the people I met. Most were strangers, and I talked to quite a lot of people. I also made a portable construction, using a plastic bag containing water and the black cloth of an umbrella. Imagine an umbrella without the metal part – a big circle with a hole in the middle – that became a black cape and I used it with the plastic bag. I put my hand in the umbrella cloth, like a glove puppet. It was appropriate that it was a black umbrella. It was appropriate to Lygia's work because she liked the basics of black, white and transparent.

It was not just the nature of outdoor interaction that connected the Brazilians to the Galaxy. It was also the intensity of the exploration of the object itself, whether through simple contemplation or through physical engagement. The important element was to experience the object absolutely and in the present tense, which was a way of fusing mystical and artistic experience.

We were making the same aesthetic discoveries at exactly the same time, but coming at it from two very different cultures. Among the many references for the Brazilian artists were Afro-Brazilian culture, the tropical environment, MPB (Brazilian popular music), the favelas, the Sertão (the arid outback of north-eastern Brazil) and the tyrannical repression carried out by five-star generals. Although constantly harassed by the police, the Londoners were not going to be bumped off or strung up on parrot perches, the de rigueur form of torture in Brazil at that time. Our original references were different: eastern mysticism, the American Beats, psychedelia, the tyranny of 'work, spend, sleep' and, above all, the ethics of wartime utility austerity.

Tropicália was the name Hélio gave to one of his artworks. Here is Caetano Veloso's description:

> ...an installation (not yet the term, but that's what it was) consisting of a winding path covered with sand, flanked by tropical plants and wooden walls, along which one was meant to walk barefoot before winding up facing a television screen tuned to regularly scheduled programs.[3]

What started as the name of a single art installation was then given as a title to one of Caetano's songs and then spread to become the name of a whole movement. Tropicália was a creative explosion and a political protest movement wrapped up into one. To me it was 'the Brazilian spring', a parallel to the Prague spring of the same era, spilling over visibly into all the arts. Caetano, in the opening chapter of his book described its thinking:

> The tropicalistas decided that a genuine blend of the ridiculous aspirations of the Americanophiles, the naive good intentions of the nationalists, traditional Brazilian 'backwardness', the Brazilian avante-garde – absolutely everything in Brazil's real cultural life would be our raw

material. Genuine creativity would redeem any aspect of it and make it transcendent.[4]

When Hélio arrived, it was decided to hold a party in his honour at Balls Pond Road. Edward made his contribution to the evening:

> My part in it was to decorate the room, which I did with crêpe paper – I just bought rolls of as many different colours as I could get and hung them so that all the walls were covered with vertical stripes of bright colour. I hadn't seen enough of Hélio's work to realise how appropriate that was to it. Some other people cooked some really fine curries, and Hélio seemed to be very happy with the evening.[5]

I met Hélio for the first time at the Whitechapel Gallery, and within a short time, he and I were close friends. He told me all about Rio, its prostitutes and its low life, how the hookers carried razor blades so they could defend themselves. In his deep Brazilian drawl, he told me in detail about the favelas and the samba schools and the drug-taking. Some of his stories were tall stories and some were not – it didn't matter much to me. Some of these conversations took place over the phone, with me shivering in a cold and urine-filled phone box near Dalston Junction, while Hélio filled my head with tales of South American gangland assassinations and with polemics.

There were anxious moments during the mounting of the exhibition at the Whitechapel, and it was touch and go whether it would happen at all. At one point, Guy, who was curating the show, was told that there were not enough 'featured' works – probably referring to Hélio's earlier suspended spatial reliefs or his glass *bólides* containing pigment.[6] Macaws, tropical plants and pebbles, constructions of untreated wood – these might lack 'plastic quality'.[7]

Guy was permanently on hand, as curator and producer of the catalogue. Paul Keeler was also in evidence, anxious that the exhibition should at last take place. Several Galaxy members, including me, paid visits to the gallery in the run-up to the opening, hanging around waiting for breaks in the preparation so that Hélio could come out and explore. The Whitechapel Gallery was in that part of London dedicated to clothes production. Around the corner were the ancient dying sheds of East and West Tenter streets, where the 'tenter hooks' for hanging dyed cloth could still be seen sunk into the ceilings. This was also the London of Jack the Ripper, where several of the Whitechapel murders took place in 1888. Hélio always loved the marginal, and the alleyways around the gallery were just that, with all the melodrama of those world-famous unsolved crimes. It was here that an African who called himself 'The Professor' invited us into a doorway and talked about magic. All of this Hélio loved.

The opening was well attended. Audrey came, wearing a tea-cosy hat, with her baby son trussed up in an extraordinary sling affair. I wore my crinoline, common to samba dancing, but unheard of in sixties London. The television cameras were present to sniff out the strangeness – in this case, Hélio's environments: I was interviewed sitting in one of his straw-filled nest-cells. Despite my cynicism towards the media, I enthusiastically delivered a little speech for the BBC, insisting that you got a better night's sleep in an artwork than on a comfortable Myers divan. With Fitz's comments about activated space fresh in my mind, I spoke with enormous confidence about the need to question the things we took for granted in our everyday life, such as furniture.

By this time in 1969, Fitz and Umiak had taken transformation of space to extremes. At their commune, people sat on conventional seating, except that they sat on sofas that had been turned upside down.

Caroline John remembers his suspended-straps sleeping area:

> One room was strung up with ropes and that kind of broad tape made of fabric you use to tie luggage on the roof rack. These ropes and tapes were strung out through the room on hooks, and that was where we slept. We didn't sleep on a bed; we slept draped in a weird disentangled hammock.

Hélio's nest-cells, like the one in which I was interviewed, were similarly challenging. In fact, his whole Whitechapel Experiment was a total environment. The participant – renamed 'participator' by Hélio – stepped barefoot off gallery flooring and onto different natural surfaces – stone chippings or coarse sand. Sections were divided off by hessian curtains and bricks, with a place to store shoes. The overall sensation was one of penetration. Yes, you entered the individual curtained-off or screened constructions called 'penetrables', but the whole gallery space had itself become a penetrable.

The non-student and non-hippie types who attended the Whitechapel show between February and March 1969 were certainly tentative, but the exhibition, despite all the previous anxiety, was a resounding success. It was becoming clear that it was perfectly acceptable to hold a totally conceptual experience in a formal art gallery setting and still be received well. Galaxy members and their friends were in there taking the lead, including Josephine, Judith and Minoushka, a Galaxy friend from the Netherlands. Audrey also participated, and particularly remembers the sand and how the local East End women with young children caught on early and brought in their kids to use the space as a playground, much to the director's disapproval: 'Because we're not a crèche!'

Of all the Galaxy members, I think it was Edward's responses to the exhibits that impressed Hélio the most. Edward kept going back to the gallery and participated more fully than anyone else who visited:

> One thing I remember is that I inhabited one of his nests. I took a very large number of pieces of paper on which were written poems I had produced in my earlier adolescence, when I was writing poems but had no contact with artists or anything like that; I was an isolated person. By the time of the Exploding Galaxy, I considered the poems very 'past it'. Well, one of the central concepts of the Galaxy, which was Gerald Fitzgerald's rather that David Medalla's idea, was what he called 'transmedia'. Whereas the psychedelic shows at the UFO club called themselves 'multimedia', where they would project some Mark Boyle-type light shows on to Pink Floyd or The Soft Machine, the idea of transmedia is that one medium becomes a metaphor for another. So, for instance, you wouldn't think of writing a poem just in black on white – you'd immediately think, 'It's made of letters, which are visual constructions,' and the sound would have a pitch, and so on. So, I thought, since all my poems were pretty

out-of-date, it would be a good thing to do with them, to make a kind of nest out of them in the Whitechapel Gallery.[8]

After the exhibition ended, Hélio came to live with my family in Putney. We had a large semi-detached home, and my parents had already housed several members of the Exploding Galaxy for various lengths of time after the police bust in Balls Pond Road. I remember that Hélio paid rent, but this was more symbolic than anything else. I very much doubt whether it covered the expense incurred for heating and food, but my parents did not mind – they adored him and were sorry when he eventually left.

Our home in Campion Road was a shabby space – cluttered and eclectic. Everything from the furnishings to the patterned wall surfaces was in some way visually busy. In Brazil, walls were refreshingly painted plain white. I wonder now how Hélio coped with the visual tangle. We had family heirlooms, but these were not carefully displayed. The 17th-century oak chest was piled high with newspapers and an assortment of things that were on their way either upstairs or downstairs, where they would eventually be put away, and the 'Chippendale' chair had been hastily covered with bright Draylon. When it came to the minimalist, or the aesthetically empty, my family just didn't get it. Unlike in Brazil, visitors were invited into the kitchen, the social centre of the house, with plenty of tea on tap. You could say that, in our kitchen, the teapot was never truly out of the picture and never entirely cold – cooling or tepid, perhaps, but always in the middle of things.

Hélio was given the largest bedroom, the one with the bay window overlooking Campion Road. As I remember, this was the least cluttered of the rooms, with just a fitted wardrobe, an Edwardian fireplace and the tubular metal wartime 'utility' bunk beds we had slept in as kids. He chose the lower of the two beds, and the room was kept, unlike the rest of the house, immaculate.

He worked flat out during his stay with us, either at his typewriter writing letters, or sketching and taking his ideas in new directions. His work seemed to become a reflection of his daily life. This became clear to me when, decades later, I read 'Nitro Benzol & Black Linoleum', a shooting script of sorts for a film project conceived while he was living with us at Campion Road. The black linoleum had been bought by my parents, who had decided to get a replacement for the tired old flooring in the kitchen. Hélio had tagged along with them to help. They all came back, really pleased with the purchase, especially my father. 'Hélio chose the colour,' he said brightly. No one chose black linoleum in those days, and it is surprising that the shop even stocked it, but the black went down on the floor and we all loved it.

Since Hélio's death in 1980, Edward and I have gone to two retrospectives of his work, separated by 11 years. Hélio has grown in stature posthumously. At the Tate Modern opening in June 2007, his name was no longer one that nobody could pronounce. We waited until the gallery attendant's back was turned before dipping our mitts into the pink pigment in one of his glass *bólides.* We adorned our foreheads with pink warpaint in homage to that great man before circulating among the party guests.

Looking back, I sometimes wonder what Hélio would have made of the media attention, the doctoral dissertations, the lectures and so forth, devoted to his work today. Perhaps he would have made one of his low, slow throwaway remarks, while loving all the analysis.

NOTES

1. These were her angular hinged constructions that appeared to stand on legs like little creatures (see the illustration on page 7).
2. The morros are Rio's hill favelas, originally settled by those who had nowhere to live. Hélio, as a dancer with Mangueira Samba School, liked to spend his time there. He encouraged the locals on the 'Morro de Mangueira' to wear and dance in his capes.
3. *Tropical Truth: a Story of Music and Revolution in Brazil*, by Caetano Veloso, Bloomsbury, 2003
4. *Tropical Truth: a Story of Music and Revolution in Brazil*, by Caetano Veloso, Bloomsbury, 2003

5. *Hélio in London*, edited by Guy Brett and Luciano Figueirdo, Tate Publishing, London, 2007
6. Hélio's *bólides* were container sculptures. To me they were like Jack-in-the-boxes, surprises that although still, would leap out and challenge. Made out of glass, wood or cardboard, they held earth, raw pigment, stones or text. The Portuguese word *bólide* means, fireball or metior.
7. *Hélio in London*, edited by Guy Brett and Luciano Figueirdo, Tate Publishing, London, 2007
8. *Hélio in London*, edited by Guy Brett and Luciano Figueirdo, Tate Publishing, London, 2007

29

Pink Brown Rice

The old that was once new, is as new as the newest of the new

AUGUSTO DE CAMPOS [1]

THE OCCASION WAS Gilberto Gil's 70th birthday. Gil and I were being filmed by the director Andrucha Waddington as we sat on the green room sofa at the Barbican, chatting about Gil's life in London. Admittedly, I was thrown into the interview suddenly and was unprepared, but *oops,* oh dear – out of my mouth popped that old phrase, so beloved of counterculture commentators, about the transformation from monochrome to bright Technicolor. It always seemed so apt – this idea of the greyness of the fifties contrasted with the new freedom of thought in the sixties in all its full kaleidoscopic glory. I was now using that same phrase to describe the arrival of Tropicália in London. The Brazilian artists were 'like a flock of exotic, brightly coloured birds, settling briefly on the monochrome world of London and then, just as suddenly, flying off'. I was serving up more of the old stereotype that many still use to describe the Brazilians and us Brits, just another version of the happy-go-lucky lover of life versus the repressed grey city gent in a bowler hat. That is not how it was at all, despite the friendly aloofness of London socialising, despite the bomb-damage and grey skies and despite the absence of vitamin D. Enough!

Let us rewind and do another take.

In fact, we had much more in common than what separated us. This was a mass, world-wide avant-garde sit-down strike. We, the youth of the world, had downed tools. We were through with repression, censorship, world conflict as status quo, and little boxes made out of ticky-tacky. The contrast was between the old attitudes and the new, and had very little to do with slight shades of cultural difference related to how close to the equator our origins were. We were all chipping away at the same monolith.

In the early sixties, London was very far from monochrome. It was energetic and particularly open to artistic expression. This was recognised by directors such as Polanski and Antonioni who both came to film in London, as did many others who were drawn to the city at the time, all of whom found the atmosphere in England conducive to creativity. On to the Swinging London of Union Jacks, Beatlemania and pop art was poured lysergic acid, and the bright colours began to swirl and merge under a fierce creative heat. Absolutely everything was questioned and turned every which way.

The event that brought the two tribes together – the Tropicalistas and the Exploding Galaxy – was the 'coup within a coup'. This occurred just before Christmas 1968 and brought to power in Brazil a regime that drove a whole generation of artistic talent out of the country to seek refuge in Europe or the US. Both Gilberto Gil and Caetano Veloso, two top Brazilian singer/songwriters, were imprisoned and then, early in 1969, forced to leave. It seemed to me that the whole world of Brazilian artistic expression – its poetry, visual arts, pop music and its fashion and style – were all fused into an indignant statement of civil disobedience. I remember meeting the Brazilian musicians soon after, at the Arts Lab in Drury Lane – Gil and Caetano, and their wives, Sandra and Dedé. They all looked cold and confused, having just arrived in England from Brazil as exiles, and were clearly traumatised.

Caetano's autobiography, *Tropical Truth*,[2] gives a moving account of just what he and Gil went through after their arrest. There is a passage in the book that describes the enormous importance to the Tropicália artists of having hair that was wildly long (*selvagemente grande*), and this reminded me of the frequent references Hélio made to the subject. The fact was that the wearing of long hair in Brazil was then seen as an act of extreme provocation. Caetano had not cut his hair since 1967, but in jail he was brought to the prison barber and given an army recruit shearing. The locks on the floor were swept up and handed in a little parcel to his wife Dedé who, not knowing what had become of him, cast them out to sea in an act in the Afro-Bahian religious tradition.

Another songwriter, Chico Buarque, was also imprisoned and then exiled. One song, written by Buarque and Gilberto Gil, contains courageous lyrics against censorship. 'Cálice' (Chalice) is the ultimate coded rebellion: 'Lord, take from me this chalice filled with blood-stained wine.' This is a play on words, with *cálice* doubling as *cale-se*, 'shut your mouth'– my translation is 'Lord, take from me this enforced silence, this chalice of blood-stained wine.' The final cryptic verse about wanting to breathe in diesel fumes flags up the story of Stuart Angel, son of the fashion designer Zuzu Angel. It is said that Stuart died while in custody when his mouth was glued to a jeep's exhaust pipe and the engine revved. Zuzu, who then dedicated her life to fighting the dictators, died in suspicious circumstances in 1976, when her car was forced off the road.

The extent of the repression in Brazil only really hit home when, at the age of 22 and newly married, I arrived in the country for the first time, at the port of Santos on a Lloyd cargo vessel. The ship was surrounded by gunboats and what seemed like gangsters with light artillery. Fellow passengers – a journalist from São Paulo, his wife and daughter – were unceremoniously taken away. At lunch, we were obliged to chit-chat with the chief agents from DOPS (the Department of Political and Social Order – the infamous repressive police organisation) who announced with satisfaction that these people were terrorists.

My impression of Caetano's vulnerability continued, although it was clear he was keen to integrate into London life and was writing songs in English from very early on. Once settled in their shared corner house off the Kings Road, Gil seemed at home in the London environment. He was interested in eastern mysticism and followed a totally macrobiotic diet. Once Balls Pond Road was sold, Edward

Pope and Rakis were frequent house guests at their home. Edward remembers how Gil often used red cabbage in his cooking, which turned his brown rice pinky-blue. Gil remembers, in turn, how Edward refused to sleep on brushed Bri-nylon sheets, rejecting synthetic fibres altogether.

Guilherme Araúju, a key figure with whom I hung out, had a fabulous eye for show business. I would describe his background and approach as parallel to Brian Epstein's as manager of the Beatles. By then I was doing evening classes in Portuguese. My first lesson in the language was a verse written for me by the poet Torquato Neto at Balls Pond Road – he was the only one among the Tropicalistas to spend the night there. Three words I remember are *ninguem* (no one), *tem* (has) and *não* (not), but I was never later able to identify the poem. While I was busy trying to understand the Portuguese on the 45 records that Guilherme had given me, Gil and Caetano were busy learning English and beginning to create lyrics in English. After Gil and Caetano visited us at Campion Road, they invited our whole family to their concert at the South Bank, where they were supporting Sérgio Mendes.

Hélio was still living with us then. We took him under our wing – when I say 'we', I mean the newly dropped-out me (I decided not to embark on my A level course at Putney High in the Autumn of 1968) and Josephine Ranken. Hélio accompanied us on many night-time outings. By the standards of the time, we looked bizarre. Josephine, the tallest of us three, wore a giant Moroccan cape whose hem swept along the pavement. I wore my usual – my father's grey army blanket get-up or a combination of oriental robes. Hélio, the shortest of us, wore an army great coat – civil defence issue, bought at Portobello Road or Kensington Market, where the Brazilian artist refugees so loved to go. If you looked at Hélio in his civil defence coat on those windy nights, you might have been forgiven for thinking, given his slight build, that it was only the heavy woollen coat that stopped him from blowing away altogether.

On those nights, we walked long distances. The streets were silent and safe and the three of us thought nothing of going on foot from the Kings Road to West Putney. One time Caetano and Gil invited their English friends over for a musical evening at their house off the Kings Road. Gil had this way of singing directly at you in his Brazilo-scat. These concert parties were intimate, and remain my favourite style of recital – a group of friends seated on somebody's front room floor with no set list, and improvisation at the heart of the rendition. Hélio did occasional demonstrations of the samba.

Josephine remembered just one conversation with Hélio. It was at the time when he went on a short trip to New York, and was astonished at the lack of censorship there and just what could be bought over the counter. 'Do you remember how low his voice was and how deliberately slowly he spoke?' she said. She attempted to imitate his accent: 'Josephine, you cannot imagine how much porn I have seen for sale in New York. I have seen a magazine called *Modern Cocks*.' He had been delighted by the absurd title.

It was after he had been in Putney some time – late spring or early summer of 1969 – that Hélio asked me if I knew anyone with an electric sewing machine. I immediately thought of the art students who lived in a vast 19th-century villa about 15 minutes' walk away, at No. 341 Upper Richmond Road. One of them, Carol, who was studying textiles at Camberwell, said Hélio could borrow her Bernina machine. It was set up in the centre of the artists' kitchen, which had remained unchanged since Victorian times and gave on to a large lawn with an ancient mulberry tree and a walled kitchen-garden beyond. A very old vine threaded its way through a balcony overlooking the garden.

Hélio arrived with a vast mound of unbleached calico. He was about to make one of his *parangolés*. These were large stretches of fabric, folded or twisted into sculptural shapes that could be worn as capes and 'experienced' by the wearer. He worked with absolute concentration and clearly had a very precise idea in his mind about the direction the construction would take. Meanwhile, I dropped a tab of acid and was out of it in not a very pleasant way for the whole afternoon. From time to time, I passed him on my way to or from the garden. Hélio remained focused throughout, oblivious to anyone else. Later, I passed by again and the kitchen was empty – Hélio was gone, the machine was gone and the *parangolé* was gone.

Over two decades later, the curator Luciano Figueiredo showed me around the Oiticica museum on the Flamengo Park road in Rio de Janeiro. I am fairly certain I recognised the *parangolé* – and I have seen it on display at exhibitions since.

Soon after that afternoon, Hélio decided that he would like to try acid for himself and he chose a day when we were due to visit Guy Brett's family home. This was a large estate with extensive grounds, including beautiful woodland, in Oxfordshire, near a place with the pretty-sounding name of Christmas Common. It was a wonderful setting for a trip, or so you might think.

There were six of us: Guy, his girlfriend Carol Laws, the poet and writer Hugo Williams and his wife Hermine Demoriane, at that time famous for her expertise on a tightrope. I don't know how many people had decided to drop tabs – I think just Hélio. I certainly wasn't planning any chemical adventure that day since by now I had a healthy fear of the stuff.

Soon after he started tripping out, our group was approached by Guy's parents. This was a disaster for Hélio, who thought they might realise his drugged state, so he attempted to hide behind some bushes as they came near. Although he may have been set on a long flirtation with the marginal, he was also a well-brought-up Brazilian when it came to introductions.

'And who's that?' asked Guy's father, the 4th Viscount Esher, and rector of the Royal College of Art. He was looking towards Hélio, who was some distance away, anxiously cowering behind some bushes. 'That's Hélio Oiticica,' replied Guy. Neither Guy nor his parents acted as though there was anything unusual about this at all. After a short chat, Lord and Lady Esher moved away.

Hélio's acid trip had started to slip downhill. He asked to be taken back to London, and since his request sounded quite urgent, it was decided that I should accompany him. Guy dropped us at the station and I spent the whole journey trying to coax him out of his hiding place in the toilet. Once in London, things sorted themselves out. Gil had arranged to meet us at the Chelsea Potter in the Kings Road and Hélio turned chirpy, enormously relieved to be back with his Brazilian friends once more.

Then, before I knew it, Hélio was gone: he had been given a one-term residency at Brighton Art College, and soon after that, he left for Brazil on a Lloyd cargo boat. Hélio had said, '*Seja marginal, seja herói*,' which means, 'Be a marginal, be a hero,' but for me there was nothing heroic about the marginality that came out of New York, where Hélio spent most of the last ten years of his life. For this reason, I could never see his later work in the same magical light as the art that had come out of Rio de Janeiro. In New York, he appeared to have immersed himself in a world which was centroclinal in the extreme. The Tropicalistas had always talked about devouring the all-pervasive outside culture. But it seemed to be New York that was devouring Hélio and not the other way round.

Guy has described the developing friendship between Hélio and the younger Galaxy members and stated how strongly Hélio felt that the Exploding Galaxy represented the kind of creative gathering he wanted to bring about in Rio, a gathering or commune which he called the Barracão. Given the level of repression in Brazil in the late sixties and early seventies, and given the extreme reaction that the Exploding Galaxy had provoked in England in what was supposed to be a democracy, he must have realised that this dream was wildly unrealistic. He had, after all, seen our document, *Planted*, and knew what had happened to us. What is clear, though, is that the inspiration exchange between the Tropicália movement and the Exploding Galaxy was mutual. These two reactive movements met, and sparks flew. We briefly joined in a miraculous union of capes, wanderings and exploration. We were all of us artists and at the same time none of us was an artist. We were all spewing out non-artworks that were also artworks. We were all living in an aesthetically mindful state and in the present tense.

NOTES

1. Augusto de Campos, quoted in *Tropical Truth: a Story of Music and Revolution in Brazil*, by Caetano Veloso.
2. Veloso, *Tropical Truth.*

30

A Galaxy Explodes

… upon every stalke standeth a floure greater than that of soccorie, but double, & thicke set together, of colour yellow, and sweet in smell, which is turned into a round downy blowball that is carried by the wind…

DANDELION, FROM GERARD'S *HERBALL* (1636)

IN THE EARLY spring of 1969, the house was in a sorry state – strangely dead, like a turned-off telly. Without the buzz and excitement, the squalor was revealed for what it was – just that.

The laws of physics tell us that entropy always has the last word. It had been working its magical transformation for at least two years on 99 Balls Pond Road. Without major expenditure on improvements, it was clear that the deterioration would accelerate – glass would shatter, roof tiles slip and damp stains spread. Major work on the house was not an option because Paul, the owner, was penniless. True, Sylvina had given him money, but this was enough to fund one concert only, and in keeping with her wishes, her money had not been used on the pursuit of the material. Paul had switched all his energy and attention to a new project, and he and Annabel were settling into a life together in which 99 Balls Pond Road no longer had any part.

Remnants of the Galaxy eventually settled back at the house, including Lizzie, David Medalla, John Dugger, Eve Ridoux and Nick Sawyer, with Judith Pertz as the most constant presence. When Paul told everyone that it was time to leave, there was a terrible feeling of loss, since we all realised that the Exploding Galaxy could only exist in a property owned freehold, without the policing of landlords or co-leaseholders. At this stage, the full implications of the emerging squatting boom in London were only beginning to be understood.

Towards the end at Balls Pond Road, as was our tradition, a meeting was called and the Galactic remnants gathered in the garden. David liked grand pronouncements. Lizzie was witness to one in India, where he had gathered everyone around him in front of the Taj Mahal and stated, as if the arrangements had already been booked and confirmed, that in exactly ten years' time they would all meet in exactly the same place. It sounded magical and, for just that moment, it was utterly convincing. Now, in the garden of 99 Balls Pond Road, Galaxy members all found somewhere to sit in order to discuss the terrible news. Lizzie remembers:

> What little common sense I had told me that, without the house as an anchor, the Galaxy could not survive and would be dispersed. We were all expressing this regret. David held up a dandelion clock and blew it so that the seeds scattered into the breeze, and he said, 'Wherever you go in the world, what is in you that is Galactic, you will transmit to others. You see, everything that you have absorbed from the Exploding Galaxy, everything that you have been given and have understood will be our fruits and our seeds.' He told us to hold no grief and no regrets and I thought that this was tremendously consoling. It was said without cynicism and I certainly took that on board.

Had a house clearance company been called in to 99 Balls Pond Road, they would have seen nothing more than market debris and other landfill and they would have binned the lot. There was little to show for two years of artistic endeavour, unless you were able to understand the significance of scrudge.

Audrey and Christian had vacated the top front room before their son was born, to live in more baby-friendly circumstances in Goldhawk Road. Once they had left, Fitz and Umiak briefly took over as 'top dwellers' and transformed the space, sinking giant eye screws into the joists above in order to suspend what they called a 'Reidinger table'. Inspired by the composition of certain 19th-century paintings where a central table appeared to be askew, the Reidinger table swung slightly, thereby creating uncertainty. After moving out, they stayed with sympathetic householders in Islington Park Street, and eventually found themselves a squat above a betting shop in Pentonville

Road, Islington, and moved in, along with their Reidinger table. This was a space that was to offer freedom for artistic transformation similar to that which we had enjoyed at Balls Pond Road.

Paul had found a purchaser for the house fairly quickly, through contacts down the road in Shoreditch. A woman found through our connections with the anti-university had plans to turn the place into a therapeutic community. At £1,000, she got the house for a snip, one sixth of what had been paid three years previously. With the proceeds of the sale of 99 Ball Pond Road, Paul flew off to Boston to organise a concert tour, while Annabel stayed with their baby son at our family home in Putney before flying out to join him.

David Medalla had a number of paintings for which he had to find homes. Audrey remembers him giving away works, some of which had been framed for display at Signals or the Lisson Gallery. She recalls:

> I chose one work for myself. It was a series of strokes, and was a little drawing about lightning conductors. There was also a box of his works which I asked someone to store. It was in their attic somewhere in Islington. Of course, I never went back for it.

It is just possible that these paintings and drawings still lie undisturbed in that Islington attic, but it is more likely that the box containing much of David's work from the years up to 1969, has gone forever. As 'the disappeared', it joins most of Fitz's early work, which was burnt after a flood, and all of Lizzie's writings, which were destroyed, and Stan's poems, which blew out of his hands one windy day. This was perhaps the only fitting end for works by artists who believed that art and life should be truly integrated.

We all went our own ways. Judith had accommodation of sorts – the Ford van she had acquired through Sylvina, which became her dwelling-cum-travelling musical show, as she toured England for some months. Later, parked up in Amsterdam, it became her student digs for the first part of her flute studies course at the conservatory there. Judith's original plan to go to Europe to study music did actually materialise.

After his return from India, Andrew settled in Paris, where he worked in restaurants and took photos. He had Sylvina to thank for setting him on his own artistic path. Through her he bought his first quality camera.

Eve, for me, became the Galaxy's nomad and permanent flower child. She travelled in India, Singapore and Malaysia, and then settled in Bali for a time. It was here in the village of Ubud that she had the first of her two daughters (at that time Ubud did not have electricity). She and her partner, the musician and painter Shane Sweeney, then moved on to a pre-tourist-destination Goa, where Eve had her second daughter. I caught up with them when they were back in France in the late summer of 1971, living in a converted fire station in the suburb of Soisy-sur-Seine outside Paris, the owner of which, actor Pierre Clementi, was in prison. Then Eve and Shane were gone again, on the road with their permanently travelling rock band.

Michael Chapman went walkabout. He describes feeling burnt out and wanting to be anonymous for a while, disguising himself as a Hassidic Jew, stuffing his hair into a tall hat and allowing a curly reddish lock to sit by each ear. After the disguise phase was over, he settled in Amsterdam. Having sunk a fortune into his printing press and lost all but £17,000 – still a fortune – he bought a barge on the Amstel river where he opened a tea shop with mixed hot tub.

The image of the dispersal of dandelion seeds is quite well suited to the post Galactic geographical distribution – something gentle. Parachute seeds can travel far and wide and their landing can put them in all kinds of extraordinary places. But this gentle image does not come close to being a suitable metaphor for the massively different and mutually exclusive belief paths taken by various members of our group. In this case, the right metaphor would most certainly be the explosion of a galaxy – dramatic and forceful. Our artistic life for the previous two years had been experienced as a spiritual journey, and it is not surprising that so many Galaxy members went on to take a spiritual path. Three immersed themselves in Tibetan Buddhism, and two became premis in the Guru Maharaji movement. Another returned to the Roman Catholicism of her childhood. Two more became Sufis. All these people have remained loyal to their chosen belief systems for nearing six decades.

I had been hearing about China's Cultural Revolution as far back as 'The 14-Hour Technicolor Dream'. Articles in *IT* suggest some degree of sympathy in the counterculture for what had been happening in China from the spring of 1966. In May 1967, Suzy Creamcheese launched into a debate with broadcaster Kenneth Allsop on BBC's *Late Night Line-Up* about the situation in China, saying that people should stop getting so uptight about the Red Guards and should look at what kind of revolution was really happening there before judging. Suzy Creamcheese was never considered a heavyweight intellectual, but the optimism she expressed was part of a general feeling held by some in the counterculture that the two mass political reactions – Flower Power and Maoism – were in some way affiliated. The astonished Kenneth Allsop said, 'But surely this is very much against your own ethics and morals. They are preaching hatred and war and violence and killing!' and then finally quipped, 'I wouldn't think you beautiful people would survive long in Peking.'

Revolutionary painters always seem to depict large harvests, showing not just bumper crops but also outsized produce. I had loved the pictures of Diego Rivera, where contented peasants carried lilies the size of small trees. By the early seventies, the same stuff was coming out of China – cabbages so big it would take two strong men to roll them down the road. I loved the pictures, but never thought the message anything other than a lie.

Some of my Marxist–Leninist friends now seemed to be active participants in this same lie. Apart from the obligatory uniforms, proudly worn, one of that circle even said that they wanted to set up a ping-pong table in their front room. At this time, a major source of information from China was Edgar Snow, who as an American journalist was flagged up by certain of my friends as an utterly reliable source. Some of these same people, although they would deny this now, openly stated that Stalin's actions were understandable given the need to protect the revolution.

It is interesting to see now how those same individuals wriggle about and make light of what they said then, when asked to discuss this subject. One old acquaintance from the Paris barricades still treasures, despite herself, the badge of gratitude given to her by a delegation from Mao Zedong, despite now knowing that, underneath it all, this was the man whose Great Leap Forward resulted in the extermination of tens of millions of people.

It has been said of David Medalla and John Dugger that they left England as Buddhists and came back as Maoists. I caught up with them in the early seventies shortly before I went off to Brazil for the first time. They were living in Cranbourn Street, next to Leicester Square tube station. They wore Chairman Mao jackets and peaked caps and carried around little red plastic-coated books from which they occasionally quoted Mao's thoughts. I was utterly horrified, remembering the fluidity and symbolism of all those untethered discussions we had enjoyed so much in Dalston. It was now just dogma, dished up as pat phrases, with lashings of moral superiority, or at least that's how it felt to me. It got easier as time went on, after the Artists Liberation Front morphed into Artists for Democracy. I liked a good deal of what came out at this later stage, especially their support for the Chilean Solidarity Campaign and their response to the Hayward Gallery's 'Sacred Circles' exhibition in 1976. This displayed magnificent examples of native North American Indian art, yet said nothing about the crisis affecting the indigenous tribes of the world whose whole way of life was under threat. Artists for Democracy launched their own counter-exhibition.

Ex-Galaxy members Rakis and Malcolm took quite another path. They had left during the Exploding Galaxy's European tour because they were unhappy with what they felt was Fitz's increasingly dominant role of both the explorations and the performances, although they were still keen to pursue the idea of kinetic drama. In spring 1968, they flew to join Malcolm's mother at the Chelsea Hotel in New York, taking the only available room, next to a woman who was really unhappy about Warhol, the way he would focus totally on people and then cut them out. Her name was Valerie Solanas and not long after that, she shot him.

At the Chelsea they rubbed shoulders with an assortment of stars and eccentrics including Jerry Garcia, whom Rakis noticed in the foyer reading the *Christian Science Monitor*. After an initial fascination, they felt that this was a menagerie containing people 'who didn't know where anything was going or what it meant'. However, Malcolm did bump into the Incredible String Band in the foyer and invited them to breakfast upstairs. They hit it off straight away, especially on the issue of untrained and intuitive performance. Within the month, Malcolm and Rakis were prancing their Arjuna stuff onstage with the String Band at the Fillmore East. This went down well, and other performances followed back in the UK. For a year or two, they operated as a troupe, drawing in other ex-Galaxy members and living together, developing performances in a commune, first in Wales and, later, in Scotland.

Had Rakis wanted to become famous after their pantomime venture collapsed in New York, he had the essential connections. His girlfriend in 1969 was the film-maker Sandy Daley, whom he describes in the following way:

> She was one of the more mysterious laid back figures who lived at the top of the Chelsea Hotel, a different world from the hell realms of the lower floors where the rock groups were billeted. Her white room was bare except for a futon and three of Warhol's floating silver pillows (he had given her four but one had flown out of the window when a careless friend left it open). Sandy had recently made *Robert Having His Nipple Pierced*, with Patti Smith's monologue as the soundtrack to Robert Mapplethorpe having a nipple ring inserted while lying in the arms of his boyfriend. Back then, both were on their uppers and visiting Sandy at the hotel for moral support and the odd shower. Sandy had a wonderful cinematic eye. One time, she 'discovered' a schoolboy in shorts and cap,

whom she had passed on a London Street. On her recommendation, he later featured as the hermaphrodite in Fellini's *Satyricon*.

Sandy, with her impeccable New York credentials and contacts that she never used for her own projects, was a little puzzled at Rakis's lack of ambition and reluctance to exploit them. He had been launched into the most prized circle of the global avant-garde, with Andy Warhol at its centre. The unfortunate truth was that Rakis found the folks down at the Factory mind-numbingly boring – a bunch of pretentious posers – and he could not wait to get away from them. In this way, he chose rural poverty over the international art world's elite and returned to Scotland, where he later did street theatre work with Malcolm and an Easter pantomime tour in a Stone Monkey revival.

Scottish ex-Galaxy members became caught up with Scientology to a greater or lesser degree. Rakis, although for a time part of Malcolm Le Maistre's Stone Monkey, which performed with the Incredible String Band, kept well away and never went through the process of 'auditing', which involved holding a lie detector contraption. The aim was to be so untroubled that you made the needle float. The down side was that you revealed all your anxious secrets. Some just paid lip service to these sessions. One of the group, who liked living in the Scientology community but not the auditing, was able to control the needle and make it float, without having revealed anything much about herself at all.

Edward signed a contract for two and a half years, which gave him financial support for Scientology courses in exchange for his participation as an auditor. He later extended this term to five years. He claims that, had he wished to join the Scientology's Sea Org, he would have signed a contract for a billion years, but joked that he might change his mind after just one million. Unfortunately, he altered his plans before his five-year contract was up and was faced with a 'freeloader bill', which meant paying in full for all the subsidised courses he had previously attended. This took him a very long time to pay off.

I didn't catch up with the Incredible String Band crowd again until May 1974, when the band were playing at the Rainbow Theatre in Finsbury Park. It must have been within days of my arrival home from Brazil, and the timing was not good. Brazil was still in the grip of a repressive dictatorship, and now I was being ushered straight into a side room at the Rainbow theatre to be 'interviewed'. It felt like an interrogation. A copy of *Dianetics* had been placed on each seat in the auditorium. I liked parts of the concert – I had always liked the String Band's openness to different ways of performing – and Malcolm was there at the front, sounding and looking good, now really integrated into the group. However, Chick Corea's talks to the audience made sure that it was Scientology that dominated that evening and not the music. As with the Maoists, I did not understand the willingness of my former companions to accept strict regulation after the freedom of thought enjoyed in the Exploding Galaxy. As far as I was concerned, if you followed Scientology, you had to accept a certain sort of pricey dictatorship; and if you were close to a follower and if you objected too loudly to what you didn't like, you were deemed a 'suppressive person' and were effectively shunned. To me, it was a question of the new boss being worse than the old.

If some post-Galaxy contingents appeared to have done an about-turn, then Fitz's direction unerringly followed the course he had set two years previously. Now unfettered by the mysticism and the *mudras* and the compromise with eclecticism, and joined by Umiak, the ideas of his new group, Transmedia Exploration, were being refined and turned into a whole new approach to treating life as an artwork.

Despite their having no visible manifesto, it was becoming increasingly difficult for the established art world to ignore Transmedia. I would describe them as a band of troubadours at this stage, and they got their gigs by continuing to use the name Exploding Galaxy, which has caused some confusion for those now trying to do research. After many attempts to gain grants, they eventually plotted to invade a meeting of the Arts Council, refusing to leave until their application-in-person had been considered. It was successful.

Although captivated by its ideas from a distance, I was not drawn to Transmedia Exploration at its height. There were no half measures here, and, to me, it felt dogmatic. I could not be 'half in' Transmedia in the way I had been on our outings to Kingsland Road market. I had been a weekend hippie and a weekend Exploder. I believed that this deal was no longer on offer.

The thing I disliked about all these new directions was their mutual exclusivity. If you were a Maoist, you could not also be a Scientologist and vice versa. The only exception was Edward Pope, who was a follower of both positions concurrently. He also kept in fairly close contact with Transmedia Exploration at this time. But then, Edward always tended to adopt a position that was exceptional.

As for me, I did not join a group or a faith. The idea of mixing movement, theatre and sculpture absorbed me for the next couple of years. I enrolled in classes at The Place and with Matt Mattox and with the Bharata Natyum teacher Balasundari, but trying to reproduce Galaxy creativity outside of the Galaxy context was meaningless. I no longer believed myself to be a poet or dancer or performance artist, since I knew underneath that I was none of these things.

Most people had gone east, to Asia. Only Hermine had travelled to the land of *bólides* and *parangolés*, and although the reports I was now getting about Brazil from Hélio were mixed, I was hatching a plan to go and live there myself one day. In the meantime, I just shuffled between London and Paris, attempting to join theatre groups like Susan Burge's or Lindsay Kemp's.

I did eventually end up in Brazil, but Hélio had upped and gone to New York well before the spring of 1973 when I arrived. By the time he got back to Rio, I was in London once more, so I never clapped eyes on Hélio again after he left my parents' home.

As far as Exploding Galaxy members were concerned, there was the occasional chance encounter. For instance, I met Rakis again in the exam room at University College in 1980 – we were both sitting our finals exams on the same day, me in Latin American studies and Rakis, his PGCE – and I bumped into Andrew Forrest and his sister Lesley in a bar called Tuttons in Covent Garden, also in 1980, and we stayed in contact from then on. But by the nineties, most Galaxy members seemed to have lost track of each other and, like those dandelion parachute seeds, had blown far and wide.

31

Towards an Evaluation

The following comments come principally from ex-Exploders and offer a range of opinions on what the Galaxy was, the nature and value of the experience of being part of it, why it broke up and what its long-term significance might be.

Evaluating the Galaxy in all its manifestations is like cutting water with a knife. I think we can only note how it changed us individually. I was no dancer (the best role I was offered in the school dance drama *The Wall* was third border guard). My body was heavily armoured by years of prep school rugby, and I was too inhibited to dance even at a party. By the end of a summer of explorations I was able to feel exhilaration and empowerment through movement. The Galaxy certainly furthered the idea that dance was not just for the audience to judge but had intrinsic value for the dancer. Marian Chace had introduced dance movement therapy into American medical practice in the 1940s, but Exploding Galaxy perfomances came long before dance therapy became widely accepted as a therapy in this country. We had our limitations… the first time I heard the word 'delusional' was when someone suggested we were the Ballets Russes of our time , with Paul our Diaghilev, Malcolm our Nijinsky. But whatever our legacy, there was a whole lot of liberation going on. The fact that most of us flew back to our cages does nothing to change that.

John Oliphant

By the age of sixteen, I had already begun to challenge the middle-class views of my parents, but meeting the Galaxy in the autumn of 1968 was exhilarating. The colourful, flamboyant, and sometimes alarming people who lived at Balls Pond Road fired my imagination with their wild clothes, strange behaviour and exciting ideas about art, music, philosophy and politics.

The possibilities this loose group of artists represented were inspiring. Their intense self-belief, intelligence and originality fuelled my own curiosity and rebellious idealism.

But beyond my own personal experience, does the Galaxy have any wider, lasting social significance? I think it does. It was pioneering, and experimental, drawing international artists from different disciplines into a collaboration of performing artists. It dazzlingly expressed the vibrancy, optimism and radicalism characteristic of the underground culture, which burst into life in London in the late sixties. The Exploding Galaxy was a one of many waves in a sea of change, contributing to a climate in which significant social and cultural shifts later occurred.

Lesley Forrest

I came into the Galaxy late, drawn by the idea of unifying art and life, and by the experience of living in the present. Strangely, it seems that when you live in the present, your memory is heightened. At one stage, I found that I could remember back, day-by-day, everything that I had done for six weeks or more. Perhaps this was because every day was surprising and different. It was part of the whole ethos of the Galaxy that you responded to things that you saw, improvising and developing a keener observation of what was around you. Something that was lying discarded in the street might hold some artistic value. This was a kind of creative recycling; but according to the Galaxy 'philosophy' it could also be a way of freeing matter from materialism, of allowing things that society took for granted to transcend their normal mundane roles. A bicycle wheel, spun round on its axis and touched lightly with a pencil, could be transformed into a gamelan orchestra.

There was freshness and optimism about this time. It was exciting to feel part of a movement, and to have a sense, at least, that you might change things. I recall a similar, but more short-lived feeling when more than thirty years later I joined the great march against the war in Iraq in 2003.

Annabel Drower

I would describe us as fairly arrogant – we really did believe that we could fix the world. It would not have taken much to turn us into a cult. However, too many opposing views co-existed for this to be a real danger. We did get some things right. Leaving aside the aesthetic question, and whether what we did was the way forward in art, the Exploding Galaxy was above all an experiment in alternative education. Ideas and themes that later influenced teaching methodology came naturally in the Galactic setting. I am thinking in particular of the way that all contributions were valued. We practised differentiation long before it became a buzz-word in teacher education. Virtually everyone interviewed who had been in the group made a point of saying that the Galaxy was their 'real' education. It is also noticeable that nearly all Galaxy members went on in later life to build careers in either education, the arts or both.

Jill Drower

David Medalla's name was on most people's lips at that time because he was, with his cultural origins, exactly representative of the era's new internationalist identity.

People tend to forget how outward-looking that era was. The sixties was the beginning of a search for a new British identity. There was a sense of us bringing home all the rich mix of cultural styles from what had been our empire. Although colonialism and imperialism have, justly, very negative connotations, on the other hand, it was our luck as British people to have had such a close contact with the art of other cultures.

David Medalla represented that cultural multi-texture, and how he showcased those cultures, free of the constraints of colonialism and imperialism, was highly significant to the way Britishness was to develop in future.

Given that we of the hippie generation were looking for spirituality free from Christian-Judaic bigotry and sexual guilt, what David Medalla showed us of aesthetics and spirituality from outside Europe was important to our sustenance. What he was bringing to Signals Gallery for us to look at and examine was, as far as I was concerned, absolutely crucial. Signals Gallery was one of the spots in the new cultural universe and Medalla hasn't been given enough credit.

There would have been a large element of racism in how the critics perceived David. Most non-white artists who were working in Britain in the sixties were, like women, ignored and excluded from the canon. For instance, Frank Bowling or Aubrey Williams...

Caroline Coon

Our art came out of a massive sense of disillusionment – from breakdown and disintegration. There was rupture within families and between generations, and there was the visible disintegration of the empire. We were in a world of young people who had all the energy, idealism and power of youth but felt lost. Like other movements in the late sixties, the Exploding Galaxy was an attempt at creating a new structure to replace the old. It was totally tribal – we had our own chieftains and shamans. The way in which Balls Pond Road developed was like a tented community, organised but with outbreaks of chaos.

Our work didn't have universality. It couldn't be embraced by a whole society because things we produced were born out of a reaction. The language we produced was understandable only to us. We were reacting against something, and in my opinion, we were mirroring the disaster that was out there. We were taking the things which were lying around, the rubbish, and we were turning it into art, on the basis that this was all that was there. We couldn't do anything else. We were dealing with what was around us and we were making a strong statement to society. For a short period, it worked. It did help to bring people together – for example, in *The Bird Ballet*, which produced that joy of being in the moment. That joy was of what was happening now, what was satisfying.

But there wasn't an answer that could have held us together. We couldn't create the separate life we wanted. We were like children on the beach, playing in the pools left by the receding sea, oblivious to all but our own imaginary world.

Paul Keeler

The Exploding Galaxy was a delightful and genuine group of people who did a number of performances that gave great pleasure to a great number of children and also adults in public situations, and this was a very beautiful activity. There was nothing wrong with it. I think the Galaxy became more complex once it started performing inside, especially in the Covent Garden clubs, because the group wasn't designed to be at the centre of conflicts with the media. That was not its purpose. So I think that made life rather difficult for people in the Galaxy.

Looking back on it, it was gloriously naïve. I say that as a compliment, not as a criticism. I think that was part of its charm: to play music and to dance and find a happiness there. It was a very naïve belief but it was a delightful one and at the time it was very pertinent.

Herzmark

The scavenge-art that the Exploding Galaxy found so absorbing was part of a wider movement, which itself came from the creative ingenuity of wartime austerity. We took nothing and turned it into something. Aesthetic meaning came out of poverty. The sudden funding of our projects removed this aesthetic meaning. If you could travel first class, what was the point in scrudge expeditions to the dustbins of Soho? I believe that both the police raids and Sylvina's generosity hastened the end of the Exploding Galaxy, but the break-up was imminent anyway, owing to the incompatibility of our two leader artists.

Jill Drower

I would say that the Exploding Galaxy were the most revolutionary people I have ever been involved with. I think this for two reasons. Firstly, we really were exploring consciousness. Sometimes, but not always, this was with the help of acid. Secondly, I remember performing with Leighana – we had no clothes on and it was quite sexual. My children and my grandchildren are still shocked by that. I think this is more revolutionary than walking down the street with a banner. Politics are from the head. They come and they go and they ignore the really important things in human beings like sexuality and feelings.

A whole lot of people at that time, in '67 and '68, went to the festivals and grew their hair and maybe they smoked the drugs and maybe they took acid once blah, blah, blah. Maybe they even went to university sit-ins and claim to have been immersed in it all. But in reality, they opted straight back in and became successful whatevers. They remained unchanged by the experience. This cannot be said of anyone from the Exploding Galaxy.

I think only a small amount of people were changed in this way at that time. John Major, for example, is our age and was brought up in London and he's a pretty straight dude. I think that it must have been significant, because otherwise there wouldn't have been such a huge backlash against it. Thatcher to me was a backlash against the sixties.

Simon Shirley

The police set out to break up the commune. This was their motive. They did this by splitting us into individuals and charging us as individuals. The raids and the street harassment were cynical attempts to end us as a way of life. I don't know what their thinking was, but certainly somebody had thought that the plants were a good way to take care of these anarchists: 'We won't even bother to look if there really are drugs in the house.'

I can't see that we were really such a threat. It happened that, in that area of London, the Angry Brigade cropped up later, but our kind of politics was much more about the freedom to be expressive – the freedom to do what you wanted within your own potential. The arrests were infringements of our liberty. It was a sledge hammer to crack a nut.

Audrey Vipond

Ours was not an organisation that was resilient enough to withstand an attack from the establishment. Speaking in political terms, we didn't have a political structure. We weren't a political group, nor a very structured theatre group for that matter. I suppose you could call us 'poetic anarchists' of a certain kind, but we did not live as anarchists. We lived in a very disciplined way. We were always very busy working at artistic projects and performances, so it is very hard to pin down exactly what we were or what we weren't.

But because of the police attack and also because of the support that Sylvina Boissonnas started giving to Exploding Galaxy members, we were a little constellation that became caught between two big black holes. These got stretched out further and further, and then just got pulled apart, and what had once had cohesiveness just got broken up into little groups. One group went off to Wales, and Fitz went off with a group to form Transmedia Exploration and a group of us went off to India.

John Dugger

To me, the value of the Exploding Galaxy lay precisely in the anonymity of key contributing members.

Only in the book *Planted*, produced at the time of the impending trial in 1968, is there any real sense of the Galaxy being a collective, with a more equal emphasis given to all the different contributors. David gave birth to the Galaxy, but like any offspring, the Galaxy grew into something quite different and had its own drives and will, independent of the parent.

To see the Galaxy as the product of any one artist, whether David Medalla or Gerald Fitzgerald, is to miss the point. We were all involved in the aesthetic experiment. In my opinion, the most exciting of the unscheduled artworks that were produced came from an exploration that doesn't even have a name or a date – perhaps we could call it the 'bakery raid', for want of a title. This was a quintessential Galactic experience – anonymous and only by chance recorded. Neither of the known artists was present at this event, and it was arguably the greatest artwork to have been created by the Exploding Galaxy. It was a product of the Galactic foot soldiers Christian Ledoux, Edward Pope, Audrey Vipond and Eve Ridoux. The photographer Mitja Hinderks happened to be present to make a visual record. If he hadn't been there to document the occasion, it would have remained unrecorded, like virtually all the artworks produced by the Exploding Galaxy, whether juniors or known artists.

Jill Drower

The Exploding Galaxy was an extraordinary explosion of ideas. It was a very creative and inspirational time for about eighteen months from mid-1967. We were a spontaneous commune, and that was one of the joys of it. Although it was unstructured, it worked for a while until gradually the manifestations of overload became too great.

We could not have existed without affluence. Benefits provided us with the means to pursue this way of life, as well as a tolerant landlord. The building was central to our creativity. We had our own space at a time when dwellings had to be paid for. The house gave us both the security of a place of our own and the freedom to explore our ideas. If we had been in a tenancy, we would have been evicted. It was only because our landlord tolerated the massive number of people who trooped in and out and who slept there that we were able to develop our ideas.

We were never professional. That was the thing about the Galaxy – we were completely amateurish. It was part of our charm. We were continuing the idea that art shouldn't be owned by private wealth or galleries and that it shouldn't be restricted to only those arenas. We believed that art ought to be a central part of life. It was almost anthropological in that sense. A lot of us had a romantic notion about past cultures and past living. It is romanticised because people who work on the land have a bloody awful time most of the time. You need to have a certain amount of leisure, and in the Galaxy, this was partly fuelled by benefits and individual wealth – mainly the wealth of having Balls Pond Road as a base.

We couldn't have survived in the commercial world because we didn't have any application in the commercial world at all. That's where its fragility lay. It was a fragile thing, which is why it disintegrated really quite quickly.

Audrey Vipond

In the context of its time and in the context of art movements, I do think that the Exploding Galaxy was important. It was bringing art to the people so that it really could be part of everyday life. It de-glamorised art and showed that it could be deeply moving and deeply significant to everybody, without needing to be hung on a wall in an antiseptic, temperature-gauged environment.

The significance of scrudge was that it symbolised the accessibility of art – how it could have meaning without being precious or commercial.

My problem is this: you get an artist and they say that art belongs to everybody – 'It should come out of galleries. It is what everybody produces, and it is a communal activity.' Then, ten years later, they say, 'Why isn't my work being recognised and why isn't it in the Tate?' Something of a double standard there really. I am very cynical about it all.

Andrew Forrest

The Dalston house epitomised their actively de-materialist philosophy. Partly out of necessity, but mostly out of principle, they recycled or readapted just about everything. They took consumer commercial waste – which they called scrudge – and made personal clothing and decoration with it, as well as serious/playful, temporary/ less temporary artworks. What made them abandon their backgrounds, at least for a while? Eccentricity, talent too big to be appreciated at home, the desire to flee dysfunctional families, personal restlessness or problems, the reluctance to take a dead-end job in a boring materialist society.

What brought them together? That within their own world, they could eliminate materialism almost entirely. That, together, their various enthusiasms and abilities could combine to create something greater than the sum of the parts, with each giving according to his or her ability. People could join the Exploding Galaxy because they wanted to; except for screening for criminals or sociopaths, they were not vetted for talent or other characteristics, like beauty. This is how many humans and animals have lived before, but voluntarily putting the group before the individual is almost unknown in human society today. For a number of years, it worked, and it was a towering achievement. One of the group's convictions was that everyone has it in him or her to create something meaningful, and that it is much easier to do so if one climbs out of the straitjacket of conditioning and convention.

Mitja Hinderks

The beauty of the Exploding Galaxy was its inclusivity and its celebration of hotch-potch expression. In a single performance, you might find Michael Chapman investigating a length of rope, Fitz having a long argument about absolutely nothing, David spouting a reconstituted tale from the *Mahabharata* and several people simply rolling around. In a way, it was representative of the early days of our counterculture, where maddeningly different preoccupations and experiments sat side by side – the old patchwork blanket again.

It seems to me that from 1966 to the early part of 1968, we were all pulling apart the old values, ideas, skills and procedures, and playing around with all the possibilities that were thrown up. In fact, a favourite Galaxy word was 'possibilities'. But by 1969 the whole thing had begun to refine itself into a series of dogmatic rule books. It is interesting that so many in the Exploding Galaxy sought structure, whether religious or political, after having been so totally at home with its absence.

Jill Drower

What I liked about the Exploding Galaxy was its amateurishness. To me, what they were doing was about 'untrained' people being creative – it was folk art.

What they were doing was redolent of ancient England, as if they were bringing countryside traditions into the town. When they performed in the open air, I thought it was like folk dancing. Because it was not classically skilled, it was accessible to all and I loved that. Their performances were something that Cecil Sharp might have looked at and been interested in. The way that they costumed themselves was very folk – I related them to morris dancing. To me, morris dancing is one of the most splendid parts of folk dance form and acting and street theatre that English culture has to offer.

Morris is also symbolic of early multiculturalism! Morris is evidence of the spread of cultural forms from India and North Africa. Blackness was in English culture centuries ago! Somebody must have written a thesis on why it became fashionable in white leftist circles to trash morris dancing... Anyway, it was through the lens of morris dancing that I appreciated the Exploding Galaxy!

The Exploding Galaxy were part of everything that our hippy new world represented, our look into the future, the space age, the international all-encompassing countryside-to-city flow across borders, boundaries and nations.

The look, the style that they represented was hippy ethnic – the soft flowing robes of the peasant countryside or of the east. It was a bringing into town of pagan or eastern spirituality, of claiming urban spaces for frolic and bucolic bacchanal – their performance of nudity was like a discarding of civilisation and connecting human beings back to nature.

For me, I felt that, if the Galaxy was there, wherever Release was, then all was well. They were emblematic of the peace and love counterculture – they were an icon of countercultural peace and love.

Caroline Coon

The Exploding Galaxy made such a strong stand against the status quo – more so perhaps than the counterculture at large and more so even than the revolutionaries across the water. This was because we spoke such a different language. We were peaceful and gentle in our forms of expression, but totally revolutionary in our advocacy of life as a total art form and our shunning of commerce and growth. Attempts to crush us, although successful in destroying the Exploding Galaxy itself, were not entirely successful in the long term. The legislation against discrimination and police corruption that was eventually enacted has been an attempt to close off that avenue.

In countries where there is a degree of democracy, the forces of evil have long needed something more powerful to crush dissent than mere repression. They regrouped and came up with a much better plan. By supporting the rebel artists, they have neutralised them. By flattering aggressive dissent with attention and the promise of out-of-this-world prices, they have effectively nobbled any real chance of protest through art.

An 'incursion' or an 'intervention' has now become something cute you might do in the basement tanks of Tate Modern. It can be as crazy as you like, provided it conforms to health and safety regulations.

Jill Drower

However you try to sum up the Galaxy, the opposite is also true. We threw out our culture's rule books but then discovered deep truths in ancient disciplines from many cultures. Trying to emulate these disciplines generated impractical ambitions that clashed with our inexperience and our wish to be spontaneous and unprofessional. The establishment saw us as filthy druggies, and it's true we were cat-and-dirt-tolerant, and many had tried LSD, but we aspired to a life of addiction-free creativity and achieved many unique ephemeral artworks with a fetish-like quality that will never reside in a museum. Each of us discovered our own path out of this conundrum. Our legacy is: return to the source and keep up the good work.

Edward Pope

The Exploding Galaxy was neither a movement nor a club. We were more a group of people who somehow, by chance, mostly by chance, got together with the aim of animating the world around us. We called it *activation*. We had tremendous fun *activating* the streets, the buses and the night clubs, and we wanted to show people how they themselves could have fun like us.

Certain performances, like *The Bird Ballet*, were extraordinary. I would not say that they were badly made, but they were certainly unprofessional, and perhaps *un petit peu n'importe quoi*. They were sweet and, of course, naïve, but within that naivety, there was a lot of intelligence. There was sharpness in many of the things we did.

The thing about the Exploding Galaxy was that we had no ambition. We did not wish to place ourselves as protagonists in the history of art. If you had ambitions, all you did was to put limits on the expression. The Exploding Galaxy was a transient thing for all of us. We lived it intensely for a while, and then, *pfff*, it was gone.

Christian Ledoux

Index

Abbreviations used:
BPR - Balls Pond Road
EG - Exploding Galaxy
JD - Jill Drower

9 780992 777524

CPSIA information can be obtained
at www.ICGtesting.com
Printed in the USA
LVHW102257301121
704874LV00015B/458

9 780992 777524